INDIA
BRIEFING

Asia Society is a nonprofit, nonpartisan public education organization dedicated to increasing American understanding of Asia and broadening the dialogue between Americans and Asians. Through its programs in policy and business, the fine and performing arts, and elementary and secondary education, the Society reaches audiences across the United States and works closely with colleagues in Asia.

The views expressed in this publication are those of the individual contributors.

INDIA BRIEFING
Takeoff at Last?

Alyssa Ayres and Philip Oldenburg

Editors

Published in Cooperation with the Asia Society

An East Gate Book

M.E.Sharpe
Armonk, New York
London, England

An East Gate Book

Library of Congress ISSN: 0894-5136
ISBN 0-7656-1592-4 (hardcover)

Printed in the United States of America

The paper used in this publication meets the minimum requirements of
American National Standard for Information Sciences
Permanence of Paper for Printed Library Materials,
ANSI Z 39.48-1984.

BM (c)   10   9   8   7   6   5   4   3   2   1

Contents

Foreword

India is viewed as a key regional power with one of the world's fastest growing economies; supported by a vibrant democracy with an electorate that is intelligent and responsive; and blessed with an educated workforce, strong industrial and manufacturing sectors, and innovative entrepreneurs who have together placed India at the cusp of a major transformation. At the same time, India's seemingly bright future continues to be challenged by enduring developmental issues—entrenched poverty, low levels of literacy, poor access to health care, inadequate infrastructure, social inequities, among others. As the title of the volume *India Briefing: Takeoff at Last?* suggests, the perception that India is finally on its way to achieving global-power status continues to be under both domestic and international scrutiny and speculation. The political will that India demonstrates in addressing these competing priorities will determine the course of its future and its place in the global arena.

India Briefing: Takeoff at Last? is the eleventh publication in a series of regular assessments of key events in Indian affairs prepared by the Asia Society. We are extremely fortunate to again have the editorial team of Alyssa Ayres and Philip K. Oldenburg whose knowledge about the region, steadfastness, and diplomatic aplomb has brought the project to successful completion. The editors have enlisted a very talented group of authors who represent the best and the brightest minds in their respective areas of expertise—Isher Judge Ahluwalia, Richard H. Davis, Niraja Gopal Jayal, Renana Jhabvala, Manjeet Kripalani, Amitabh Mattoo, Irawati Parnerkar, and Mary Rader. We thank them all for producing such high caliber pieces and readily adhering to the Asia Society's stringent editorial procedure and timetable.

It is particularly heartening to highlight the diversity of topics covered in this volume. Readers should note that some of the chapters were completed prior to the defeat of the National Democratic Alliance government led by the Bharatiya Janata Party (BJP) in the 2004 Lok Sabha elections. However, the themes that emerge from the chapters remain relevant—India is undergoing a tremendous change culturally, economically, socially, and politically. India's economic promise, geo-strategic importance, social development, and cultural status in the world will be determined by how the Indian leadership tackles these changes. If India fails on this account, it will continue to be relegated to what the co-editors have pointed to in the introduction, as a "yes, but" country.

We are also thankful to Lisa J. Hacken and Chris Reeves, the returning Managing and Copy Editor team. Lisa's attention to detail and watchful eyes steered the volume from manuscript through production, and Chris painstakingly copyedited the entire volume. We hope to be able to continue working together in the future.

This is Asia Society's fourth *India Briefing* published in collaboration with M.E. Sharpe's East Gate Books imprint. We thank Patricia Loo, Amy Albert, and Angela Piliouras from M.E. Sharpe and we look forward to continuing this important partnership in the coming years.

Last but certainly not the least, no part of this volume would have been possible without generous funding from the GE Foundation. This is the third *India Briefing* that has benefited from the GE Foundation's support. We are most grateful to R. Michael Gadbaw and Scott Bayman of the General Electric Company and Robert L. Corcoran and Roger Nozaki of the GE Foundation. Their encouragement and continued support over the years have enabled the Asia Society to further its mission—fostering a better understanding of Asia and enhancing communication between Americans and the peoples of Asia and the Pacific. We know that *India Briefing* fulfills that larger goal in its own unique way.

As always, *India Briefing* is intended as an educational resource for students and interested general public. We are interested in making this series relevant to our readers and welcome comments and suggestions via email: policy@asiasoc.org.

Vishakha N. Desai
President
Asia Society

Robert W. Radtke
Senior Vice President for Programs
Asia Society

CENTRAL ASIA
CHINA
Boundary claimed by India
Aksai
Chin
Cease-fire Line
Kabul
Kashmir
AFGHANISTAN
Islamabad
Srinagar
Boundary claimed by China
TIBET
Lahore
Lhasa
McMahon Line
PAKISTAN
New Delhi
NEPAL
BHUTAN
Kathmandu
Indus
River
Brahmaputra River
Karachi
Ganges
River
BANGLADESH
INDIA
Calcutta
Dhaka
BURMA
Bombay
Arabian
Sea
Rangoon
Bay of
Bengal
N
Madras
Andaman and Nicobar Islands (India)
Palk Strait
Colombo
SRI LANKA
Indian Ocean
MALDIVES

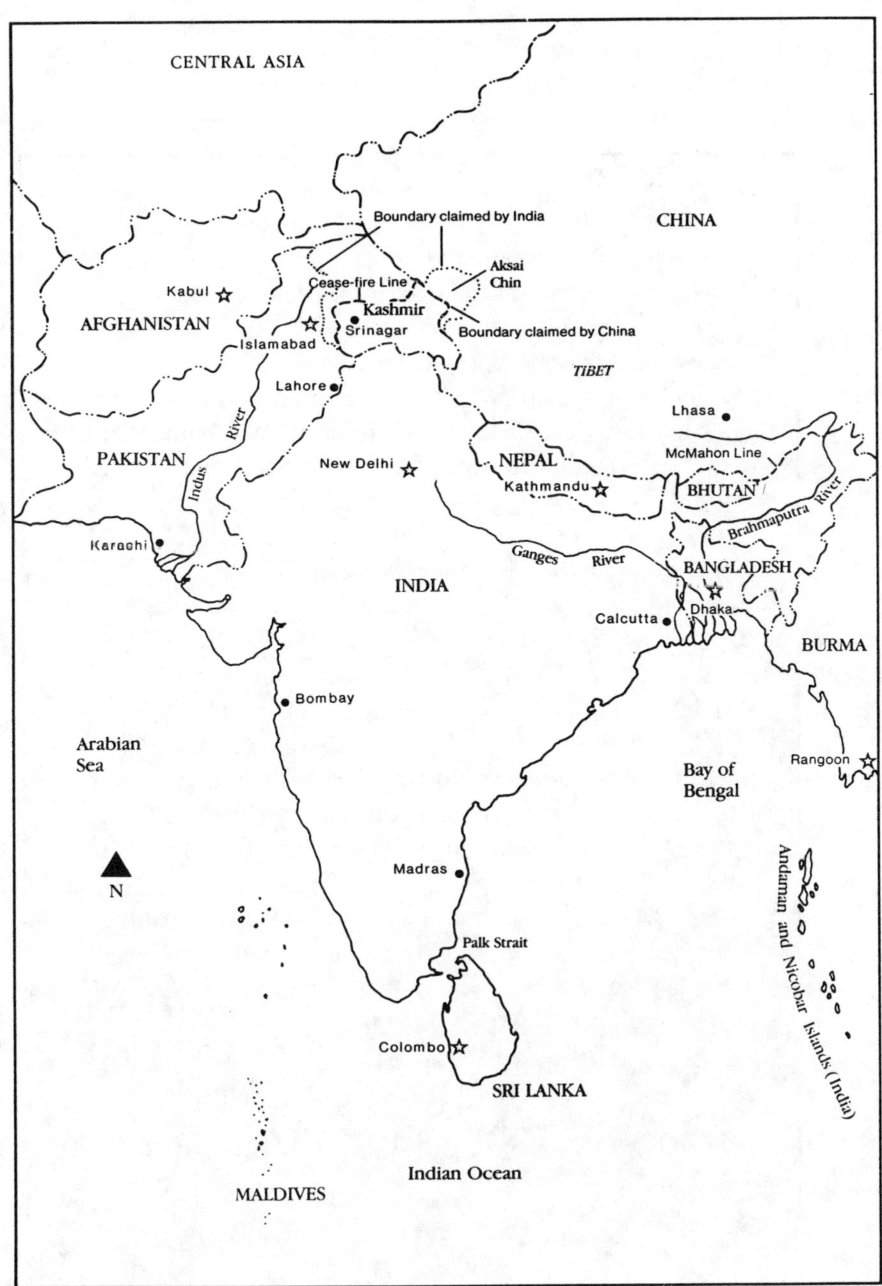

South Asia

KYRGYZSTAN
TAJIKISTAN
AFGHANISTAN
Kabul
Islamabad
Srinagar
Amritsar
Lahore
PAKISTAN
PUNJAB
Chandigarh
HARYANA
New Delhi
Aligarh
Jaipur
Agra
RAJASTHAN
Boundary claimed by India
Cease-fire Line
Aksai Chin
JAMMU AND KASHMIR
HIMACHAL PRADESH
Chinese Line of Control
UTTARANCHAL
CHINA
TIBET
Lhasa
Boundary claimed by China
McMahon Line
ARUNACHAL PRADESH
Thimpu
NEPAL
SIKKIM
BHUTAN
Kathmandu
ASSAM
Lucknow
UTTAR PRADESH
BIHAR
Patna
MEGHALAYA
MANIPUR
BANGLADESH
JHARKHAND
Ahmedabad
GUJARAT
Bhopal
INDIA
MADHYA PRADESH
WEST BENGAL
Dacca
MIZORAM
Calcutta
CHHATTISGARH
TRIPURA
MYANMAR
ORISSA
MAHARASHTRA
Bombay
Bhubaneswar
Hyderabad
ANDHRA PRADESH
Bay of Bengal
Yangon
GOA
KARNATAKA
Bangalore
Madras
Port Blair
Kavaratti
TAMIL NADU
KERALA
LAKSHADWEEP
Polk Strait
ANDAMAN AND NICOBAR ISLANDS
Trivandrum
SRI LANKA
Colombo
MALDIVES
Indian Ocean

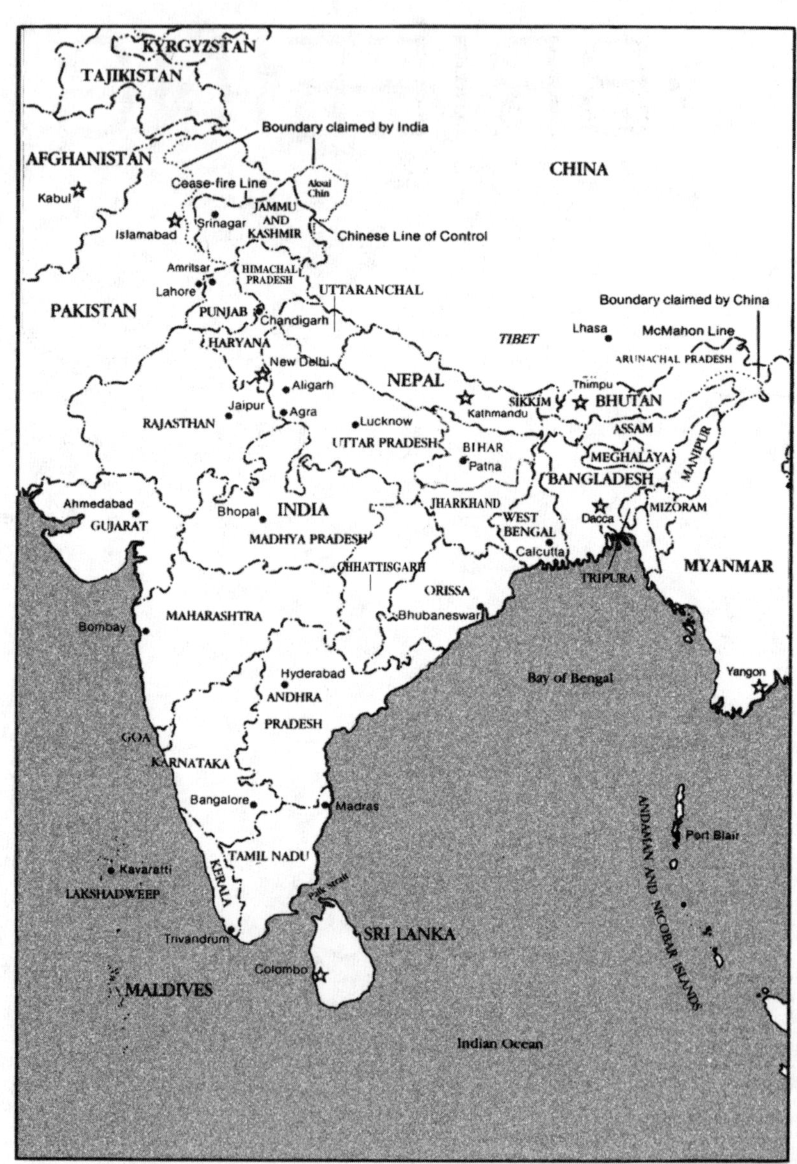

India

INDIA
BRIEFING

Introduction
India Briefing: Takeoff at Last?

Alyssa Ayres and Philip K. Oldenburg

Even by the standards of a rapidly changing world, over the past three years India has set a scorching pace. Our last volume of *India Briefing* was subtitled *Quickening the Pace of Change*—an assessment which could not have been more appropriate. Since then, India has been swept by continuing change and tumultuous events in virtually every sphere: politics, the economy, foreign relations, society, and the arts.

The economic historian W.W. Rostow, writing more than forty years ago, defined "takeoff" as "the interval when the old blocks and resistances to steady growth are finally overcome. . . . The forces making for economic progress . . . expand and come to dominate the society. Growth becomes its normal condition."[1] According to Rostow's linear stages of economic growth, India launched takeoff around 1952 and would reach its "maturity," or the state in which technological and entrepreneurial skills would provide the ability to produce anything of India's choosing, after some twenty years.

Whether or not one subscribes to the notion of neatly packaged stages of development, Rostow's words merit some reflection today. A change that was predicted for years but never quite came about is now under way in India. The country has become one of the fastest growing economies in the world. Foreign exchange reserves are at an all-time high. India's knowledge industries have become global models of excellence. Yet another free and fair national election, India's fourteenth, has produced a change of government, which has taken power with no fuss. Moreover, there is a newfound confidence in the way Indian leaders

---

1. W.W. Rostow, *The Stages of Economic Growth: A Non-Communist Manifesto* (Cambridge: Cambridge University Press, 1960), p. 7. Rostow later (p. 57) defines "takeoff" as "an industrial revolution, tied directly to radical changes in methods of production, having their decisive consequence over a relatively short period of time."

speak of their country—demonstrated by the calm with which the new Indian prime minister, Dr. Manmohan Singh, asserted in a September 2004 address at the Council on Foreign Relations in New York that the architecture of the global order was anachronistic, and that it is time to recognize "India's due place in global councils."[2]

But even now some observers doubt that India is completely airborne. These critics expect a forced landing in the not too distant future—perhaps a result of global market forces, such as competition from China or rising oil prices; a health crisis brought on by the HIV/AIDS epidemic; a paralyzing political turn either to a revived and divisive Hindu nationalism or to a left-wing anti-globalization populism wary of notions of neo-colonialism; or the dependency they say globalization will bring. Other observers, unconvinced that India's time has come, point to continuing high levels of poverty, corruption, and domestic violence; the very slow progress in increasing the reach and standards of education; and the slowing down of improvements in health care as factors hindering India's full potential.

The chapters in this volume will not settle the issue. As always, India remains a "yes, but" country. Yet the balance has tipped: one would be *surprised* if the economy were to stop growing at the substantially higher rate of the last twenty years, let alone crash into stagnation or decline. We have come to expect a smooth transition as one party (or coalition) replaces another in Delhi and in the states, and we are used to the substantial overlap in policy that is revealed each time, once political rhetoric has to be fit into the realities of governing. And it is taken for granted that not only will India be increasingly integrated into the global economy, but it also will play an increasingly important role in it. In international affairs, India has become a motivating force, a presence that will make things happen, rather than a pure recipient of economic aid, diplomatic pressure, and global cultural trends. It is in these expectations that India's takeoff—the term remains current and probably encompasses Rostow's "maturity" stage in common understanding—has been accomplished.

In politics, the change of government after the parliamentary election in spring 2004 was unexpected. The ruling National Democratic Alliance (NDA) government, headed by the Bharatiya Janata Party (BJP), went into the elections confident of a return to power, dissolving Parliament and calling for elections six months ahead of schedule in order to

---

2. See http://www.cfr.org/pub7407/richard_n_haass_manmohan_singh_vishakha_desai/russell_c_leffingwell_lecture_with_manmohan_singh.php.

capitalize on what it believed to be soaring public confidence. Indeed, the coalition government had made history of sorts by becoming the first non-Congress government to complete a five-year term in office. Prime Minister Atal Behari Vajpayee had established himself internationally as a senior statesman, someone seeking a legacy of economic prosperity, self-confident foreign policy, and peace in the subcontinent through his overtures to Pakistan. Virtually all political commentators and media pundits predicted an easy majority for the NDA. Yet a coalition led by the Congress and supported by communist and regional parties was able to form a new government when the BJP and its allies lost a significant number of parliamentary seats.

Some blamed the BJP-led government's attention to the glamorous information technology sector, perhaps at the expense of the working poor. Others suggested that voters had not forgotten the appalling anti-Muslim pogrom in Gujarat in March 2002. Still others suggested that it was not the poor's *resentment* of the new globalization-led prosperity, but a cry for a greater share of it that led to the election results. In the first chapter of this volume, "The BJP Falls from Power," Niraja Gopal Jayal situates the political fortunes of the BJP against a broader canvas of the evolution of the party system and Indian democracy. Jayal reexamines conventional wisdom on coalition governments and the erosion of ideological differences between the major parties, and also looks at the increasingly important role of identity in Indian politics.

Identity has become a frontline concern in India. Perhaps the most salient of contemporary India's "identity faultlines" concerns the role of religion in Indian public life. This issue is at the heart of the difference between competing ideas about India: its tradition of secular politics versus the increasingly popular appeal of Hindutva, or Hindu nationalism. Even though the BJP-led coalition lost power, the party has successfully placed the core notion of Indian secularism on the public agenda and has called for its reinterpretation. This question will not vanish simply with a change of government, which makes it all the more important to understand the deeper history of Hindutva and what it means to so many. Richard Davis's chapter in this volume, "The Cultural Background of Hindutva," provides exactly that. Davis takes a long view of the strands of intellectual history that have forged today's modern Hindutva. He places the political rise of the BJP and the Sangh Parivar against a much larger backdrop of public philosophy and debates over the past century about what it means to be Indian and what it means to be Hindu.

India has also been making global headlines in the business world—especially in information technology and what are called "IT-enabled services," ranging from call centers and data processing to advanced financial services and biotech research. The explosive growth of this sector is likely to continue. One measure of this new international prominence was the emergence of India as a campaign issue in the 2004 U.S. presidential politics. Along with China, India has become the focus of resentment over job losses as a result of globalization. Despite evidence that the outsourcing of knowledge work has not led to overall job losses in the United States (by some measures, new categories of work have been created), the issue remains a live one politically. What is now undeniable is that it has brought India to the attention of Americans in a new way. Major corporations can no longer afford to be without an "India strategy," and business schools have begun taking students to India to witness the outsourcing phenomenon firsthand. This shift suggests that a new and powerful constituency in the United States will likely become more engaged with India, will seek to learn more about it, and will continue to further its economic growth.

Despite the optimism, there's still cause for caution. Isher Judge Ahluwalia explains why in "Indian Economy: New Pathways to Growth and Development." Ahluwalia surveys India's recent macroeconomic trends, particularly with respect to the ongoing process of economic reforms. The reforms that began in the 1980s and sharply accelerated in 1991 have deepened to include the privatization of public sector undertakings in the face of considerable political obstacles. The tendency of politicians to make fiscally unsustainable promises has impeded reform, and in sectors such as power, blocked it entirely. Thanks to the failure of Indian politicians to build a national constituency for further reforms, subsidies of various kinds have increased since the mid-1990s, contributing to a steep increase in the country's fiscal deficit when looking at the center and the states combined. Ahluwalia suggests that despite soaring economic growth and record foreign exchange reserves, concerns remain.

In a complementary chapter, Renana Jhabvala takes a bottom-up look at economic realities from the perspective of Indian workers in the informal sector. In "Work and Wealth" Jhabvala examines the significant—though often ignored—contribution of those in insecure and unorganized jobs to the country's wealth. Despite its much-lauded success, India's IT sector employs only a tiny percentage of the country's workforce.

Most Indians make their living through daily labor, in an economy that lacks a safety net for the unemployed, pensions for the elderly, and health insurance for the sick. Though their voices often go unheard in economic literature and the glossy stories of the business press, in terms of sheer numbers these workers are the backbone of India's economy. Jhabvala's chapter provides a powerful argument for the necessity of an "economic voice" for them.

Over the past three years India has ridden an international relations rollercoaster, particularly with respect to Pakistan. Following a suicide attack on the Indian Parliament in December 2001, the Indian and Pakistani armies went "eyeball to eyeball" for almost a year. For much of 2002, one million troops faced off at the border, raising the possibility of a nuclear exchange between the armed neighbors. A flurry of diplomatic activity by the United States, United Kingdom, and Russia attested to global fears. Following that state of near-war in 2002, however, the two countries met during the South Asian Association for Regional Cooperation meeting in 2003 and have now embarked on a far-reaching set of dialogues, which has included some limited progress on the Kashmir issue.

India's relations with the United States have also entered a new phase. The terrorist attacks of September 11, 2001, turned U.S. foreign policy on its head, and one result was the virtual elimination of a sanctions regime that had dogged the bilateral relationship since India's testing of nuclear devices in May 1998. Of course, the geopolitical repercussions of 9/11, in which the United States re-energized its relationship with Pakistan to fight its war on terror, complicated the notion of the United States and India as "natural allies." Yet the two countries have moved forward on joint military exercises—something unimaginable just a few years ago—and have formalized intelligence sharing. Amitabh Mattoo explores these issues in his chapter in this volume, "India's International Relations: The Search for Stability, Space, and Strength." Mattoo also takes a closer look at the Kashmir conflict. As India seeks to extend its sphere of influence in Asia and beyond, it seeks new kinds of relationships with East and Southeast Asia. Mattoo explains why these developments will be worth following.

In many parts of the world, Indian popular culture has long been prominent. Its giant film industry, "Bollywood," holds sway not only throughout India but also over large parts of the Middle East, Africa, the former Soviet Union, and Southeast Asia. And in recent years, Indian culture has attained a higher profile in the United States, with Bollywood films showing in major U.S. cities, Indian-inspired Broadway musicals (*Bombay Dreams*), and Hollywood's own Bollywood-influenced films (*Moulin Rouge* and *The Guru*). In "The Business of Bollywood," Manjeet Kripalani explores how the Indian film industry works and details the structural changes under way. For example, with the passage of legislation recognizing Bollywood as a formal industry, filmmakers can now raise capital through official channels, including credit from banks. This change is leading Bollywood producers out of the arms of an organized criminal enterprise (too often a financial mainstay in the past) and guiding the industry to reevaluate its management practices. It is already changing the global profile of Bollywood as a business sector, and may well lead to the industry's rise as a potential investment opportunity.

Our final chapter provides an overview of the growing number of online resources about India. Mary Rader outlines how the Web has expanded access to a wide range of sources beyond the confines of a handful of research libraries in the United States, United Kingdom, and India. In "Downloading India," Rader examines the proliferation of Web sites featuring India-related content and also gives a roadmap to what has become available on the "deep Web" (subscription databases and proprietary sources). New initiatives such as the Digital South Asia Library, the JSTOR (Journal Storage) project, and the electronic conversion of Asia-focused indexes create opportunities for students, researchers, or the casually interested to access knowledge about India.

How fast India will continue to change is anyone's guess. The underlying premise of these chapters is, however, that a new trajectory of change is present in India. This change may well mean recurring crises of one form or another, coming in quicker succession than previously but with none likely to change the basic direction in which the country is moving. There is also considerable momentum, a demonstrated capacity to handle crises and challenges, and a resilience of society, economy, and polity, all of which suggest that India's future may at last resemble the hopes so many had for it a half century ago.

Politics:
The BJP Falls from Power

Niraja Gopal Jayal

Introduction

Politics in India in 2003 is best viewed as the dress rehearsal of the Bharatiya Janata Party ("Indian People's Party," or BJP) for the grand performance of 2004 that never happened. The BJP's misfortune was that it came to believe in a myth of its own making: the myth of invincibility that it had so aggressively and assiduously fostered and that eventually consumed it. Buoyed by an intoxicatingly high economic growth rate, the resumption of peace talks with Pakistan (resonating in the popular imagination through a successful cricket tour of that country), and a series of landslide victories in the December 2003 state elections, a self-assured, even complacent, BJP called for an early election[1] in the hope of garnering a more decisive majority in the fourteenth general election to the lower house of India's Parliament.

As it turned out, this optimism was misplaced. Contrary to the predictions of psephologists and astrologers and the analyses of salon and studio alike, the Indian electorate delivered a verdict that astonished even its beneficiaries. The election ushered into power a government of the Congress Party in alliance with a number of small regional parties that had, over the last five years, given the impression of being a fragmented, feeble, and ineffectual opposition.[2] Within days of the election results, Congress Party President Sonia Gandhi announced her decision to decline the post of prime minister, nominating Dr. Manmohan Singh, who

---

1. Technically, its term should have ended eight months later but, with the BJP riding the crest of a victory wave in the state elections, Prime Minister Vajpayee exercised his prerogative to advise the president to dissolve the lower house in February, calling for general elections in the summer of 2004.

2. This impression was only strengthened when, in August 2003, the Congress Party initiated a no-confidence motion that proved to be a damp squib.

served as finance minister in the last Congress government (1991–96).[3] Though the new government appeared anything but new in terms of the number of faces from past Congress cabinets, it was distinctive in being the first-ever coalition government with Congress participation. The Congress had long resisted the politics of strategic alliances and coalitions in favor of a dominant role in the polity. Its current achievement, however, clearly could not have been possible without the coalition.

The previous government, the BJP-led National Democratic Alliance (NDA), a coalition of some twenty-seven parties, was the first non-Congress government in the history of independent India to have completed a full term.[4] In December 2003, the BJP won resounding victories in three of four state assemblies that went to the polls. In these elections, the BJP had experimented with a rather different platform from its tired Hindu nationalist anthem. The new slogan of development and growth enabled it to successfully slay three incumbent Congress governments. This success was interpreted as a positive sign that the BJP's efforts over the past year in consolidating and reinventing itself had borne fruit.

Indeed, the last few months of its term revealed not only hitherto unimaginable skills in the technocratic management of politics, but also the attempt to repackage the BJP itself, from its past image of a party locked into a revivalist vision of a glorious ancient past, to a party of economic modernization proclaiming its commitment to development and its intent to make India a superpower. There was a certain incongruity about the BJP, with its nostalgic attachment to a Hindu past and its rather conservative cultural symbolism, flaunting the vision of a future in which India's economic and technological achievements—arguably,

---

3. Sonia Gandhi's "foreign" origins—she is Italian-born—have been consistently targeted by the BJP, whose personal campaign against her acquired greater shrillness after the election results were declared. Her own party had earlier split on this issue, with a splinter group led by Congress Party veteran Sharad Pawar leaving and forming a new party, the Nationalist Congress Party. For the 2004 election, Pawar—whose party has since been in partnership with the Congress in the Maharashtra government—entered into an alliance with Sonia Gandhi's Congress and is now minister for food and agriculture in the new government. Sonia Gandhi's own party has consistently supported her candidature for prime minister, asserting that the Congress could not have won back as much of the popular vote as it did without her tireless campaigning across the country. The BJP's tirades against Sonia Gandhi are obviously polemical and have no legal foundation, for the Indian Constitution permits no discrimination between citizens on the basis of birth, and a naturalized citizen has the same rights as any other, including the right to contest and hold political office.

4. By one reckoning, since the 2004 election was called a few months early the NDA government almost served a full term. By another, the previous government of thirteen months should be added to the count, and the NDA government served more than a full term.

including its nuclear capability—would take it to the status of a world superpower and a *vishwaguru* (world guru) in the sciences, the arts, and the economy.[5] The electorate apparently found this vision neither appealing nor convincing.

The coalition that came to power in May 2004 is led by the Congress Party and supported by various smaller regional parties, as well as the two communist parties. While the Congress itself won just 145 seats in the Lok Sabha ("House of the People," or lower house) out of a possible 543, it emerged as the single largest party, with seven seats more than the BJP's 138. At 26.69 percent, the Congress's vote share was also higher than the BJP's 22.16 percent. The margin between them may have been slender, in terms of both seats and votes, but the big difference lay in the expectations with which the parties had gone to the polls. The BJP had expected to improve upon its 1999 score of 182 seats, while the Congress began with a severe handicap of just 114 seats in 1999. Thus, while neither party performed spectacularly well, the Congress's gain was made the more dramatic by the BJP's loss.

In policy terms, the BJP-led coalition government had been committed to Hindu nationalism,[6] on the one hand, and privatization and liberalization in economic policy, on the other. The Congress-led coalition, under the newly minted label of the United Progressive Alliance (UPA), is predictably committed to secularism and minority rights, along with a commitment to economic reforms. If the BJP-led NDA was seen by the core constituency of the BJP as not quite nationalist enough—in culture as in economics—the Congress's reformist economics is also being closely monitored by its allies among the communist parties, which threaten to rein in any excesses of market fundamentalism. Quite apart from the issue of numbers, then, how substantially has the replacement of one coalition by another signaled a shift in the polity? A macro view of Indian politics

---

5. BJP chief Venkaiah Naidu, quoted in *Outlook* magazine (March 8, 2004).

6. On Hindu nationalism, see Richard Davis's "The Cultural Background of Hindutva" in this volume. Some observers have interpreted the defeat of the BJP in the 2004 election as a rejection of Hindutva. However, the evidence on this is as yet ambiguous, with too many exceptions to sustain a neat single-factor explanation in these, or indeed any other, terms. The BJP's Modi government in Gujarat did, after all, win the Assembly elections of December 2002 despite the riots of February of the same year. The loss of support for the BJP in Gujarat in the 2004 election is not so much a verdict on Hindutva, as a manifestation of dissatisfaction of the Bharat Kisan Sangh (the RSS's farmers' unit) with Modi, as also the dissent within the Gujarat state unit of the BJP on the autocratic leadership style of the chief minister. The BJP's own allies—including the Trinamool Congress, the Telugu Desam Party (TDP), and even the Shiv Sena—have however attributed the defeat to the Gujarat riots.

in 2004 suggests two important long-term trends in the political land-scape and party system, both of which call for careful evaluation.

Coalition Politics

The first of these trends is the persistence of coalition politics that has characterized the polity since 1996. Possibly the most striking outcome of the 2004 election has been the fact that, for the first time ever, the Congress Party is cast in the role of the leader of a coalition government. This appears to lend credence to the argument that Indian politics has entered a decisively new phase—coalition politics—in which no party can afford to entertain hopes of forming a government entirely on its own. However, since the Congress's ability to lead and sustain a coalition is yet to be tested, this claim has largely been made on the basis of the BJP's record since 1998, and it is in that context that it must for the present be judged.

Coalition government in India represents a deviation from the standard model of executive coalitions. It is almost inevitably, and certainly since 1998, characterized by the clustering of a number of small parties around one larger dominant party. The small parties invariably occupy subsidiary positions; the smaller numbers of seats they bring to the coalition are reflected in the less important ministerial portfolios they get as well as their overall marginality to the process of policy-making. This was true of the BJP-led NDA coalition that governed from 1998 to early 2004 and could very well be true of the Congress-led UPA, keeping in mind the initial distribution of ministerial portfolios and the Congress's historical predisposition to a centralized style of ruling.

Ideological Consensus

The second trend relates to the perception that the ideological polarity that characterized the political scene over the last decade has dissolved into an ideological consensus, or at least that the ideological distance between the major parties has been reduced. On the question of economic reforms, the difference between the BJP and the Congress has indeed been negligible. It is on the question of religious diversity in Indian society, and the proper orientation of the state toward it, that there has been a fundamental difference between the two parties. In the 2004 campaign, the BJP tried—albeit too late, too unconvincingly, and therefore with limited success—to broaden its appeal, conveying the impression that it had moved closer to the center of the ideological spectrum. Indeed, the claim of a shift in the ideological center of gravity of the political system depends substantially upon the BJP's campaign (and considerable success) in the December 2003 state assembly elections, which the party sought to replicate in the 2004 election. These attempts to broaden its appeal suggested that the BJP had finally been "normalized," as its main platform in the elections was not Hindutva (the ideology of Hindu nationalism) but development and governance, as embodied in the party's slogan: *bijli*, *sadak*, *pani* (electricity, roads, water).

The greater success of the BJP, however, lies in the fact that the terms of the political discourse on culture have shifted quite decisively, with even some Congress leaders demonstrating an alarming eagerness to flirt with Hindu nationalism. As such, while the BJP is far from forsaking its Hindu nationalist agenda, the fact that the Congress is not averse to experimenting with it either is perhaps a sign of the former's success in shifting the terms of discourse on the question of cultural pluralism in Indian society. However, the Congress's move in this direction is necessarily tempered by its need to prove itself as the natural leader of the secular parties, and it may be easy enough for the Congress to reclaim its ideological inheritance of pluralism despite some recent episodes of minor infidelity to it. In a sense, then, in 2003 and 2004 the major political parties appeared to be experimenting with each other's core strength, signaling both parties' readiness to make expedient compromises with ideological purity.

Section two of this chapter will examine and qualify the coalition politics claim, which recently has acquired the status of a cliché. In addition, section two will propose a distinction between coalition politics and coalition government that applied to the BJP-led coalition and is likely to apply to the new Congress-led coalition as well. Section three will attempt to nuance the ideological consensus argument by showing that the center of gravity of the political system itself is in a state of flux. Evidence regarding the new ideological consensus—based quite substantially upon the BJP's so-called normalization—will be examined to argue that the party has certainly been normalized in terms of internal factionalism and a propensity to corruption, neither of which can be construed as strictly ideological. In terms of its newfound passion for inclusivism, the normalization of the BJP is more wishful thinking than fact—and an eminently reversible trend that already shows some signs of reversal.

It is in this context that section four discusses the shifts in the core constituencies of the two major parties, especially the astonishing support that the Rashtriya Swayamsevak Sangh ("National Volunteers' Association," or RSS) and Vishwa Hindu Parishad ("World Hindu Council," or VHP) have managed to mobilize for the BJP among the tribal populations of central India. Section four also comments upon the absurd lengths to which caste was pushed by the logic of Indian politics in 2003. Section five looks at the party-neutral phenomenon of corruption and the lowering of the threshold of its acceptability in politics and society. The visibility and acceptability of the nexus between crime and politics are of a piece with this development. However, some institutions in the constitutional system have proved to be reassuringly robust, and section six draws attention to some verdicts of the Supreme Court and the performance of the Election Commission as evidence of this. The work of these institutions is reinforced by various civilian organizations that are serving as monitors and watchdogs, as well as certain crusading individuals, including the leaders of social movements now entering the electoral fray. Finally, section seven comments upon the significance of a new phenomenon encountered in Indian politics: the importance of image management and marketing. While this may seem unsurprising given the large number of young people in the Indian electorate, there does appear to be a disturbing disconnect between, on the one hand, the election campaign in terms of both its content and its packaging and, on the other, its presumptive market.

Coalition Government Versus Coalition Governance

It is true that coalition government at the national level—viewed through the 1990s as an alarming sign of chaos and instability—has become an accepted norm, not only in public opinion but equally in the practice of all political parties. The frenzied search for alliance partners in the run-up to the parliamentary election of 2004 was clearly underwritten by the implicit assumption that no single party would obtain a majority, and that the outcome would surely be a coalition.[7] Even the Congress, which

---

7. The last two decades have witnessed the emergence of a number of regional parties which rose to challenge the hegemony of the Congress Party in the states. Some of these parties were offshoots of either the Congress (e.g., the Trinamool Congress and the Nationalist Congress Party) or the Janata family of parties (e.g., the Rashtriya Janata Dal and the

had historically adopted a snobbishly aloof attitude toward coalitions, forged winning alliances with nine regional parties, without which it would not be in government today. Indeed, for many, this was the secret of its newfound success at the hustings. On the whole, the smug "we will go it alone and decide on alliances *after* the polls" attitude of yesteryear was for the most part[8] replaced by an eager soliciting and receiving of overtures to future partnerships, leading political analysts to authoritatively proclaim that this is "a time of coalitions."[9]

Coalition government undoubtedly has many virtues: greater representativeness, a lower possibility of domination by a single party, and a built-in system of checks and balances. None of these, however, is the *raison d'être* of coalition government in India, which is entirely an unintended outcome of a particular political configuration in which ethnic mobilization by a proliferating number of political parties (there were thirty-eight political parties represented in the last general election in 1999, and 169 parties put up candidates in that election)[10] has fragmented the vote to the point where its effects can no longer be contained by the majoritarian first-past-the-post electoral system. As such, the particular quality of coalition government that so exercised and worried political analysts through the 1990s was its presumed inherent instability. The experience of a stable coalition government since 1999 has laid those fears to rest, and so imparted to coalition government a new and quite unearned sheen.

Biju Janata Dal), while others, such as the Telugu Desam Party or the Akali Dal, were specifically regional in nature. While most of these are single-state parties, there is a difference between those that can succeed only at the level of one state and those that identify themselves more or less strongly with the regional culture and language of the state. Together with older existing regional parties such as the Dravidian parties, the Dravida Munnetra Kazhagam (DMK) and All India Anna Dravida Munnetra Kazhagam (AIADMK) in Tamil Nadu, they contributed to a major transformation of the party system beginning in the late 1980s, with the fragmentation of parties leading to a higher fragmentation of the vote and therefore the necessity of coalitions. On the decentering of India's polity, see John Echeverri-Gent, "Politics in India's Decentered Polity," in *India Briefing: Quickening the Pace of Change*, ed. Alyssa Ayres and Philip Oldenburg (Armonk, NY: M.E. Sharpe, 2002), 19–53.

8. With exceptions like Mayawati's Bahujan Samaj Party, whose unpredictability is now seen as mercurial and unreliable rather than clever and strategic.

9. *A Time of Coalitions: Divided We Stand* also happens to be the title of a recent book by Paranjoy Guha Thakurta and Shankar Raghuraman (New Delhi: Sage, 2004), which argues that coalitions are not a temporary aberration, but are here to stay.

10. These included, as per the categorization of the Election Commission, 7 national parties, 40 state parties, and 122 registered parties. In the Fourteenth Lok Sabha, 37 parties are represented.

But a distinction needs to be made between the form and substance of coalition government, for rather like Indian democracy, the coalition phenomenon in India too is *sui generis*. The political system today certainly resembles a coalition in form, but it is only nominally a coalition of substance. Each of the smaller parties in the coalition has a fairly narrow social or regional base, and their coming together is necessitated by the peculiar requirements of a majoritarian political system. In form, the coalition government will endure for the foreseeable future. In substance, however, it is worth extrapolating from the experience of the last NDA coalition, which was very much a government of, for, and by the BJP, making it dangerous, if not foolish, to impute virtue to what is little more than a necessity. All of the important policy initiatives—whether concerning ideologically sensitive history textbooks or economically consequential disinvestment—were piloted by BJP ministers, which was hardly surprising given that most of the important ministerial portfolios were retained by the BJP. Other than the Defense Ministry (led by George Fernandes of the Samata Party)[11] and the Ministry of Railways (headed by Nitish Kumar of the same party), no major portfolio was, at the end of its term, in the hands of a BJP alliance partner. It is for this reason important to distinguish between coalition politics and government formation, on the one hand, and coalition governance, on the other, to the extent that the politics makes possible the formation of a multiparty government, even though one party claims and obtains inordinately greater power in the actual processes of policy-making and governance.

In the Cabinet reshuffle of May 2003, the BJP succeeded in offending the leader of one of its alliance partners, Trinamool Congress Chief Mamata Banerjee, by failing to include her in the Cabinet. Likewise, the Dravida Munnetra Kazagham (Party for the Progress of Dravidam) wanted to retain for one of its own members the important commerce portfolio that had fallen vacant on the death of its leader, Murasoli Maran, but the ministry was transferred to the charge of Arun Jaitley, the BJP law minister. The key position of minister of state for home affairs was filled by inducting the saffron-robed Swami Chinmayanand, a candidate supported by the VHP. It is a telling commentary on the nature of

---

11. The Samata Party, which had pulled out of the Janata Dal (U) in 2000, formally merged with it again in October 2003. However, this merger was rejected by the Election Commission chiefly on account of representations made to it by disaffected and expelled members of the Samata Party. In any event, members of the erstwhile Samata Party contested the 2004 election under the JD(U) banner.

coalition *dharma*, as some have called it, that at the end of its term in office, the BJP held a disproportionate share of ministerial positions: twenty-two out of thirty-one Cabinet ministers, four out of seven ministers of state holding independent charge, and thirty-five out of forty-two minister of state positions.

The common minimum program of the NDA in the last general election of 1999 had noticeably underplayed one area of disagreement between the alliance partners: that of the normative and political value of secularism in the Indian polity, and the oft-heard claim of the BJP's allies to be secular.[12] However, the BJP leadership's endorsement of rank communalism and the complicity of its government in Gujarat in the brutal communal violence of February 2002[13] put the coalition to the test—and called the bluff of the alliance partners quite effectively. At critical moments such as these, the allies did not desert the ship of state. Or, to mix metaphors, the loaves and fishes of offices of state kept them from doing so. As such, though the BJP was only the dominant partner in the alliance, it was clearly the glue that held it together. It remained, until the end, the unrivaled captain of this ship, with all passengers inclined to stay on board in the hope of handsome dividends.[14] In popular as in political discourse, there had occurred a certain blurring of the boundary between the BJP and the NDA. The achievements of the government at the center were perceived and indeed claimed as the achievements of the BJP. Equally, for critics of the BJP, its failures also

---

12. Much of the contestation in Indian politics over the last decade and a half has been over the meaning of secularism, a fight between those who believe in the importance of minority rights and those whose agenda is, at its core, defined by a majoritarian and exclusivist politics. Some view secularism as synonymous with a state policy of equidistance from all religions, while others see it simply as an injunction to treat all religions equally. In politics, all sides claim that *their* interpretation of the principle of treating all religions equally is the correct one. The Indian Constitution provides for the freedom to practice and propagate one's religion, along with cultural and educational rights for minorities; it prohibits discrimination on the basis of religion. However, the BJP describes the Congress Party's protective attitude toward minorities as "pseudo-secularism" and "minority appeasement" and, generally, as somehow shortchanging the majority community of Hindus by treating other religions as deserving of special privileges, and therefore unequally.

13. In February 2002, one carriage in a train carrying pilgrims from Ayodhya was set afire in a small town called Godhra in Gujarat. The death of approximately forty people in this incident became the pretext for some of the most horrific violence seen in independent India: the brutal killing of an estimated two thousand Muslims, the rape of women, and the plunder and destruction of the property of Muslim citizens.

14. Halfway through the general election, Vajpayee surprised his allies by issuing a public appeal for a mandate for his party alone. Admitting that a coalition of more than twenty parties was too unwieldy, he said that the BJP would be more effective at governance if it secured a majority on its own. Once again, the remark apparently did not ruffle any feathers among the allies.

redounded to the discredit of all members of the coalition, who appeared to be in serious danger of losing their identities except in the regions from which they were elected.

The Congress-led UPA government that came to power in May 2004 may well reproduce this trend, if the Congress has the required ability to stay in command. The Council of Ministers has forty-two ministers from the Congress Party and twenty-five ministers from eight other parties, of which three parties have only one ministerial berth each. The ministers of Cabinet rank number twenty-eight, and the Congress accounts for seventeen of that number. As with the previous government, the major portfolios—in this case, home, external affairs, finance, defense, and human resources development—remain with the Congress itself.

This account of the ministries in both the former and present governments is consistent with the reading of the political equilibrium that at the federal level there is a multiparty system organized around essentially two poles, represented by the BJP and the Congress, and the minor parties group and regroup around these poles. At the state level, what prevails is an essentially bipolar system, and the two major parties are the principal contenders for power in only seven states: Madhya Pradesh, Rajasthan, Gujarat, Himachal Pradesh, and the three rather small states of Delhi, Chhattisgarh, and Uttaranchal. The total number of members of Parliament (MPs) returned to the Lok Sabha from these states is 107, or less than 20 percent of the total number of seats. In the remaining twenty-three states (of a total of thirty), the contest is not between the Congress and the BJP, but rather between the Congress *or* the BJP as one of the principal contenders, with a state party representing the other pole. Jharkhand is the only state in which the BJP is the polar opposite of a non-Congress party. By contrast, the Congress provides the polar opposite to non-Congress parties in six states (Orissa, Punjab, Assam, Haryana, Andhra Pradesh, and, as the major party in a coalition, Kerala). These account for a total of 120 seats. In most of these states, the BJP is at best an ally or a junior partner of the main party opposing the Congress. In the states of West Bengal and Tamil Nadu, which together account for a substantial eighty-one seats, neither the Congress nor the BJP has any effective presence. A substantial 196 seats in the Lok Sabha are shared between Uttar Pradesh, Bihar, Karnataka, and Maharashtra. In the first two, neither the Congress nor the BJP has any substantial support, while in the latter two, both parties are partnering with the major contenders for power, suggesting that a degree of polarity may be emerging.

At the national level, therefore, India has a nominal multiparty system in which there are only two serious contenders, neither of which is capable of coming to power on its own. In the most recent Lok Sabha, the BJP and the Congress together accounted for just over 50 percent of the vote share and a total of 296 seats, just over half of the total number of seats in the house. In the recent elections to state legislatures, the combined vote share of these two parties was in the region of 75 percent, suggesting that even in these largely bipolar states, approximately one-fourth of the voters favor other parties. In the 2004 general election, the BJP and the Congress together accounted for 283 seats, a little more than half the total strength of the lower house. The combined vote share of the two parties was just 48.85 percent.

In the course of the 2004 election, even as television analysts debated endlessly the issue of whether exit polls would have a "bandwagon" or an "underdog" effect, the voters registered utter contempt for television analysts and sundry pundits alike and voted confidently for the best local or regional alternative, suggesting that the national polity today is merely an aggregation of the regional. The persuasiveness of this argument lies in the fact that no party can entertain hopes of coming to power on its own, and that "the map of party competition has to be read not at the national level but at the state level."[15] There can be little disagreement about this, as with the phenomenon's effect upon the strategies of smaller parties, which no longer seek to be as encompassing and aggregative as possible but instead identify a niche constituency from which they seek to maximize returns. The incentive to have a clear-cut ideological position has clearly been reduced.

However, the valence of the regional parties depends crucially upon their affiliation with a nominally national (though not necessarily pan-Indian) party, and hence the regional and the national are bound together in an intimate dynamic characterized by interdependence and mutuality. As such, the Congress's success in the 2004 election was substantially the result of clever electoral arithmetic and strategic alliances with the right regional parties. None of these state-level parties have any independent valence at the national level, except through affiliation with a national party. The definition of "national" party has of course changed over time, and having a substantial presence in every state across the

---

15. Suhas Palshikar, "Revisiting State Level Parties," *Economic and Political Weekly* 39, nos. 14 and 15 (April 3–10, 2004): 1477.

country has less and less to do with it: the Congress remains a national party mainly for historical reasons, while the BJP is a national party partly because it is the successor to another national party, the Jana Sangh, and partly because its electoral successes are not limited to a couple of states, encouraging it to entertain pan-Indian ambitions.

The End of Ideology?

The second trend that deserves careful evaluation is the apparent shift in the center of political gravity to the right, as ideological differences are perceived to have dissolved. There is some merit in this characterization, though it is at least partially based upon an argument about the normalization of the BJP that is exaggerated and must be questioned. It has been said that the BJP has undergone a process of "congressization," in that it has absorbed many of the features considered characteristic of the Congress. These include opportunistic inclusivism (as seen in the desperate pre-election attempts to patronize and co-opt Muslim politicians in search of a saleable pluralist image), factionalism (in contrast to the BJP's earlier image of being a disciplined cadre-based party),[16] and corruption (vitiating and exposing the hollowness of its claim to be a party that stood for a clean public life, free of corruption). Most recently, the normalization of the BJP has come to be seen not so much in terms of its acquisition of Congress-like proclivities, but rather in the perception that it has forsaken its Hindu nationalist agenda. This perception was fueled in the state assembly elections of December 2003 by the fact that the campaign platform was overtly developmental, focusing on the failures of incumbent Congress governments to provide development, encapsulated in the devoutly aspired-for trinity of electricity, roads, and water. The one state election that the BJP lost in that round was Delhi, where the Congress chief minister, Sheila Dikshit, was seen to have actually delivered on these fronts. The election campaign of 2004 witnessed another unusual development that strengthened the per-

---

16. Elements of factionalism in the party have been noted by Christophe Jaffrelot's study of the Madhya Pradesh unit of the BJP in the 1990s. Factionalism here, Jaffrelot showed, was different from that in other parties, as it expressed a tension between the party-building style of the RSS-trained *sanghatanists* (organization men) and others who were recruited into the party but did not possess a committed RSS background. This tension, of course, had everything to do with struggles over power and offices and led to a decline in party discipline. Cf. Christophe Jaffrelot, "BJP and the Challenge of Factionalism in Madhya Pradesh," in *The BJP and the Compulsions of Politics in India*, 2d ed., ed. Thomas Blom Hansen and Christophe Jaffrelot (New Delhi: Oxford University Press, 2004), 267–90.

ception that the BJP was becoming a moderate—because less communal—party. The BJP leadership actively courted the Muslim vote. Despite the obvious spuriousness of this phenomenon, however, it generated a debate in which the pronouncements of Muslim community leaders, the opinion of the Urdu press, as well as the responses of other political parties are significant. Let us examine each of the elements of the supposed normalization of the BJP: its apparent inclusivism, factionalism, and corruption.

Inclusivism

Deputy Prime Minister L.K. Advani's campaign for the parliamentary election of April–May 2004 took the form of the *Bharat Uday Yatra*,[17] crisscrossing India from Kanyakumari in the south to Pathankot in the north, and from Porbandar in western India to Puri in the east. The *yatra* covered close to eight thousand kilometers, with visits to 121 parliamentary constituencies, spread across twelve states and union territories. At its launch in Kerala—where the BJP is conspicuous by its absence from the political stage—local Muslim clerics and (in a state which has a substantial Christian population) some Christian priests shared the platform with Advani and the BJP's handful of token Muslim leaders. On this campaign Advani frequently claimed that he cherished the diversity of India, but equally often—depending upon the location, as in Ayodhya itself[18]—he emphasized his party's continued commitment to

---

17. The *rath yatra* in Hindu religious practice refers to a chariot in which a temple idol is taken out in a procession thronged by worshippers. Advani had undertaken a notorious *rath yatra* in 1990, before the demolition of the Babri Masjid in 1992, which was believed to be largely instrumental in creating a wave of popular opinion in favor of the demolition. This *rath yatra* was intended to convey a more consensual image of a "national" leader of a plural society. *Bharat Uday* is a literal translation of India Rising, a name uncannily similar to that of the controversial advertisement blitz that the NDA government ran before the electoral code of conduct came into force. "India Shining," an expensive campaign in the electronic as well as print media, sought to project the economic successes of India. It was widely criticized for using taxpayers' money to subsidize what was practically an advance election campaign for the BJP/NDA. It was also criticized for ignoring the very real issues of poverty and farmer suicides in the countryside.

18. Ayodhya, a small town in the state of Uttar Pradesh, is believed by devout Hindus to be the birthplace of the Hindu god Rama. The claim, advanced in a strident campaign led by the BJP, was that the Babri Masjid (a mosque believed to have been built by a nobleman in the reign of the Mughal Emperor Babar) was the precise site of the birth of Rama, and it was to reclaim this site that the mosque was forcibly torn down by members of the BJP, RSS, and VHP in December 1992.

the building of the Ram temple in Ayodhya, a commitment described in greater historic detail in Richard Davis's chapter in this volume. It is significant that even before the election manifesto of the NDA alliance was launched, the BJP released its "Vision Document" on March 30, the Hindu festival of Ramnavami. The document promised Ram Rajya, literally "kingdom of Rama" and metaphorically a "paradise of good governance."

The attempts by the BJP to recruit important Muslim leaders scored some ostensible successes, especially with the induction of Arif Mohammed Khan, the Congress MP who famously resigned from the Rajiv Gandhi cabinet on the issue of the *Shah Bano* case[19] and spent the intervening years in the largely *Dalit*-oriented Bahujan Samaj Party. Najma Heptullah, great-niece of Maulana Azad (a prominent Indian Muslim nationalist who championed a plural and secular India), four times Congress MP, and until recently deputy chairperson of the Rajya Sabha (upper house), also left the Congress and appeared to be cozying up to its rival. The BJP had certainly improved upon the stature of its token Muslims. Nevertheless, Arif Mohammed Khan and BJP minister Shahnawaz Khan, two of its leading Muslim candidates, lost the election, and it became clear that the party is a long way from being genuinely inclusivist and an even longer way from convincing voters that it is. A glance at the BJP's vision document alongside the NDA manifesto is instructive in this respect.

The first part of the vision document suggested the BJP's continued —albeit muted and indirect—commitment to some of the contentious issues that has long characterized its anti-minority and communal agenda: construction of the Ram temple at Ayodhya (on the site of the Babri Masjid, or "mosque of Babur," destroyed in December 1992 by BJP storm troopers), enactment of a "uniform civil code," and abrogation of Article 370 of the Constitution. On the Ayodhya issue, the vision document emphasized the importance of the judicial verdict and dialogue in an atmosphere of mutual trust and goodwill as the way forward. Similarly, it no longer called for a uniform civil code, a document that would

---

19. In the *Shah Bano* case, the Supreme Court had ruled in favor of an elderly Muslim woman divorcee receiving maintenance, thereby upholding the distinction between the criminal law of the land (which applies to all citizens equally) and the civil law (in which respect Muslim personal law provides an exemption). Less than a year after the judgment, Rajiv Gandhi's government passed a controversial law undoing the effect of the judgment. This was a blow not only to Muslim divorcees, but also to the cause of gender justice and equality, and the prominent Congress MP, Arif Mohammed Khan, resigned from Rajiv Gandhi's cabinet on this account.

eliminate the differential laws governing marriage and property rights on the basis of religion and replace them with one common legal framework for all Indian citizens. Instead, the BJP appropriated the vocabulary of gender justice to argue the need for social and political consensus on this issue. Because Muslim personal law can be discriminatory to women, one argument—indeed, one employed by feminists, including some Muslim feminists—calls for its elimination in the name of gender equality. This subtle shift in the manner in which these issues were projected led commentators to suggest that the BJP was seeking to occupy a centrist space and had moved from a hard-line position to a softer approach based on consensus. The abrogation of Article 370, which gives a special status to the state of Jammu and Kashmir, has long been one of the most controversial features of the BJP's political program. Instead of mentioning Article 370, the vision document identified the challenges in that state as those of terrorism, development, and the strengthening of governance. Interestingly, the vision statement was followed by "The BJP Agenda for the Next Five Years," a chapter that maintained a scrupulous silence on all these issues, hinting at a distinction of substance between its "vision" and its short-term "agenda." The only plausible explanation for the release of a vision document in the weeks leading up to an election, even as the common manifesto of the NDA alliance was yet to be announced, is that the BJP felt compelled to reassure its fraternal organizations in the Sangh Parivar ("Joint Family" of like-minded Hindu nationalist civic, religious, and political organizations) of its unwavering commitment to their common ideals—and to remind at least its core constituency in the electorate that it had not forsaken these altogether in the pursuit of power.

If the vision document tried to suggest that the BJP was moderating its stance on these controversial issues, the NDA manifesto accomplished exactly the opposite. For the first time, it actually brought on board the Ayodhya temple issue, though with the same caveats about the judicial verdict and the dialogue based on mutual trust and goodwill. Thus, even as the BJP sought to reinvent itself as a mainstream party, its alliance partners signaled their willingness to partake of some of its controversial core agenda. An unmistakable and telling family resemblance linked the two documents.

In the last month of the 2004 election campaign, the BJP actively courted Muslim voters, particularly in the state of Uttar Pradesh. A committee of Muslim intellectuals and clerics, the Atal Bihari Vajpayee

Himayat Caravan (Sympathizers' Committee), undertook a seventeen-day bus tour to mobilize support for the prime minister. Addressing the committee, the prime minister claimed that he (note, not his party) had always believed that the country could not progress unless Hindus and Muslims learned to live together, and it was in this spirit that he was appealing for votes, not out of greed for short-term political benefits. In a politically incorrect turn of argument, he also cited the success of his peace initiative with Pakistan as an example of his good intentions. The BJP also succeeded in getting an endorsement from the influential imam of Delhi's Jama Masjid, Syed Ahmed Bukhari. The imam generally issues a *fatwa* on the eve of an election, advising Muslims on how they should vote. This time, he expressed the view that the parties supported by Muslims in the past had taken their votes without giving anything in return, accounting for the appallingly low presence of Muslims in public employment as well as their rather low levels of educational attainment. The BJP, he argued, is different from the other parties in that it is what it seems to be—its animosity toward Muslims has never been concealed—and, therefore, its promises (in the form of a development package for the Muslim minority within six months of coming to power) could be taken at face value.

The most obvious explanation for the BJP's sudden decision to court the Muslim vote is rooted in the peculiarity of the political situation in Uttar Pradesh. The Muslim vote in Uttar Pradesh traditionally went to the Congress Party, until the demolition of the Babri Masjid during the premiership of the Congress's P.V. Narasimha Rao. A sense of betrayal sent the Muslim voter scurrying to the Samajwadi Party (SP) and the Bahujan Samaj Party (BSP), each of which had come to represent the interests of different disadvantaged caste groups. As a result of the fracturing of the vote, Uttar Pradesh has faced a series of hung assemblies in recent years. The electoral contest is invariably three- or four-cornered, with the BJP, the Congress, the SP, and the BSP contesting the elections. The BSP can fairly safely bank upon a core constituency of Scheduled Castes, while the SP has traditionally depended upon the combined strength of the Muslim and Yadav vote.[20] The BJP's efforts to woo Mus-

---

20. The Yadavs form part of the Other Backward Classes (OBC), an official category that describes the middle castes, as opposed to the higher castes on one extreme and the Scheduled Castes and Scheduled Tribes on the other. In the 1970s and 1980s, the backward castes, many of whom were farmers who had benefited from the land reform program, became politically assertive. The characterization of these groups as "backward classes" by

lims may be interpreted as a clever strategy to split the Muslim vote and so prevent it from consolidating in favor of another party.

The Muslim voters of Uttar Pradesh found themselves in an unenviable position. The SP's loyal Muslim constituency, for instance, was disturbed by two developments: first, the circumstances under which the SP government was installed in Uttar Pradesh in 2003 and its apparent willingness to do business with the BJP, and second, an ill-advised campaign poster comparing party leader Mulayam Singh Yadav with the son of the Prophet in terms of the sacrifices he had made during the Karbala tragedy 1,400 years ago. This advertisement, published in Urdu newspapers, naturally angered clerics and others by its egregiousness and impudence. Despite this, the SP succeeded in obtaining the largest share of the Muslim vote, presumably because it was perceived as the most likely guarantor of the security of Muslims.[21] The BJP's unconvincing attempts at inclusivism failed to counteract the enduring, chilling effect of the 2002 riots in Gujarat, the state which contributed the most to its failure in 2004. Prominent leaders of NDA parties as diverse as the Shiv Sena and the Trinamool Congress have gone on record to state that the Gujarat violence lost them the election.

Factionalism

The second attribute that encouraged the view of the BJP's normalization is the accumulating evidence of differences within what has always been known as a highly disciplined cadre-based party. The most striking example of this was the June 2003 proclamation by party spokesman

---

official commissions was a reference to their "social and educational backwardness," on the basis of which they were granted a quota in public employment and education in 1990. The OBCs are far from being a homogeneous group, and the differences between the upper (such as the Yadavs) and lower backwards can be substantial, with a category of the Most Backward Castes also appearing on the political landscape. The Scheduled Castes are the former "untouchable" castes, so called because of the official schedule that lists the various castes that are eligible for the policies of affirmative action. The Scheduled Tribes category includes tribal communities that are similarly eligible. In today's political discourse, it is the terms *Dalit* (the oppressed) and *adivasi* (original inhabitant) that are used, following the self-definition of the latter two groups.

21. This is confirmed by the initial findings reported by the National Election Survey 2004 (CSDS), which suggest that while Muslims in many states voted overwhelmingly for the Congress Party, where there was a strong regional alternative, they chose the latter. Thus, while 72 percent of Muslims in Maharashtra and 85 percent of those in Rajasthan voted Congress, only 15 percent of Muslims in Uttar Pradesh did the same. See Sanjay Kumar and Alistair McMillan, "Caste Matters, but So Do a Whole Lot of Other Things," *The Hindu*, May 20, 2004.

Venkaiah Naidu that the next election would be fought under the joint leadership of Atal Bihari Vajpayee, the *Vikas Purush* (development man), and his deputy, L.K. Advani, the *Loh Purush* (man of iron) of the party. To the extent that this suggested an undermining of the preeminence of the prime minister, it was interpreted by agitated Vajpayee supporters as insolence, if not heresy. Vajpayee, who was abroad at the time, snubbed Naidu upon his return, saying he was "neither tired nor retired." Vajpayee's image, which had been carefully cultivated to project him as a moderate liberal in a right-wing party, initially helped to make the BJP acceptable to political allies. His admirers described him as the right man in the wrong party—even as his detractors described him as a mask that concealed the real face of the BJP. By contrast Advani, with his grip over the cadres and organizational apparatus of the party, has always represented the authentic, tough face of the BJP.

More evidence of differences within the party surfaced when, following the special court's verdict on the demolition of the Babri Masjid at Ayodhya to frame criminal charges against him (though not against Advani), the human resource development minister, M.M. Joshi, resigned from the Cabinet. The resignation was cleverly timed, as the prime minister was in the United States at the time. However, the anticipated chorus of support from the RSS—whose agenda the minister was known to conscientiously advance—was not forthcoming, and the minister found that his attempt to claim the high moral ground vis-à-vis Advani (the actual leader of the Ayodhya movement) had failed. In these instances—and numerous others—the BJP's image as a tightly controlled party of disciplined cadres has been dented, and it can be assumed that the desire to hold on to political power was strong enough to overcome any discomfiture about compromises with ideological purity.

Corruption

Finally, the BJP demonstrated conclusively that it was not quite "the party with a difference" on the issue of corruption. In 2001 the party president, Bangaru Laxman, was videotaped accepting a bribe of Rs. 100,000 (approximately US$2,200; $10,000 in PPP terms) in a sting operation by *Tehelka*, an Internet magazine. The same operation had led to the resignation of the defense minister, George Fernandes, who subsequently rejoined the Cabinet. A sting operation in the run-up to the December 2003 Assembly election targeted the BJP's candidate for chief minister of Chhattisgarh, Dilip Singh Judeo, who was also the union minister for environment and forests. The sting, organized by the son of the Congress chief minister of Chhattisgarh, Ajit Jogi, resulted in an incriminating video of Judeo accepting a cash bribe for allowing mining leases in proscribed forest areas. A red-faced BJP was compelled to send Judeo packing. However, just days before the election Judeo retaliated by producing a letter, signed by Jogi, offering bribes to opposition (BJP) members of the legislative assembly to defect to his party. Despite these dramatic developments just before the election, and amidst allegations of corruption flying thick and fast in both directions, the election results from the relatively remote tribal areas of the state showed that the BJP had managed to muster support from this section of the people.

Saffronization of Political Discourse

The BJP has certainly become normalized in terms of its propensity to factional infighting and corruption. The claim of inclusivism, however, is deceptive. While there has been a "congressization" of the BJP, there is also evidence of what could be termed a "BJP-ization" of the Congress. This is not to suggest that ideological consensus prevails, although that is broadly true in the matter of economic reforms. For the rest, the defining difference between the Congress (and its affiliates) and the BJP (and its partners) has been their position on pluralism in Indian society. Over the last decade, this crucial issue has been routinely brought out of the cupboard and dusted up before elections, but it had begun to look a trifle moth-eaten in recent months and, indeed, was not a central issue in the 2004 poll. The core importance of the issue has been sordidly compromised by its cynical manipulation and even abuse by a host of political parties that have assumed the rather unlikely mantle of the torchbearers of secularism in India. For instance, Laloo Prasad Yadav, the leader of the Rashtriya Janata Dal (National People's Party), the ruling party in Bihar, has long claimed to be the protector of secularism and minorities. However, he apparently saw no contradiction in fielding, from his party, an RSS candidate who was actively involved in the demolition of the Babri Masjid and another candidate who has been a local leader of the Vishwa Hindu Parishad, a particularly rabid organization belonging to the Sangh Parivar.[22]

---

22. The first was Rajesh Kumar Majhi, a former BJP leader who is also a *Dalit*, while the second was Bhagwanlal Sahni, a former VHP leader who has been fielded against Defense Minister George Fernandes.

As far as the Congress is concerned, this shift could be traced back to its cautious and measured responses to the February 2002 Gujarat riots. Congress President Sonia Gandhi visited Ahmedabad in the wake of the riots but—in a political *faux pas* of some magnitude—failed to call on the bereaved family of a veteran Muslim congressman, Ehsan Jafri, who had been murdered during the riots. In the election campaign for the Gujarat state assembly elections in December 2002, reluctant to alienate an electorate with heightened Hindu sensibilities, Congress leaders were not particularly forthright in their condemnation of the violence against Muslims. Indeed, Sonia Gandhi chose to launch the Congress campaign from the precincts of the Ambaji temple. This attempted appeal to Hindu sentiment did not fetch the votes, but it did win the party the epithet of "the B Team of the BJP."

Congress governments in the states too were not averse to flirting with Hindu nationalism. In 2003, Digvijay Singh, the Congress chief minister of Madhya Pradesh, wrote to the prime minister, calling upon the central government to ban cow slaughter. Cow slaughter is banned in many Indian states;[23] by attempting to make a national issue of it, Singh was evidently trying to outdo his electoral rival (and eventual successor) Uma Bharati, a *sanyasin* (female renunciant), in proving his Hindu credentials and appealing to a Hindu constituency through an argument very much in the mold of "we are better Hindus than you." In a rather similar vein, Singh wrote to the RSS chief professing shock at the organization's reluctance to donate (as opposed to sell) a piece of land in Ujjain, the sacred site of the Simhastha Kumbh, for a religious fair scheduled for March 2004. In his letter, Singh claimed that, as a devout Hindu himself, he was surprised that the RSS would ask Rs. 200 million—five times the market price—for sacred land. Neither attempt at playing the Hindu card succeeded in getting Singh reelected for a third term.

Most recently, there have been a series of attacks on *Shivaji: A Hindu King in Islamic India*, a new book on the seventeenth-century Maratha king, Chhatrapati Shivaji, written by American historian James Laine and published by Oxford University Press. Here, the Nationalist Congress Party (formed by the former Congress dissident Sharad Pawar, now a minister in the central government), which rules Maharashtra in alliance with the Congress, wrested the initiative from the BJP and the

---

23. Some Indian states have had such a ban for several years, though even here it does not affect the routine killing of cows for personal consumption, as in Tamil Nadu or Andhra Pradesh.

Shiv Sena by banning the book on the grounds that it contains derogatory references to Shivaji's parentage and so hurts Maratha pride. Members of an organization called the Sambhaji Brigade, allegedly supported by Pawar, vandalized the Bhandarkar Oriental Research Institute, a library of rare books and invaluable manuscripts in Pune, where Laine had consulted reference materials. Once again, in a contest to prove their greater loyalty to Maratha identity, depths of absurdity were plumbed when a BJP leader demanded a ban on Jawaharlal Nehru's *Discovery of India*, claiming that it too contained defamatory remarks about Shivaji—even as the ruling party called upon Interpol to arrest James Laine! Despite apologies from the author and the publisher, the state government refused to drop the charges.

By contrast, the Congress's position on economic reforms has remained more or less consistent. The reforms were in fact launched during the premiership of Narasimha Rao of the Congress Party (1991–96). At this time, the BJP—consistent with *its* cultural nationalist agenda—had opposed the entry of foreign capital and advanced the idea of indigenous capitalist development. In subsequent years, particularly under the United Front government of 1996–98, the Congress attributed its loss of mandate partly to the reforms process and—at a party conclave at Pachmarhi in September 1998—even paid halfhearted lip service to its old socialist agenda. In 2004, seeing its thunder stolen by the gung ho liberalizers of the BJP, the party finally decided to reappropriate the reforms, claiming first authorship by foregrounding the contribution of Dr. Manmohan Singh and suggesting that if elected it would aggressively pursue the reform initiatives already under way. The Congress also tried to recover its lost constituency among the poor by speaking of reforms with a human face and safety nets. On economic issues, as on secularism, the Congress seemed to be attempting a difficult balancing act, running with the BJP hare and hunting with the ghost of the old Congress hound. Its relative success in the election seems to have been a function of smart alliances with regional parties rather than a skillful balancing of contrary ideological tendencies. The latter task will in fact be its major challenge in a government dependent upon the support of the parties of the left.

Caste and Tribe: Shifting Political Loyalties

The foregrounding of issues of development in recent election campaigns at the state and the center generated some optimism that the heyday of caste and community is over, as the essentially secular impulse to power dominates. This is actually an illusion, partly because it is well known that political parties have, over the years, themselves aided and abetted the construction of ethnic identities in the search for votes in an intensely competitive polity. However, in Uttar Pradesh and Bihar—where this phenomenon has been most marked—ample evidence suggests that there is little scope for a further fragmentation of the vote, with most caste groups in these states being more or less permanently identified with an individual or a political party. This ossification reduces the number of the floating vote that can cause an electorally significant swing. Of course, the parties in question do not invariably put up candidates belonging to the core constituency of the party. For instance, Mayawati's BSP is known to eagerly field upper-caste candidates. The choice of candidate depends upon the caste composition of the constituency, the degree of polarity in the contest, and the strategies of rivals. It is all too easy to overstate the role of caste in determining the way people vote. It has been demonstrated, for instance, that support for the BJP may be higher among the upper castes but also increases with a higher class position regardless of the caste to which the voter belongs. Similarly, the *Dalit* vote of the Bahujan Samaj Party declined from 59.2 percent in 1996 to 50.5 percent in 1998, and it has begun to attract upper-caste candidates (this vote share having increased from 3.6 percent in 1996 to 10.2 percent in 1998).[24] Clearly, a properly nuanced picture of voters' preferences can only emerge from a combination of caste, class, education, and occupation.[25]

One of the most intriguing political developments in 2003 was the demand, by an organization called the Social Justice Front led by Devi Singh Bhati, for the inclusion of the poorer sections of the upper-caste Rajputs and Brahmins in the list of backward classes in Rajasthan. In terms of the caste-politics nexus, this demand was an attempt to counter Jat domination in Rajasthan with a Rajput-Brahmin combine that could arguably influence the outcome of the elections in at least two-fifths of Assembly constituencies. The Congress chief minister of Rajasthan had already recommended such a quota, and the BJP, which could hardly be

---

24. Rajendra Vora, "Decline of Caste Majoritarianism in Indian Politics," in *Indian Democracy: Meanings and Practices*, ed. Rajendra Vora and Suhas Palshikar (New Delhi: Sage, 2004), 287.

25. Subrata K. Mitra and V.B. Singh, *Democracy and Social Change in India* (New Delhi: Sage, 1999), 139.

seen lacking in sensibility toward what has been *its* core constituency of upper castes, immediately stood up to be counted as well. However, this took the overall quota percentage (for all backward castes and classes) in Rajasthan to 63 percent, well over the 50 percent limit laid down by the Supreme Court. This demand was referred by the Union Cabinet to the attorney general, who recommended the establishment of a new Commission on Backward Classes to consider the matter. Meanwhile, as the 2004 election campaign gathered momentum, the Social Justice Front found itself upstaged, with various upper-caste associations, such as the Brahmin Samaj, voicing support for the BJP in the 2004 election. Eventually, Devi Singh Bhati himself joined the BJP.

In Uttar Pradesh, the state where caste politics matters most, there was some evidence of gotra-based (subcaste-based) politics. This was apparently fueled by the recognition that the affirmative action in the post-Mandal period has benefited mainly the Yadavs (among the "Other Backward Classes" represented by the Samajwadi Party) and the Jatavs (among the *Dalits* dominant in the Bahujan Samaj Party). A new, though relatively insignificant, phenomenon became evident: parties based upon the support of a single caste or a subcaste such as the Kurmis, Khushwahas, or Mallahs. Most of these were parties led by single individuals. Both developments—the proposal for upper-caste reservation as well as the gotra-based parties of Uttar Pradesh—could suggest that caste politics has reached not only a plateau but also perhaps a point of trivialization and cannot be redefined much further.

What does this imply for the core social constituencies of the two major parties? Historically, the social base of the Jana Sangh, the organizational predecessor of the BJP, was dominated almost exclusively by the Brahmin and Bania (commercial) castes, leading some to deride it as the party of traders and merchants. This appellation has tended somewhat to stick, with the BJP attracting more urban voters than rural. In class terms, it is the middle class that is most likely to vote BJP. Data (from surveys conducted before the general elections of 1996, 1998, and 1999)[26] regarding the occupational patterns of voters show that the BJP is supported by people of a higher occupational status, such as professionals or white-collar workers, and that the BJP has consis-

---

26. The data in this paragraph are taken from V.B. Singh, "The Rise of the BJP and the Decline of the Congress," in *Indian Democracy: Meanings and Practices,* ed. Rajendra Vora and Suhas Palshikar (New Delhi: Sage, 2004), 313–22.

tently enjoyed much greater support from male voters than from female voters.[27]

On the other hand, the Congress has enjoyed the support of unskilled workers, agricultural workers, and artisans, a fact that is also reflected in its traditional social base, which consists of disadvantaged groups such as religious minorities (primarily Muslims), *Dalits* (Scheduled Castes), and *adivasis* (Scheduled Tribes). Though this base has been eroded, fragmented, and redistributed across the many regional and caste-based parties which have come into existence over the last decade, the Congress retains its pre-eminence as "the party of the downtrodden."[28] The BJP's traditional image of an upper-caste party has, on the other hand, been further strengthened by its image as an upper-class party, supported by prosperous social groups rather than the poor. This was reinforced by surveys conducted before the December 2003 Assembly elections that suggested that younger and more educated voters are more likely to support the BJP. A recent survey of eighteen- to twenty-four year olds has reaffirmed this, even as it registers a rather worrying trend in terms of opinions about minorities, with 79 percent of young people stating that they are not comfortable with neighbors from other communities.[29] This is an alarming sign of the ideological impact of the BJP over the last decade and a reminder that urban and prosperous young Indians are not necessarily liberal or secular.

The BJP also managed to mobilize an astonishing degree of support among the *adivasis* (tribals) of central and western India. While the Scheduled Castes in northern India have moved their support from the Congress to parties like the Bahujan Samaj Party (of mostly north Indian provenance) that claim to authentically represent them, the Scheduled Tribes have no party—other than small state-specific ones like the Jharkhand Mukti Morcha—to which they could be said to have a natural affinity. The BJP's affinal organizations in the Sangh Parivar have been working zealously in tribal areas to counter what they describe as the sinister propaganda of Christian missionaries in these regions. The Chris-

---

27. The BJP has repeatedly proclaimed its commitment to the passage of the draft Women's Reservation Bill, which would reserve 33 percent of seats in Parliament and state legislatures for women. However, the bill has been hanging fire for seven years already, in the absence of what is politely termed a political consensus. Despite the fact that five states presently have women chief ministers, all parties continue to propose pitifully few women candidates.

28. Yogendra Yadav, "The New Congress Voter," *Seminar*, no. 526 (June 2004): 68.

29. *India Today*, May 3, 2004.

tian organizations—some of which have been running schools and providing health facilities for the tribes for more than a century—are accused of large-scale religious conversions and subjected to hate mail, abuse, and violence. The strategy of the RSS has been to obtain the support of the *adivasi*s by invoking an inclusive Hindu tradition, in which these tribal peoples—*vanvasis* (forest dwellers) in their lexicon—are invited, in so-called homecoming programs, to return to the Hindu fold from which they have been alienated. Another affiliate in the Sangh Parivar, the VHP, has also joined hands in this effort. The RSS runs institutions like the Sewa Bharati, the Saraswati Shishu Kendra, and the Vanvasi Kalyan Ashrams, which provide basic educational and health services and also organize self-help groups. The activities of these institutions are heavily inflected by storytelling from the epics, exposure to the Hindu religious tradition, and, of course, a strong message of political support for the BJP.[30] These activities partially explain the unusual participation of tribals in the February 2002 anti-Muslim violence in Gujarat. Ample evidence of the considerable penetration of the BJP in tribal regions was provided by the results of the 2003 state Assembly elections, especially those in Chhattisgarh, Madhya Pradesh, and Rajasthan, in which it has been estimated that the Vanvasi Kalyan Ashrams helped the BJP win seventy-seven out of the ninety-nine seats reserved for the Scheduled Tribes.[31]

The creation of the new state Chhattisgarh in 2000, carved out of Madhya Pradesh, was based upon its predominantly tribal population, and its first administration was a Congress government headed by Ajit Jogi, a former bureaucrat from the elite Indian Administrative Service and himself a tribal.[32] The presumption of Chhattisgarh as a Congress citadel was called into question by the electoral verdict of December 2003, which somewhat unexpectedly swept the BJP to power in this state. This was at least partly made possible by the support base created by the RSS and VHP in tribal regions of the state. The rest of the work was done by the autocratic and self-aggrandizing regime of Jogi, and the unrestrained exercise of power by his son, who held no formal position in the government.

---

30. "Saffronising the Tribal Heartland," *Frontline* (March 26, 2004): 19–26.

31. Mahesh Rangarajan, "Advantage Vajpayee," *Seminar*, no. 533 (January 2004): 37.

32. Ajit Jogi was himself embroiled in a controversy about whether he was genuinely a tribal or had managed to fake a certificate to this effect.

Crime, Corruption, and Politics

The propensity of all political parties to corruption and the nexus between crime and politics were amply demonstrated in 2003, as was the lowering of the threshold of its acceptability in society. Undoubtedly the biggest scandal of the year was the counterfeit stamp paper scam,[33] also referred to as the Telgi scam after Abdul Karim Telgi, its mastermind. Undetected for ten years as it thrived in eighteen states, the stamp paper scam led to a loss of revenues totaling approximately $7 billion at the initial official estimation. In collusion with officials from the Indian Security Press in Nasik, Telgi illegally manufactured and supplied to vendors a variety of official paper in short supply, including judicial court fee stamps, nonjudicial stamps, notarial stamps, share transfer certificates, and insurance policies. As the scandal began to be uncovered, the involvement of the Mumbai police commissioner and the Maharashtra deputy chief minister (home minister) also became apparent. The former was removed from office, and the latter resigned. While the case is still under investigation, it is clear that the Telgi operation was made possible by the active involvement of numerous politicians belonging to various political parties and of civil servants, especially police officers, who helped stall every previous investigation that could have led to its uncovering. The case demonstrated convincingly the blurring of boundaries, not just between political parties, but also between the political and the permanent executive and between the mafia and the state at all levels, from judiciary to police to elected ministers.

Even the Bahujan Samaj Party, which claims to represent the poorest sections and lowest castes of Indian society, has not remained untainted by allegations of corruption. Uttar Pradesh Chief Minister Mayawati, who uses only one name, was compelled to resign as evidence appeared of her personal financial interest in the Taj Heritage Corridor Project. Initially, this project was investigated for procedural irregularities and financial malpractices. Gradually, it emerged that while the state government had obtained central permission to beautify the Taj Mahal (by building green pathways around it) and link it with other monuments in Agra, its actual intent was to construct shopping malls and entertain-

---

33. Stamp paper is a legal instrument/document that can be used as evidence in courts. Sworn affidavits, sale deeds, cases filed in court, and other contracts and transactions must be recorded on stamp paper. Stamp paper denominations range from a few rupees for simple documents to several thousands for law suit submissions, in which they represent a percentage of the amount involved. Following the British tradition, stamp paper provides a major source of state revenue.

ment complexes in such close proximity to the monument as would be an aesthetic travesty.

While cases investigating powerful and wealthy politicians are wont to be endlessly prolonged, open assertions of closeness between politicians and criminals do attract attention. When D.P. Yadav—a well-known don, implicated in twenty-five criminal cases of murder and kidnapping, whose son was the prime accused in a high-profile murder in Delhi only a few months earlier—joined the BJP in February 2004, the resulting outcry was enough to embarrass the party into announcing, the very next day, that his membership stood withdrawn. However, there is also the phenomenon, most recently commented upon by the Patna High Court, of people charged with serious criminal offenses, and sometimes even imprisoned, contesting and with a reasonably good past record of winning—elections. In response to a public interest litigation filed by NGO Jan Chowkidar, the Patna High Court directed the Election Commission to consider countermanding elections in constituencies where criminals are contesting from the jailhouse. In the state of Bihar alone, there were seventeen such candidates, most of whom are fearsome criminals facing dozens of charges, including organized robbery, kidnapping, and murder. There were several others in Maharashtra, Uttar Pradesh, Jharkhand, and Gujarat, supported by parties as diverse as the Rashtriya Janata Dal, the Samajwadi Party, the Congress, the BJP, the Nationalist Congress Party, the Communist Party of India (Marxist-Leninist), and the Janata Dal. Existing law has no provision for debarring such individuals from contesting an election (since they are not yet proved guilty, but awaiting trial), though it does deprive them of the right to vote.[34]

Checking Excess: Public Institutions and Civil Society

Outside the mainstream political process, there are still reassuringly robust institutions such as the Supreme Court, the Election Commission, and the presidency.[35] These three institutions have been identified as

---

34. This has become a controversial provision in the Representation of People Act 1951, because in India there are an estimated 300,000 "undertrials," that is, prisoners who have not yet been proved guilty or convicted of any crime.

35. The president in India is the titular head of state, while the prime minister is the head of the government. The role of the president is essentially the same as that of a president in any parliamentary democracy: a republican variant of the constitutional monarchy.

signifying the shift from an interventionist to a regulatory state.[36] Consistent with its behavior over the last few years, the Election Commission fiercely asserted its independence as the supreme watchdog of the conduct of political parties during the election of 2004, and in its enforcement of the law regarding the declaration of their assets by candidates. The commission forced the government to suspend a government-run advertising initiative touting the country's accomplishments with the tagline, "India Shining," on the grounds that it was a case of taxpayer money being used to subsidize a political campaign that would give the BJP-NDA an electoral advantage. It also disallowed the Narmada Pujan Yatra (a political procession masquerading as a pilgrimage to the Narmada River, considered to be sacred) of Narendra Modi, the Gujarat chief minister, to celebrate the decision of the Narmada Control Authority to increase the height of the dam. This was in response to a Congress Party petition that this *yatra* was intended to get political mileage. India's president, the former nuclear scientist Dr. A.P.J. Abdul Kalam, also departed from convention to persuade people, through a radio and television broadcast, to cast their vote fearlessly; as also to openly upbraid the governor of Haryana for making partisan comments in favor of the BJP.

It is however the Supreme Court that remains, above all others, the custodian of constitutional values in India. Its most striking verdict in recent times has been that in what is popularly called the *Best Bakery* case. This case arose out of a petition to the Supreme Court by the National Human Rights Commission—an agency with little teeth, but one that was admirably forthright in its condemnation of the violence in Gujarat—regarding the acquittal (by the Gujarat High Court) of all the accused in what was one of the most brutal incidents of carnage in the Gujarat violence of February 2002. The acquittal was justified by lack of evidence, which in turn was made possible by a suspicious development during the trial, when most of the prosecution witnesses resiled from the statements they had earlier given to the police. In August 2003, a Supreme Court bench headed by Chief Justice V.N. Khare decided that the case must be retried and issued notices accordingly to the central and state governments. In April 2004, the court

---

36. Lloyd I. Rudolph and Susanne Hoeber Rudolph, "Redoing the Constitutional Design: From an Interventionist to a Regulatory State," in *The Success of India's Democracy,* ed. Atul Kohli (Cambridge: Cambridge University Press, 2001).

made this case an occasion to comment on the distortions in the criminal justice system in the country, and the partisan nature of the Gujarat High Court. It raised issues of inadequate witness protection, the improper conduct of the trial by the public prosecutor, and, above all, the role of the courts, which "are not expected to be tape recorders" but should "control the proceedings effectively so that [the] ultimate objective (i.e., truth) is arrived at."[37] The judiciary was forthright in asserting collusion between the prosecution and the accused and making this case a critical exemplar of the justice delivery system in the country.

In some cases, the Supreme Court, the Election Commission, and civil society organizations reinforced each other's efforts. A judgment of the Supreme Court in March 2003, along with an order of the Election Commission, made it mandatory for candidates to disclose under oath their material assets, educational qualifications, criminal records, and the money they owe government (in terms of unpaid bills for electricity, telephone, and accommodation). The Election Commission also made all this information available on its Web site and allowed rival candidates the right to file information that was contrary to the sworn affidavit. Several civil society organizations and the media zealously disseminated such information to citizens, in particular publicizing information about candidates with multiple criminal charges against them.[38] The Election Watch campaign—which works by bringing together a number of NGOs in individual states—was active in monitoring the Lok Sabha election in thirteen states.

The 2004 election also witnessed a greater participation than ever before of crusading individuals like Medha Patkar, the charismatic leader of the Narmada Bachao Andolan, the movement against the construction of the Sardar Sarovar dam in the Narmada Valley in western India; Arun Bhatia, the civil servant who spent a twenty-six-year career battling corruption in the public domain; and D.P. Ojha, the former Bihar policeman who had the courage to take action against mafia dons and strongmen but paid the price for performing his duty by be-

---

37. *Zahira Habibulla H. Sheikh and Another v. State of Gujarat and Others*, Supreme Court order by Justices Doraiswamy Raju and Arijit Pasayat (April 12, 2004), reproduced in *The Indian Express*, April 14, 2004.

38. In the December 2003 Madhya Pradesh Assembly elections, for instance, the Election Watch Committee found that 152 candidates had criminal records—one candidate had as many as sixty-three criminal charges filed against him.

ing ousted from office. That none of them was successful in getting elected is of course unsurprising.

Brand Marketing: The New Language of Electoral Politics?

If the increasing watchfulness of civil society organizations signifies one type of change in the electoral process in India, there is also another quite different respect in which change is apparent, in the techniques and skills being brought to bear on election management. In the December 2003 Assembly elections, the BJP had already experimented very successfully with micromanagement of the polls. Describing the campaign in Madhya Pradesh, James Manor writes:

> This writer gained access to a pre-election strategic survey of the state, developed for the BJP by professional analysts at a think tank. In thirty-one years of studying state elections, he has seen nothing to rival it. It runs to 452 pages, excluding an extensive introduction and annexes. It contains extremely detailed information—constituency by constituency—on caste composition, local conditions and problems, other parties, voters' perceptions, and the party's chances of winning. The BJP used this formidable resource systematically in candidate selection and throughout the campaign.[39]

Of course, it was the RSS that played a key role in this process, using its cadres for canvassing. In the parliamentary election, Pramod Mahajan combined micromanagement with the latest developments in communication technology. His team consisted of media and creative experts, people who compiled a vast database of recipients of SMS (mobile phone text messages) and e-mail messages, and a group that closely monitored all television channels, including music channels. The technology that Rajiv Gandhi's backroom boys once sought to harness had been successfully appropriated by the BJP. The use of GIS mapping yielded detailed information on constituencies, including the total area of a village, the number of houses in it, the number of men and women voters, and how the population had voted in past elections. All this computed data was supposed to be just a click of the mouse away to facilitate campaign strategies. While the Congress Party set up similar systems, along with

---

39. James Manor, "The Congress Defeat in Madhya Pradesh," *Seminar*, no. 534 (February 2004): 21–22.

a Web site connecting its party workers across the districts in the country, the decline of the party organization in the hinterland meant that it lacked a cadre such as that of the committed RSS workers that the BJP could depend upon. In the ultimate analysis, however, the electorate proved to be impervious to spin, and not particularly enamored of local campaign managers either.

The BJP also employed "brand managers," professionals with Ph.D.s and MBAs from American and Australian universities, working on how best to brand and market even the elderly Atal Bihari Vajpayee. The Congress's answer to this was Team 100, a group of technology-savvy youngsters to assist Rahul Gandhi to victory. The team included graduates from the London School of Economics, Leeds, and the University of California at Berkeley, apart from others who hold degrees from reputed Indian institutions and some political experience as well. Professional public relations firms made competitive bids for party accounts, and the enthusiasm with which the election came to be perceived as just another challenging marketing opportunity is perhaps partly explicable in terms of the age profile of the Indian electorate. In the 2004 election, almost half of the 675 million citizens eligible to vote were between the ages of eighteen and thirty-five years, with one hundred million of these being first-time voters. This found some reflection in a larger number of young candidates, but was also simultaneously a reminder of the entrenchment of the dynastic principle in Indian politics. It has been estimated that in 250 of the 543 constituencies, candidates belonged to political families, most often sons or daughters and sometimes spouses and siblings of politicians. This connects every sixth candidate in the election with a political family, with over one hundred families represented in the contest.[40] From the Congress, the son of Rajiv Gandhi, the son of Delhi Chief Minister Sheila Dikshit, as well as the sons of Madhavrao Scindia and Rajesh Pilot (two of the most talented Congress leaders, both of whom died young in accidents) were only a few of the political offspring who contested and won the election.

With such a large number of second-generation (and sometimes third- and fourth-generation) politicians, the dynastic principle has been not merely entrenched, but also proved its popularity well beyond the Nehru-Gandhi family to include members of all the important regional parties from all parts of the country. The entrance of so many privileged young

---

40. Prabu Chawla with Priya Sehgahl and bureaus (Cover story, Political Power). *India Today*, April 12, 2004.

people into the political arena perhaps explains the fact that, for the first time, image management and spin doctoring became the preferred techniques of doing politics, and the election—curiously, without any irony—became more about event management and marketing than substantive political issues. Indeed, even the bread-and-butter issues were clothed in spin, as in an advertising campaign popularly referred to as the "India Shining" campaign that was launched by the government in December 2003. Government advertising made a quantum leap from the usual poorly produced Directorate of Audio-Visual Publicity (DAVP) advertisements to slick films produced by the multinational advertising agency Grey Worldwide.[41] The "India Shining" campaign attempted to highlight the economic achievements of the country through a lyrical video showing economic growth, the slashing of interest rates, the availability of loans for small businesses, price stability, expanding road and telecommunication networks, and so forth.

The Election Commission banned the airing of the campaign on the ground that it was paid for with taxpayer money but was likely to give an unfair advantage to the BJP. While there is no reliable estimate of the amount of money spent on the campaign, it appears that it was part of a Rs. 100 crore (US$22 million) India Development Initiative, provided for in the official budget of 2003–2004 to promote trading and other business opportunities for India abroad. However, eventually only Rs. 87 million (nearly $2 million) of a total of Rs. 48.33 crore (more than $11 million) spent in the first phase was spent on advertising in the foreign media.

All the gloss and glamour of the "India Shining" campaign could not conceal the dismal poverty that persists and endures. Perhaps its most tragic manifestation was the sari stampede in the sitting prime minister's constituency of Lucknow, when Lalji Tandon, Vajpayee's election manager and a prominent leader of the BJP's Uttar Pradesh state unit, decided to celebrate his birthday by distributing saris to 20,000 poor women. Quite apart from this being a questionable and corrupt practice on the eve of the election, it led to a stampede in which twenty-one women were killed and many others were injured. The BJP leadership responded with insensitive excuses rather than an apology for the tragedy.

---

41. The DAVP is part of the Ministry of Information and Broadcasting, the official agency through which all government advertising is meant to be routed.

The sari episode was only one example of the desperate poverty that exposed the hollowness of the claim of "India Shining" and the utter disconnect between the prosperity experienced by the middle and upper classes in the metropolitan cities, on the one hand, and the grinding poverty that characterizes the condition of a large section of the electorate, on the other. Farmers' suicides were stark reminders of those for whom India does not yet shine, as was the demand of poor voters in the most backward districts for the "below poverty line" cards that would entitle them to subsidized food from the public distribution system. The promise of India's democracy is still far from being realized, and the voters made no secret of their awareness of this as they exercised their franchise.

The next five years will be decisive in determining the future evolution of the party system in India. If the Congress is successful in managing and sustaining a coalition, politics at the national level could well move toward replicating the experience of Kerala, where two stable coalitions have been alternating in power for some time now. This could mean the evolution of neither a two-party nor a multiparty system, but rather of a two-coalition system. However, it is still too early to discern a definite pattern of this kind, which remains, at the present moment, more a possibility than a trend.

In more substantive terms, what are the issues that are likely to drive the political process in the foreseeable future? An optimistic view would interpret the recent election result as indicating that Hindutva has lost its ability to garner votes, but this must be qualified by two caveats. The first relates to the perception that power within the BJP has moved decisively into the hands of L.K. Advani and his supporters. The recent reorganization of the party shows that those considered responsible for the BJP's defeat have nevertheless retained their positions of preeminence within the party. The more extreme elements in the Sangh Parivar in any case attribute the defeat to the BJP's abandonment of hard-line Hindutva in this election. Whether a recovery of this agenda would be in the long-term electoral interest of the BJP or would be politically suicidal for it is an issue upon which the BJP leadership will doubtless reflect, and which will determine the shape of the party in times to come. A second caveat is that although the efficacy of Hindutva in garnering votes may have declined for the present, a societal trend that is discernible, and could work to the long-term advantage of the BJP, is the greater legitimacy of

42

Table 1

Seats and Vote Share, Lok Sabha Elections 2004; by Party Grouping and State

Seats (Vote share [%])	BJP		BJP allies[a]		Congress		Congress allies[b]		Left parties[c]		Other parties[d]		Inde-pendents	
	S	VS	S	VS	S	VS	S	VS	S	VS	S	VS	S	VS
Totals	138	22.2	51	11.0	145	26.7	75	7.9	62	8.4	70	19.6	2	4.2
South														
Andhra Pradesh (42)	0	8.4	5	33.1	29	41.6	5	6.8	2	2.4	1	3.6		4.2
Karnataka (28)	18	34.8	0	1.9	8	36.8					2	24.2		2.3
Kerala (20)	0	10.4	1	1.7	0	32.1	1	6.3	18	46.1		0.9		2.5
Tamil Nadu (39)	0	5.1	0	29.8	10	14.4	25	37.2	4	5.8		4.4		3.3
Other (2)*			1				1							
Central														
Chhattisgarh (11)	10	47.8			1	40.2						8.1		3.9
Jharkhand (14)	1	33.0			6	21.4	6	19.8	1	5.8		13.1		6.9
Madhya Pradesh (29)	25	48.1			4	34.1						13.8		4.0
Rajasthan (25)	21	49.0			4	41.4						6.9		2.7
North														
Bihar (40)	5	14.6	6	22.4	3	4.5	26	39.8	0	1.9		10.2		6.6
Chandigarh (1)	0	35.2			1	52.1						9.3		3.4
Delhi (7)	1	40.7			6	54.8						3.2		1.3
Haryana (10)	1	17.2			9	42.1					0	37.6		3.1
Himachal Pradesh (4)	1	44.2			3	51.9						2.2		1.7
Jammu and Kashmir (6)	0	23.0			2	27.8	1	11.9			2	29.9	1	7.4
Punjab (13)	3	10.5	8	34.3	2	34.2			0	4.4		13.8		2.8
Uttaranchal (5)	3	41.0			1	38.3					1	17.8		2.9
Uttar Pradesh (80)	10	22.2	1	0.8	9	12.0					60	61.2		3.8
East														
Assam (14)	2	22.9	1	7.8	9	35.1			0	1.3	2	26.1		6.8
Orissa (21)	7	19.3	11	30.0	2	40.4					1	5.8		4.5

Tripura (2)	0	7.8	0	5.1	0	14.3			2	68.8	1.6	2.4
West Bengal (42)	0	8.1	1	21.0	6	14.6			35	50.7	2.3	3.3
Other (10)**	2		4		3							1
West												
Gujarat (26)	14	47.4			12	43.9	0	1.1			4.1	3.5
Maharashtra (48)	13	22.6	12	20.1	13	23.8	10	21.1			8.5	3.9
Other (4)***	1				2						1	

Sources: Spreadsheet courtesy of the Data Unit, Centre for the Study of Developing Societies (CSDS), New Delhi; Election Commission of India, *Provisional Statistical Report on General Elections, 2004, to the 14th Lok Sabha*, vol. 1, pp. 151–68 (accessed August 18, 2004 at http://www.eci.gov.in/archive/ls2004/Vol_I_LS_2004.pdf). The nuances of alliance, given in fine detail in the CSDS spreadsheet, are not reflected in this table.

* Other Southern states: Lakshwadeep (1), Pondicherry (1)

** Other Eastern states: Andaman and Nicobar Islands (1), Arunachal Pradesh (2), Manipur (2), Meghalaya (2), Mizoram (1), Nagaland (1), Sikkim (1)

*** Other Western states: Goa (2), Dadra and Nagar Haveli (1), Daman and Diu (1)

Note: Figures for parties with more than 10% of the vote are in brackets when the category has more than one party.

a BJP allies: Telugu Desam Party (Andhra); Janata Dal (United, Karnataka, Bihar, U.P., Assam); Indian Federal Democratic Party (Kerala); All India Anna Dravida Munnetra Kazhagam (Tamil Nadu); Shiromani Akali Dal (Punjab); Biju Janata Dal (Orissa); All India Trinamool Congress (Tripura, West Bengal); Shiv Sena (Maharashtra)

b INC allies: Telangana Rashtra Samithi (Andhra); Kerala Congress (Mani) (Kerala); Muslim League (Kerala); Dravida Munnetra Kazhagham [16 seats, 24.6%]; Pattali Makkal Katchi (Tamil Nadu, Pondicherry); Marumalarchi Dravida Munnetra Kazhagam (Tamil Nadu); National Congress Party (Bihar, Maharashtra [9 seats, 18.3%], Manipur); Lok Jan Shakti Party (Bihar); Rashtriya Janata Dal (Bihar [22 seats, 30.7%], Jharkhand); Jharkhand Mukti Morcha (Jharkhand [4 seats, 16.3%]); People's Democratic Party (Jammu and Kashmir); Janata Dal (Secular) (Maharashtra); Republican Party of India (A) (Maharashtra); Republican Party of India (Maharashtra); People's Republican Party [PRBP] (Maharashtra)

c Left parties: Communist Party of India (Andhra, West Bengal, Jharkhand, Kerala, Punjab, Tamil Nadu); Communist Party of India (Marxist) (Andhra, West Bengal [26 seats, 38.6%], Tripura [2 seats, 68.8%], Jharkhand, Kerala, Punjab, Tamil Nadu); Communist Party of India (Marxist-Leninist) (Assam); MCC (Jharkhand); Kerala Congress (Kerala); Janata Dal (Secular) (Kerala); IND (LF) (Kerala); Revolutionary Socialist Party (West Bengal); All India Forward Bloc (West Bengal)

d Other major parties: MIM (Andhra); Asom Gana Parishad (Assam [2 seats, 20.0%]); Indian National Lok Dal (Haryana [0 seats, 22.4%]); HVP (Haryana); Jammu and Kashmir National Conference (Jammu and Kashmir [2 seats, 22.0%]); JD (S) (Karnataka [2 seats, 20.5%]); PWP (Maharashtra); BBM (Maharashtra); Manipur People's Party (Manipur); Federal Party of Manipur (Manipur); Jharkhand Mukti Morcha (Orissa); Shiromani Akali Dal (Simranjit Singh Mann) (Punjab); Bahujan Samaj Party; Samajwadi Party (U.P. [35 seats, 26.7%]), RLD (U.P.), Samajwadi Janata Party (Rashtriya) (U.P.), National Loktantrik Party (U.P.)

political argument based on religious majoritarianism and a denial of pluralism.

Be that as it may, issues of material well-being and development will remain crucial to Indian politics in the coming years. The middle classes have already tasted the fruits of prosperity and clearly aspire to the furtherance of the reform process. But it will not be enough for the new United Progressive Alliance government to sustain a high rate of economic growth. It will also have to prove its ability to spread the benefits of growth more widely and address the basic needs of the poor. On this will depend not just the future of the new alliance in government, but also the potential of Indian democracy to respond to the needs of its citizens.

Indian Economy: New Pathways
to Growth and Development

Isher Judge Ahluwalia

The parliamentary elections of May 2004 saw the largest electorate in the world voting to replace the ruling coalition of the National Democratic Alliance (NDA), led by the Bharatiya Janata Party (BJP), with the United Progressive Alliance (UPA), led by the Congress Party. The vote raised concerns about India's prospects for continued reforms and its ability to maintain good economic performance. India's economic reforms, unlike those of many Asian economies, were in any case viewed as too hesitant to ensure robust growth. Added to this was the additional fear that the new government, which depends upon the left parties, may not be able to maintain even the modest pace of reform witnessed over the past decade. These fears are best addressed against the background of a closer look at the evolution of policies and economic performance in India in the past decade and a preliminary assessment of the Common Minimum Program (CMP), which was adopted by the government and has been endorsed but not signed by the Left.

The elections have brought to the surface a debate on how far economic reforms have improved economic conditions in the country. Claims and counterclaims were made with regard to the overall social and economic development and distribution of the gains—across income groups, between rural and urban areas, and across regions. Whatever may be the reasons behind the electoral verdict, it is clear that the "India Shining" campaign of the ruling coalition backfired in an environment of rising expectations and resulted in a strong anti-incumbency message from the electorate. The current debate on what is a feasible and sustainable pace of reforms for India, especially given the increased hope for better economic conditions, needs to be addressed in this context. The true challenge for India lies in its ability to work democratically to generate the economic growth necessary to eradicate poverty and improve economic and social conditions.

The Indian economy has recorded a respectable rate of growth of gross domestic product (GDP) over the past twenty-five years: 5.6 percent per annum. This is a significant improvement over the earlier record of 3.5 percent per annum growth from 1950 to 1980. Indeed, the growth performance of the past two decades places India in the set of the ten fastest growing economies in the world. The significantly better growth performance after 1980 was also associated with some success in lowering the growth rate of the population from over 2 percent per annum to 1.7 percent per annum. This has implied an average growth in per capita income of about 4 percent per annum over the past two decades. By contrast, the increase in per capita income over the preceding three decades was about 1.5 percent per annum. The proportion of the population in poverty, which fluctuated around 50 percent for much of the period before 1980, has now come down to about 25 percent. On human development, the progress has been substantial but not adequate to meet the millennium development goals, let alone the more ambitious goals set in the Tenth Plan, which covers the period from 2002–2003 to 2006–2007. Although India's Five-Year Plans have decreased in importance since the first one began in 1951–52, they have all along provided goals for economic and social development. The new UPA government, with its emphasis on infrastructure, health and education systems, and programs for poverty alleviation, has brought the Tenth Plan more into the forefront of policy discussions.

The economic transformation of India is being accomplished through gradual and at times complex changes in policies in the direction of market orientation and greater integration with the world economy and without any big ideological U-turns.[1] The process has been carried forward through a slow building of consensus within a noisy atmosphere of vested interests in what is the largest democracy in the world. The fact that an

---

1. While providing an overview of the process of economic reform, Montek Singh Ahluwalia spells out the rationale behind the gradualism at work; see "Economic Reforms in India since 1991: Has Gradualism Worked?" *Journal of Economic Perspectives* 16, no. 3 (Summer 2002). For reviews of India's economic reforms, also see John Williamson and Roberto Zagha, "From Slow Growth to Slow Reform" (paper presented at the CREDPR Annual Conference on Indian Economic Policy Reform, Stanford, CA, June 3–4, 2002); and T.N. Srinivasan, "Indian Economic Reforms: A Stocktaking" (paper presented at the CREDPR Annual Conference on Indian Economic Policy Reform, Stanford, June 5–7, 2003).

enterprising private sector has all along been an important feature of India's economic landscape meant that reform efforts were directed at reenergizing this sector by widening its field of operation and challenging its energies through greater competition and better regulation.

Since 1991, various political parties at the center and states have taken turns moving the economic reform process forward, albeit in a haphazard manner. The underlying objective has been to hasten economic growth to facilitate alleviation of poverty. Most recently, until they were voted out of power in May 2004, the NDA was very vocal in espousing the cause of pro-market economic reform to boost economic growth. This was partly because the alliance was led by the BJP, which has been traditionally a party of the right of center, and partly because they felt that the cumulative effect of the policy reforms of the past decade was now showing results and they could benefit from building this constituency. The Congress Party, on the other hand, which had initiated the reforms and was more cognizant of the distributional aspect of the change during the transition, was watching from the sidelines and waiting its turn. In any event, the pace of reform continued to be gradual. There were also occasions when both the major parties came together to push the pace of liberalization further as in the case of the passing of the Insurance Act in 1999, which allowed a larger role for private investment, particularly foreign investment. Admittedly, the opening was still too little, with a cap of 26 percent on foreign investment. It is not surprising therefore that the private sector accounts for less than 20 percent of the insurance business, although the induction of competition has brought about an expansion in the size of the total market, offered a wider range of insurance services, and created substantial employment. The new government has proposed an increase in the cap for foreign investment in insurance from 26 percent to 49 percent.

It is worth noting that private investors, while lauding the reforms of all the governments in the past decade and particularly of the NDA in the past four years, have come forth with little by way of new investments after 1995–96 despite their repeated assertions that the climate for private investment in India is improving. Fixed investment of the private corporate sector responded strongly in the early years of the reforms, rising to 10 percent of GDP in 1995–96, but the subsequent period has seen a long and drawn out slide. This overall picture clearly obscures the strong dynamism of industries such as pharmaceuticals and auto components, or the new dynamic sectors such as biotechnology and the export-oriented information technology (IT) sector. It may also reflect inadequacies of data collection for the new emerging sectors so that the actual picture is better than what the data show. However, it also reflects to some extent a general risk-aversion on the part of Indian industry, which is still getting used to the muscle of the marketplace and the global forces. The strong growth in the domestic production of the capital goods sector in the past two years and substantial increase in the imports of capital goods in 2003–2004 also suggest that the latest investment data (yet to come) for 2003–2004 may well be the leading indicators of resurgence in private investment.

India's demographic position today places it among the countries with the largest share of working age persons in its population. While this raises India's potential growth rate in the coming years, it also points to the urgent need for creating rapid growth in productive employment so that the higher potential for growth can be realized. The emphasis by the UPA government on agriculture and rural development on the one hand, and on agro-based industries and labor-intensive exports on the other, has to be seen in this context. In order to reap the demographic dividend, larger public spending on education and health has to be combined with better administration in these areas and public-private partnership to ensure improved social conditions, which would facilitate higher growth.

The first part of this chapter presents a brief overview of the policy reorientation and performance with respect to economic growth and poverty reduction during the 1980s leading up to the balance of payments crisis of 1990. The second part outlines the broad contours of economic reform since 1991 with its distinct phases and their discernible effects on growth and the overall effect on poverty reduction. The third part takes a closer look at the major areas of reform since 1991. Against this background, the fourth part sets out the major challenges in policies and institutions if India is to attain the goal of 7–8 percent growth, let alone the more ambitious target of 8–10 percent growth, to meet the rising expectations of the population.

Deregulation, Productivity Improvement, Poverty Reduction, and Fiscal Profligacy during the 1980s

The 1980s marked a departure from the dirigiste policies of the earlier decades, which had significantly constrained the growth of the industrial sector. The reorientation of industrial and trade policy during this period involved hesitant experimentation with domestic deregulation within the confines of a closed economy and dominance of the public sector. The reforms of the 1980s were driven not by any crisis but by the frustration that the old regime of command and control had delivered neither growth nor social justice, and by the compulsion to explore alternative means to achieving greater economic and social development.

In agriculture, the primary responsibility for development is assigned by the Constitution of India to the state governments. Nevertheless, there is room enough for the center to play a catalytic role in pushing reform in these areas. The agricultural policy reform in the late 1960s was driven by new technology (imports of seeds of a high yielding variety of wheat) and its promotion through research and extension. While this strategy paid handsome dividends in the form of the Green Revolution in cereals, the new challenges facing Indian agriculture have been inadequately addressed. Agricultural policies in the 1980s continued to be directed at spreading the Green Revolution by providing input subsidies, including those to fertilizer and irrigation, a price support and procurement system, and a public distribution system for availability of subsidized food grains. The technology mission of the mid-1980s emphasized the development of dry land agriculture through national programs of integrated dry land development. Special task forces were set up for the development of pulses and oilseeds. While the production of pulses and oilseeds increased, the productivity levels remained low.

A central focus of the policy reforms in the 1980s was the improvement of industrial productivity by providing a larger role for market forces and infrastructure development through more public investment and better efficiency and coordination among the government departments and public sector enterprises (power, energy, railways, and transport). Some important features of the reforms included domestic deregulation, simplification of trade policies and procedures, and reorientation of the direct foreign investment regime, which facilitated the modernization of the capital goods industry as well as access to intermediate goods.[2]

The impact of the reorientation of the policy regime on productivity growth in Indian industry has been extensively documented in Isher Judge

---

2. For detailed discussions of the policy regime prior to 1980, see J.N. Bhagwati and P. Desai, *India: Planning for Industrialisation—Industrialisation and Trade Policies Since 1951* (New Delhi: Oxford University Press, 1970); Isher Judge Ahluwalia, *Industrial Growth in India: Stagnation Since the Mid Sixties* (New Delhi: Oxford University Press, 1985); and Isher Judge Ahluwalia, *Productivity and Growth in Indian Manufacturing* (New Delhi: Oxford University Press, 1991).

Ahluwalia (1985) and Isher Judge Ahluwalia (1991). The extent of the positive response in the form of acceleration in GDP growth in the 1980s (to 5.6 percent per annum) and reduction in poverty (decline in the percentage of the population below the poverty line from 50 percent during 1950–80 to 36 percent by the end of the 1980s) was also firmly established with the passage of time.[3]

It was the fiscal profligacy of the central government that proved to be the villain of the piece in generating macroeconomic imbalances and checking the sustainability of the high growth rates of the 1980s. Worsening fiscal deficit in the course of the decade resulted from the rapid increases in subsidies, interest payments, defense expenditures, and other items of government consumption. The government's efforts to promote exports through export subsidies within the confines of an import substitution regime were also unsuccessful, as the anti-export bias continued to make Indian exports uncompetitive although the depreciation of the real effective exchange rate in the latter half of the decade helped to generate rapid export growth.

The growing macroeconomic imbalances resulted in government borrowing at home and abroad, and the government also started to incur more short-term debt on commercial terms. By 1990, about a third of the external debt of the Government of India was owed to private creditors. Political uncertainty in 1989–90 with the change in government at the center created further vulnerability. The Gulf War of 1990–91 and the resulting surge in oil prices was the last straw. With the consolidated fiscal deficit reaching 9.4 percent of GDP in 1990–91, and erosion of confidence in the ability of the government to manage the macroeconomic environment, the result was a balance of payments crisis in which the foreign exchange reserves of India dipped to below $1 billion in May 1991, amounting to less than two weeks' worth of normal imports, and India was on the brink of default on its external debt obligations.

Economic Reform, Continued Growth, and Poverty Reduction since 1991

The decade of the 1990s began with a balance of payments crisis, but the crisis was turned into an opportunity for reform. There have been

---

3. Based on the Ministry of Finance, *Economic Survey* (various years) and the Reserve Bank of India, *Annual Report* (various years).

three distinct phases of reform since 1991, and a fourth began in June 2004. The first phase began after the balance of payments crisis of 1991 and continued for about five years. This period saw, besides policies to ensure macroeconomic stabilization, a number of radical economic reforms directed toward making the Indian economy more competitive and releasing the forces that would tap the potential for higher economic growth. With the approach of parliamentary elections in 1996, reforms slowed down and India entered the second phase. A number of coalition governments were formed at the center, supported by a number of regional political parties, which are playing an increasingly important role in making or breaking the coalitions. While the successive coalition governments that came to power continued with economic reforms, the pace of market-oriented reforms slowed between 1996–97 and 2000–2001.

At the turn of the century, economic reform gained momentum once again, this time with emphasis on privatization and foreign investment. With the change in government after the elections in 2004, a new phase has begun with much more focus on agriculture, social sectors, and poverty alleviation, while infrastructure reforms continue to remain at the top of the agenda.

Agriculture, education, and health are sectors for which state governments hold the principal responsibility. They have suffered from problems of inadequate allocation of resources from the center and the states as well as ineffective and inefficient delivery mechanisms. Only some states have come along on the path of reform to reinforce the process of economic and social development. One consequence of this is that regional disparities have widened.[4] The UPA government at the center is now promising to pursue reform "with a human face." It requires as much a change in policies at the central government level as facilitating change in the state governments' approach to economic and social development. It is still too early to tell how policies and institutions will be designed for GDP growth of at least 7–8 percent per annum while ensuring that the fruits of growth are widely shared and social development finds a prominent place in the agenda of reform.

---

4. Montek Singh Ahluwalia, "State Level Performance under Economic Reforms in India" (Working Paper No. 96, Center for Research on Economic Development and Policy Reform, Stanford University, March 2001).

1991–92 to 1996–97: Crisis and Response

The immediate task in 1991 was to bring the fiscal deficit under control and correct the macroeconomic imbalances built up over the preceding decade. The macroeconomic policy reforms during this period were certainly driven by the urgency of the crisis, and the consolidated fiscal deficit of the center and the states declined from 9.4 percent in 1990–91 to 6.4 percent in 1995–96. The policy makers were also emboldened by the favorable experience of the market-orientation of the industrial and trade policy regime in the 1980s. In addition, the increasing awareness of China's economic transformation and of the Southeast Asian economies helped policy makers address the challenge of improving the competitiveness of the economy by opening it up to domestic as well as foreign competition. Financial sector reforms were also initiated in India much before the Asian financial crisis put them on the agenda of the emerging markets, although public sector dominance in financial institutions has continued with its adverse effects on competition and efficiency. An important factor influencing the radical break with past policies was the powerful effect of the break-up of the Soviet Union, which greatly weakened the Left's traditional resistance to economic reforms. However, while a beginning was made with fiscal policy reform and the industrial and trade policy regime was made more market-oriented to create better conditions for economic growth, little attention was paid to reforming the public sector (both at the center and in the states), particularly in crucial areas of social development such as education, health, and direct programs of poverty alleviation.

The impact on growth was higher than was foreseen even by the change makers themselves. The growth of GDP between 1992–93 and 1996–97 (the period of the Eighth Five-Year Plan) averaged 6.7 percent per annum compared with 5.6 percent as the plan target. The acceleration in growth during the Eighth Five-Year Plan period was across the board. Compared with their growth rates of 3.5, 7.1, and 6.7 percent per annum in the 1980s, GDP in agriculture, industry, and services grew at 4.7, 7.6, and 7.5 percent per annum, respectively.

1997–98 to 2001–2002: Slowdown of Reforms and Growth

Notwithstanding the better growth performance, fiscal and trade policy reforms slowed down after 1996–97. This was partly because the end

Figure 1   Fiscal Deficit: 1990–91 to 2003–04

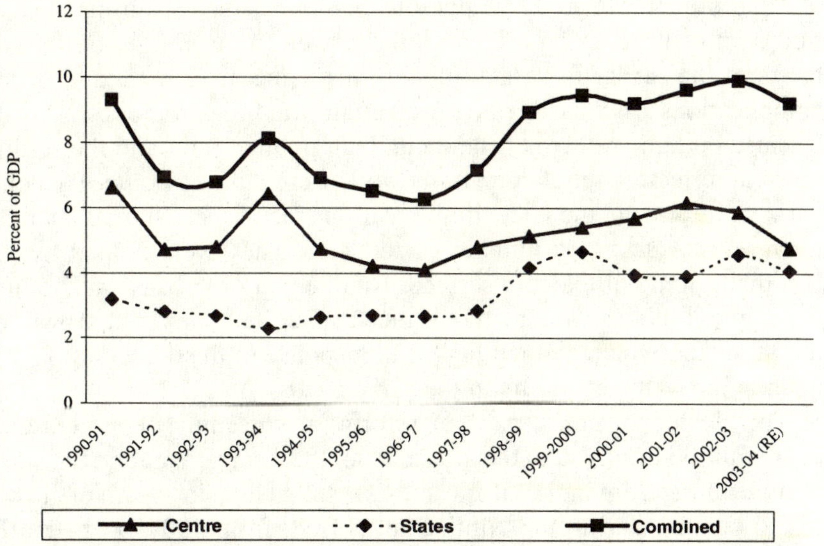

Source: Economic Survey 2001–2002, 2002–2003, and 2003–2004, Ministry of Finance, Government of India.

of the crisis brought some complacency and also because changes in government brought new actors on the scene who were not entirely convinced of the need to reform.[5] As the competition began to bite, Indian industry also became less supportive of change, including especially external liberalization. There was some going back on the opening of the economy to competition from imports as the weighted average of import duty rates, which was 73 percent at the beginning of the reforms and had been reduced to 25 percent in 1996–97, reached 36 percent in 2000–2001 before declining again to 18 percent in 2004–2005. There was also a significant deterioration in the fiscal deficit during the period from 1997–98 to 1999–2000 and again in the two years after 2000–2001. (See Figure 1.)

Infrastructure sector reform became a major focus of attention during this second phase of reform, although actual progress in reforming

---

5. For an early diagnosis of the slowing down of the reforms and its implications, see Shankar Acharya, "Macroeconomic Management in the 1990s," *Economic and Political Weekly* 37, no. 16 (April 20, 2002).

the sectors such as power, transport, and roads was slow. The complexity of the issues and the diversity of the interest groups stood in the way of rapid policy reform. Considerable energy was spent during this period on how to redesign reform in the power sector in light of the setbacks of the earlier fast-track model for private investment and of the complications arising from the Enron affair. But little progress was made because both the reform of the incumbent public sector and the setting up of an effective regulatory framework were slow to come. By comparison, reforms in the telecommunications sector were started later but moved faster despite a number of setbacks. They were helped by the fact that pricing of telecom services (unlike that of power) was not uneconomic. Policies were also designed to facilitate the rapid growth of the IT sector, which had sprung up in response to the deregulation and opening up of the economy in the early 1990s.

The slowdown in the pace of reform, a worsening of the external economic environment in the aftermath of the Asian crisis, and the sanctions resulting from India's nuclear tests resulted in a slowdown of growth to 5.6 percent during the Ninth Plan period, from 1997–98 to 2001–2002, compared with the plan target of 6.5 percent. Both agriculture and industry grew at rates slower than in the 1980s, 1.9 and 4.5 percent per annum, respectively. By contrast, the services sector was the principal driver of growth, reflecting the strong performance of IT and large increases in salaries to government employees. The IT boom continued throughout the 1990s. The take-off in the Indian IT industry and the export boom associated with it were a direct consequence of the economic reforms that were launched in 1991. Besides its own contribution to the growth of GDP, the IT boom created a new brand image for India in world markets.

Taking the decade as a whole, GDP growth increased marginally to 5.7 percent per annum in the 1990s compared with the 5.6 percent of the 1980s. However, it is significant that the growth was attained in a more competitive environment when tariff and nontariff barriers were much lower, Indian industry was still restructuring, infrastructure constraints were rampant, and the external environment in the latter part of the 1990s was less favorable.

Poverty Reduction and Human Development in the 1990s

As in the 1980s, higher growth performance of the 1990s was also associated with a substantial reduction in poverty. Trends in poverty incidence in the 1990s have been the subject of much debate[6]—as discussed in detail by Renana Jhabvala in the chapter in this volume—mainly because the estimates derived from various thin samples of the National Sample Survey (NSS) between 1993–94 and 1998–99 appeared to show no decline in poverty despite robust growth. The large sample estimate for 1999–2000, which was comparable in size to the 1993–94 sample, showed a marked reduction in the percentage of the population below the poverty line from 36 percent in 1993–94 to 26 percent in 1999–2000. This appeared to vindicate the advocates of reform who had argued that sustained high growth would have a direct positive effect on poverty reductions, but the results were questioned on the grounds that the period of recall over which consumption was measured had changed in the later survey. Subsequent studies attempting to put the two estimates on a comparable basis have concluded that poverty not only declined in the 1990s but did so at a faster rate, albeit not as fast as the government had intended—a conclusion that advocates of reform would readily accept since the growth rate was actually below target.[7]

Progress in human development seems to have slowed in the 1990s. This is particularly true of health indicators, which have slowed significantly. The infant mortality rate (IMR) had shown significant improvement from 115 per thousand in the 1980s to 79 in 1992, but since then the improvement has been at a much slower pace, so that the IMR declined to only 68 in 2001. The mortality of children under five appears to have shown no improvement in the 1990s. A new and fast increasing threat to the health system is posed by the sharp increase in the incidence of HIV-AIDS in the 1990s. Estimates of incidence—the number of new cases contracted in a twelve-month period—range from four million to eight million in 2002. In education, the official estimates of literacy and net enrollment rates have been improving, but there are wide disparities across states, gender, and caste in completion of primary education. In the area of gender inequality, India lags far behind countries with much lower per capita income, and female mortality rates have been increasing in some states with each successive census. Progress in the social sectors is impeded not only by low levels of spending but also by poor availability of services, low priority by state governments,

---

6. For a summary of the debate, see *Economic and Political Weekly* 38, no. 4 (January 25–31, 2003).

7. Angus Deaton, "Adjusted Indian Poverty Estimates for 1999–2000," *Economic and Political Weekly* 38, no. 4 (January 25–31, 2003).

low absorption of allocated funds, and lack of availability of personnel such as doctors and teachers.

Regaining Momentum

By 2000–2001, India was regaining its earlier momentum of change in policies toward improving the environment for private investment, opening the economy to foreign competition by lowering tariffs, and infrastructure development. The resumption of tariff reductions was particularly significant when viewed against the *Swadeshi* (inward looking and nationalistic) rhetoric of the election campaign (1999) of the BJP, the principal party in the NDA coalition. However, macroeconomic policy continued to fail to address the weaknesses that would undermine the achievement of sustainable growth at high rates, and growth performance continued to fall below the government's own targets. A "feel good" factor was, however, emerging. It is not surprising therefore that the change in government at the center in 2004 has created significant apprehension about the prospects for reform. It is important to recall that the change in government has brought the team of the original reformers back in the saddle. The prime minister, Manmohan Singh, was finance minister in 1991 when India's economic policies made a radical break with the past. In 2004 Singh heads a coalition government that is dependent upon the support of the Left parties. The current finance minister and the current deputy chairman of the Planning Commission are also part of the team that worked with Dr. Singh in the first phase of reforms. However, this time the economic team is functioning in the company of the Left parties, which are an important part of the coalition. The Common Minimum Program announced by the new government and the budget presented in July 2004 have reaffirmed the need to accelerate growth to 7–8 percent per annum through economic reform, but has highlighted the importance of the social agenda.

After ten years of attempts by successive central governments to disinvest government shareholding in some of the public sector enterprises, it was the NDA government which put privatization of public sector enterprises explicitly on the agenda of reform. Some undertakings were indeed privatized during the three years from 2001–2002 to 2003–2004, the most important being the privatization of Bharat Aluminum Company (BALCO) to a "strategic" private investor (i.e., a company chosen in a transparent manner on the basis of its ability to meet the strategic needs of the company for restructuring and growth). Other significant privatizations included a major car company, Maruti; a computer maintenance company, Computer Maintenance Corporation (CMC); and a bakery, Modern Bakery. However, the process ran into insurmountable resistance from within the NDA government itself when the privatization of two oil companies was attempted. The new government has put further brakes by announcing in the Common Minimum Program that no profit-making public sector enterprise will be privatized.

The period since 2000–2001 saw some major policy initiatives in infrastructure development, and the new government has also set up a task force on infrastructure under the chairmanship of the prime minister to push the reform further in this area. Reform in telecommunications has led to better service at lower prices for significantly larger numbers of customers. Road development has received a long overdue thrust during the past few years, and the new government has strongly endorsed further progress in this area. As in infrastructure, policies of the new government toward opening up the economy to foreign trade and investment also represent continuity with the earlier regime. While further opening up of the economy to trade and investment and accelerated reforms in infrastructure sectors are very much on the agenda of the new government's reform, there is heightened concern that the reforms should help the poor and that the benefits of higher growth be widely shared. Emphasis has shifted from privatization of public sector enterprises to reforming agriculture, health, and education. The character of the reform process is likely to change but the growth orientation remains at the forefront for the success of the reforms of this government.

It is worth noting that the doubling of the rate of growth of GDP from a low of 4 percent in 2002–2003 to 8.1 percent in 2003–2004 reflected not only a strong rebound in agricultural growth (from 5.2 to 9.1 percent) but also modest recovery in industrial growth and continued resurgence in the services sector (now accounting for about half of the GDP). While this rebound was projected in an exaggerated manner as the basis for "resurgent" India during the election campaign of 2004, there is increasing evidence that the Indian economy is poised to move from the present growth rate of GDP of 5.5–6 percent per annum to 6.5–7 percent per annum if government policies do not get in the way. The present government is committed to move to a sustainable trajectory of 7–8 percent growth with emphasis on reforming health, education, agriculture, and infrastructure so that the growth is broad-based and the fruits are widely shared. Attaining these goals would depend on the ability of the government to push through the critical and complex reforms, which are more difficult today than in 1991.

Major Areas of Reform: A Closer Look

This section will review closely the reform effort and performance since 1991 in the areas of macroeconomic management, infrastructure, integration with the world economy, agriculture, and private investment. It provides a basis for making an assessment on future prospects of reform and its implications for economic and social development on a sustainable basis.

Macroeconomic Management

Analysis of the macroeconomic management since 1991 leads to the conclusion that the Indian economy has been on an unsustainable path and the situation is made worse by the fact that the vulnerability is not easily discernible for a number of reasons, discussed below.

One of the principal tasks of policy reform in 1991 was to reduce the fiscal deficit of the general government (center and states) with a view to providing a macroeconomic environment that would be conducive to sustained high growth of GDP. The performance over the decade has been highly disappointing, with deterioration in the overall fiscal deficit, revenue deficit, and the primary deficit. As mentioned earlier, some progress was made in lowering the consolidated deficit of the center and the states from 9.4 percent of GDP in 1990–91 to 6.4 percent in 1996–97, principally through lowering the fiscal deficit of the center. But there was consistent and significant deterioration afterward at both levels of government, such that by the end of the decade in 2000–2001, the consolidated deficit at 9.5 percent exceeded that in the pre-crisis year of 1990–91. Further deterioration in the last three years has brought the deficit to 10 percent of GDP in 2002–2003, a level far higher than in most other developing countries. The budget of July 2004 proposed lowering the consolidated deficit to 9.4 percent by reducing the deficit for the center as well as the states. It remains to be seen if the reduction can be attained amidst increasing pressure for more spending on health, education, agriculture, infrastructure, and poverty alleviation programs.

Public investment has borne the brunt of fiscal adjustment in the 1990s. While the stabilization objective of the early reformers took its toll on public investment in bringing the fiscal deficit down, the period after 1996–97 saw further declines in the rate of public investment—even though the fiscal deficit continued to increase because of increases in government consumption. Thus, public investment as a percentage of GDP declined from 9.3 percent of GDP in 1990–91 to 7 percent in 1996–97, and further to 5.8 percent by 2001–2002. This sharp slowdown has taken its toll on infrastructure development.

The deterioration in the fiscal deficit after 1996–97 was reflected in a major decline in public saving from 1.7 percent of GDP in 1996–97 to –2.7 percent in 2001–2002. As the government borrowed to finance the rising fiscal deficits, interest payments mounted, accounting for over 50 percent of government revenues. But this was only part of the problem. Governmental expenses, including an oversized administration, food and fertilizer subsidies, and the budgetary burden resulting from the government's inability to introduce user charges for public services continue to take their toll on scarce public resources. For example, financial losses of the power sector alone reached Rs. 332 billion in 2001–2002, amounting to 1.4 percent of GDP. Food and fertilizer subsidies together accounted for another 1.4 percent of GDP in 2002–2003. In spite of the policy decision to phase out the subsidies in the petroleum sector, even these subsidies amounted to 0.3 percent of GDP in 2002–2003.

If expenditure reforms failed to take off, tax reforms were not associated with the much needed buoyancy of tax revenues either. The strategy of lowering tax rates was successfully implemented during the 1990s, but a broadening of the tax base did not materialize, and the tax/GDP ratio declined from 15.4 percent of GDP in 1990–91 to 14.8 percent in 2002–2003. The ratio of direct taxes to GDP actually increased from 1.9 percent in 1990–91 to 3.4 percent in 2002–2003, reflecting the reforms in personal as well as corporate taxes. But reform in the indirect tax regime failed to keep pace. The trade policy reforms were expected to lead to a decline in the ratio of customs duty to GDP. The major failure lay in the inability to reform the domestic indirect tax regime. While moves to a limited Valued Added Tax (VAT) principle for excise duties and simplification in excise rates by the central government have made some progress, reform is urgently needed in extending the coverage of the VAT regime for central excise duties, integrating the state sales tax regimes with the central VAT regime, and reducing exemptions. The taxation of some services in recent years and the first attempt to integrate indirect taxation on goods and services in the budget of July 2004 are steps in the right direction. However, the budget has left the custom duty rates largely intact with no lowering of even the maximum rate of tariff. The domestic indirect tax regime for goods and services must be overhauled to ensure greater buoyancy of revenues and better efficiency of resource allocation, particularly since further reform in custom duties could otherwise be constrained by revenue considerations.

The cumulative impact of the large and rising fiscal deficits has been to raise the public debt to GDP ratio over a short period, from 66 percent of GDP in 1996–97 to 85 percent by 2002–2003, exceeding the levels of this ratio at which many countries have experienced currency crises. The actual picture is even worse because of the rising debt of the central public enterprises and guarantees provided by the central government and the state governments on this debt. If the debt of the public-sector utilities (PSUs) is included, then the ratio may well exceed 90 percent.[8] It is worth noting that in the recent period even when the interest rates declined, the public debt situation has continued to deteriorate.

Buiter and Patel, in their empirical study applying the primary gap approach to the Indian data, had concluded that India's government debt was unsustainable (i.e., that the expected present value of future surplus was inadequate to pay off the debt as of 1990).[9] In a subsequent analysis for the year 1999–2000, Shome used the same approach and came to much the same implication for debt unsustainability.[10] In a recent paper, Roubini and Hemming use a balance sheet approach to reach the same conclusion.[11] Martin Feldstein in his "L.K. Jha Memorial Lecture" at the Reserve Bank of India points not only to the danger of insolvency in a situation of a continuing rise in the ratio of debt to GDP but also to the serious adverse effects of even a stable but high ratio of debt to GDP in "crowding out private capital formation and imposing a higher tax burden to service the debt."[12] Pinto and Zahir argue that fiscal ad-

---

8. Brian Pinto and Farah Zahir, "Why Fiscal Adjustment Now," *Economic and Political Weekly*, March 6, 2004.

9. Willem H. Buiter and Urjit Patel, "Solvency and Fiscal Correction in India: An Analytical Discussion," in *Public Finance: Policy Issues for India*, ed. Sudipto Mundle (New Delhi and New York: Oxford University Press, 1997).

10. Parthasarathi Shome, *India's Fiscal Matters* (New Delhi: Oxford University Press, 2002).

11. Nouriel Roubini and Richard Hemming, "A Balance Sheet Crisis in India?" (paper presented at the NIPFP-IMF Conference on Fiscal Policy in India, New Delhi, January 16–17, 2004).

12. Martin Feldstein, "Budget Deficits and National Debt" (L.K. Jha Memorial Lecture, Reserve Bank of India, January 12, 2004).

justment is needed not so much to stave off an imminent crisis but because postponing reform would place sustained growth in the long run in jeopardy.[13]

Public sector banks have played an important role in supporting the high levels of government debt. The banks have been increasing their holdings of government securities and have used the sovereign bonds to improve their balance sheets. The debate continues on whether the high interest rates have pushed out private investment, or whether the low demand from private investors and stronger prudential norms have driven the banks toward government securities. In any event, the higher interest rates will take a toll on economic growth. The recent Development Policy Report of India by the World Bank draws attention to the risk that rising interest rates may cause to the financial institutions, including insurance companies and pension funds, which have been making trading profits as interest rates have been falling. State pension funds have also invested heavily in bonds issued by the Special Purpose Vehicles and guaranteed by state governments. The Reserve Bank of India and the central government are working to establish clear policies for such guarantees, recognizing their potential risk should the gap between state government bonds and central government securities widen.

A significant positive development for macroeconomic management has been the passage in 2003 of the Fiscal Responsibility and Budget Management Act, which mandates reduction in the fiscal deficit and elimination of the center's revenue deficit by March 2008. Five states have passed similar acts and others are likely to follow suit.[14]

India's vulnerability to an external financial crisis is apparently significantly tempered by three factors: low levels of external debt in general and short-term external debt in particular, the presence of capital controls, and huge accumulation of foreign exchange reserves. After the experience of the balance of payments crisis of 1991, Indian policy makers have consciously and successfully moved toward a low level of short-term external debt. Its ratio to foreign exchange reserves fell precipitously from 77 percent in 1990–91 to 19 percent in 1992–93, and then declined to the 2003–2004 figure of 6 percent. The extensive capital controls reflect the consistent policy of the Government of In-

---

13. Pinto and Zahir, "Why Fiscal Adjustment Now."
14. The five states are Karnataka, Kerala, Punjab, Tamil Nadu, and Uttar Pradesh.

dia to move cautiously on this front in the face of changing fashions in the developing world. The large accumulation of reserves partly reflects a sharp increase in private capital inflows to India in the aftermath of September 11, 2001. But it is also the result of a stagnant rate of fixed investment, which has constrained the demand for imports.

In his analysis assessing India's vulnerability to external crisis, Montek Singh Ahluwalia has presented a mixed picture highlighting the dangers from the poor fiscal performance and incomplete reforms in the banking sector if the capital account were more open.[15] The weaknesses of the financial system arise largely from the dominance of the public sector in banking and other financial institutions. Even the NDA government, which owed no allegiance to the Left, had committed to uphold the "public sector character" of the banks, while lowering the government's share of their equity. A recent paper analyzing the strengths and weaknesses of the Indian macro policy environment concludes that this system "helps India remain stable and crisis-free at levels of debt that would get other countries into trouble, but the absence of early symptoms removes the warning signs that would force the political system into resolving fiscal imbalances until the debt is that much larger. Moreover, volatility is likely to increase as India becomes more globally integrated."[16]

An interesting feature of India's experience in recent years has been the sharp accumulation in foreign exchange reserves, which increased from less than $30 billion at the end of March 1998 to $118 billion at the end of July 2004.[17] In one sense the accumulation of reserves is a demonstration to the critics of liberalization who repeatedly warned of the dangers of liberalization in provoking a foreign exchange crisis. Scarcity of foreign exchange and the need to allocate it carefully have been the obsessive preoccupation of the government in the period prior to the reforms. The experience of liberalization has been quite the opposite, with a steady piling up of foreign exchange reserves. This is also not due to an excessive foreign exchange inflow on the capital account. Underlying this phenomenon is the fact that the Indian

---

15. Montek Singh Ahluwalia, "India's Vulnerability to External Crises: An Assessment," in *Macroeconomics and Monetary Policy: Issues for a Reforming Economy*, ed. Montek S. Ahluwalia, Y.V. Reddy, and S.S. Tarapore (New Delhi: Oxford University Press, 2002).

16. Ricardo Hausmann and Catriona Mary Purfield, "The Challenge of Fiscal Adjustment in a Democracy: The Case of India" (paper presented at the NIPFP-IMF Conference on Fiscal Policy in India, New Delhi, January 16–17, 2004).

17. Reserve Bank of India, *Bulletin* (October 2004).

economy has not run the current account deficit that was expected. In 2002–2003 and again in 2003–2004, India had a current account surplus of 0.2 and 0.8 percent respectively. This raises the question as to why private investment has not expanded—a question to which we shall return.

Infrastructure

The importance of the infrastructure challenge for a faster growing economy was recognized early in the reform process, but progress has been much slower than either desired or expected. A strategy for infrastructure development was first articulated in the Eighth Plan at the end of 1992. In an early volume which reviewed the ongoing reform process in India, attention was drawn to the fact that "contrary to the impression conveyed by many critics that the reforms relied excessively and unrealistically upon private investment for development of infrastructure, the strategy outlined in the plan envisaged a continuance of public sector dominance, with the private sector playing only a supplemental role."[18] This in itself was a radical break from the past. As late as in the Seventh Plan, there was no mention of private investments in infrastructure, and the latter had all along been an almost exclusive reserve of the public sector.

The cautious transition to a larger role for the private sector in the provision of infrastructure services was to some extent conditioned by a worldwide shift in attitude with regard to the public sector being a natural supplier of infrastructure services, but it was also driven by the growing disillusionment with the performance of the public sector in India. The problems arising from the poor productivity of the public sector enterprises and government departments such as railways were compounded by the inability of these enterprises and departments to levy and collect appropriate user charges for the delivery of infrastructure services.

Private entry into power, telecommunications, ports, transport, and so forth was seen as a way to bring additional resources as well as competition through the newly created Foreign Investment Promotion Board

---

18. Montek Ahluwalia, "Infrastructure Development in India's Reforms" in *India's Economic Reforms and Development: Essays for Manmohan Singh*, ed. Isher Judge Ahluwalia and I.M.D. Little (New York: Oxford University Press, 1998).

and improve the quality of services. Foreign investment was actively encouraged to help relieve the critical bottlenecks in these sectors. The Government of India constituted an expert group in October 1994 to consider issues related to the commercialization of infrastructure projects including institutional arrangements, legal frameworks, and financial arrangements that would facilitate the investments in infrastructure sectors. The group submitted its report in June 1996. Policy toward the infrastructure sectors has evolved in the past ten years, and there has been a lot of learning by doing. The performance has varied across sectors, telecommunications being the best example of success and the power sector showing the most disappointing performance.

The power sector attracted early attention of the reformers in the 1990s because of its crucial importance. Private investment in general and foreign investment in particular were actively encouraged through fast-track routes to power generation. However, in the absence of reforming the distribution network, which remained largely in the public sector (the state electricity boards), the financial viability of the private ventures was questionable.

The weak and worsening financial health of the state electricity boards (SEBs) was principally due to the very low tariffs for agriculture and residential consumers and inability to collect even the low tariffs because of the increasing theft of power through connivance with the distribution staff. In 2000–2001, the average tariffs for the SEBs recovered less than 70 percent of the average cost of supplying power.[19] The increasing tendency of state governments to either heavily subsidize or make power available free of cost to farmers has also taken its toll on the finances of the SEBs. The latest states to join this bandwagon are Andhra Pradesh, Tamil Nadu, and Maharashtra after the recent general elections. Against this background, the commercial losses of the Indian power sector have been growing steadily and are estimated at 1.5 percent of GDP in 2001–2002.

Since the fundamental problem of the financial viability of the SEBs remained unaddressed, and the potential private investors in power generation demanded payment guarantees from state governments and counter guarantees from the central government to mitigate risks of nonpayment from the SEBs, it is not surprising that most of the private proposals failed to reach financial closure. Of the over 200 memoranda

---

19. Expert Group Report, "Power Sector Reforms 2001: Onetime Settlement of SEBs' Dues" (Ministry of Power, under the chairmanship of Montek S. Ahluwalia, 2001).

of understanding (MOUs) signed by potential investors with the respective SEBs, not even a dozen reached fruition.

For kick starting the process of private investment in power generation, the Central Government had agreed to extend sovereign guarantees to eight selected projects, of which Dabhol Power Project was one. This notorious project of the Enron Corporation ran into serious difficulties after its Phase-I started delivering electricity to the Maharashtra State Electricity Board (MSEB). Tariff levels proved to be too high because naptha prices rose unexpectedly and the rupee also depreciated, and both risks were borne by the power producer. The high tariff levels coupled with the continued ill health of the MSEB led to a breakdown of the payment mechanism where both the MSEB, which was the primary obligor, and the Maharashtra state government, which was the counter guarantor, failed to make payments. Since there were also disagreements on the amounts due, the sovereign counter guarantee of the Government of India, which was limited to amounts validly due, could not be invoked. As a result, the project is not functioning and the matter is in dispute. This project served to demonstrate the crucial role of the tariff setting framework and the financial viability of SEBs for private participation to succeed.

In more recent years, attempts have been made to depoliticize the process of fixing power tariffs. Following the lead of the central government, a number of state governments have set up independent regulatory commissions for this purpose. As of May 2004, sixteen state governments have started functioning within a regulatory framework and are in different stages of setting up regulatory commissions. Policies are also being directed at improving efficiency of distribution, both through reforming the existing utilities and selective privatization. The Electricity Act of 2003 lays out a broad legal framework of regulation for the sector. Its provisions for open access to the transmission grid offer investors the potential for creating a national market for power. The act effectively empowers state governments to accelerate power sector reforms through fostering greater competition, increased involvement of the private sector, and better governance. But many details remain to be put in place.[20] While the bold principles laid out in the act should form the basis of reforming the power sector in the medium run,

---

20. See J.L. Bajaj, "Some Light at the End of the Tunnel: Ingredients of Power Sector Reforms in India" (paper presented at the CREDPR Annual Conference on Indian Economic Policy Reform, Stanford, June 5–7, 2004), for a discussion of transitional issues.

the current phase of transition in which different state governments are implementing reforms at different speeds needs to be steered effectively by the central government. The Common Minimum Program of the new government has expressed a commitment to review the Electricity Act, but the review must ensure that the forward movement in power reform is only accelerated.

In contrast to the power sector, reforms in telecommunications have moved relatively fast—although they were sometimes perceived as being unfair to some players. The transition from a fixed license fee to revenue sharing for license holders of mobile phones and the redefinition of the regulatory powers of the Telecom Regulatory Authority of India were controversial policy measures, but regular consultations with the different stakeholders and quick decisions in responding to the emerging problems during the transition have helped to create an environment in which several private sector service providers of fixed line and cellular telecommunications are in operation and provide effective competition to the incumbent public sector provider. A feature that distinguished the telecommunications sector from the power sector was that payment risk was not significant. While power has been perceived in India as a basic necessity and therefore has an implicit claim for subsidization, telephones have been seen more as luxury items for the upper income groups. Ironically, this difference in perception has enabled the policy makers to reach out with the telephone to the common man. Indeed, telecommunication has emerged as a powerful symbol of what could be achieved with reforms in a short time. Mobile phones have become identified with better quality and lower price service to increasing numbers of people; likewise, they are visible proof that economic reforms can improve the life of the common man.

India's transport infrastructure (roads, ports, civil aviation, and railways) is in urgent need of overhaul. The long overdue reforms in the road sector were begun in recent years under the explicit and direct leadership of the former prime minister, Atal Bihai Vajpayee, who employed new institutional arrangements and self-financing revenue models to start programs for building high quality highways, North-South and East-West corridors, and rural roads. The current prime minister, Manmohan Singh, has expressed his government's strong commitment to bring about greater connectivity in the road sector, particularly in rural areas. In the port sector, corporatization, increased participation of the private sector, and an independent tariff regulatory authority make berth capacity less of a constraint. But the efficiency of the existing port capacity, particularly in the older ports, needs to be significantly improved. In the domestic civil aviation sector, greater competition has lowered rates for domestic air travel and improved the quality of service. By contrast, the international segment of civil aviation continues to be dominated by Air India in the public sector. Reforms have hardly touched the railway sector.

Integration with the World Economy

A significant feature of the economic reforms of the 1990s was the opening up of the Indian economy to competition from imports. This was a direct repudiation of the import substitution strategy and worked toward removing the anti-export bias that was the hallmark of the old regime. Import liberalization itself, by increasing the availability of capital goods, intermediate products, and technology needed for exports, as well as by reducing the costs of these components, played a crucial role in creating a level playing field for exporters. In addition, the reduction in barriers to imports, particularly on consumer goods later in the reform process, subjected domestic industry to external competitive forces with beneficial results for efficiency and for product and process innovation. Nonetheless, as discussed below, the process has been slow and at times reversed, and India still continues to be one of the most highly protected economies in the world.

Import licensing for capital goods and intermediate goods was abolished relatively early during the reform process, but it was only in April 2001, ten years after the beginning of reforms, that quantitative restrictions on the import of consumer goods and agricultural products were phased out to meet India's multilateral trade commitment. As regards tariff protection on imports, as mentioned above, the period up to 1996–97 saw a consistent reduction in custom duty rates. However, beginning with 1997–98, surcharges and special customs duty rates were used, which had the effect of reversing this process. Tariffization of imports which were earlier subject to quantitative restrictions had the same effect. As a result, the import-weighted tariff increased to 35 percent in 2001–2002. With the resumption of the reduction in import tariffs, the import-weighted rate was brought down to 25 percent in 2003–2004. This was still above the rate attained in 1996–97 and the highest among the developing countries. For example, in 2000 the import-weighted tariff rate was 14.7 percent in China, 10.1 percent in Malaysia, 5.2 percent in Indonesia, and 3.8 percent in the Philippines.[21]

The opening to trade has paid good dividends. India's export share in world markets has increased in recent years, and the exports of software, pharmaceuticals, and auto components have performed exceptionally well. As the roadblocks of poor infrastructure, reservations for small-scale sector, labor market rigidities, and other domestic constraints are eased, Indian industry should be able to compete better in world markets. A major impending challenge is from the dismantling of the Multi Fiber Arrangement (MFA) on January 1, 2005, when the Indian garment and textiles industry will face world competition for the first time. While there has been a lot of domestic concern about the preparedness of Indian industry for this challenge, the emerging conventional wisdom is that India will be among the gainers in the post-quota world, particularly in ready-made garments. A lot will depend on the policies and institutions that will enable the industry to exploit the huge opportunity in the world market.

The second key component of global integration is the integration of the capital and financial markets. Here the reform process has been much more cautious, based on the belief that while the benefits of outward trade orientation are clear, those of capital account liberalization are much less so. The repeated crises in many other emerging markets only served to reinforce the caution. There was concern that unfettered movement of portfolio capital flows could lead to significant volatility, particularly given the state of the domestic financial system and the requirements for financing the large fiscal deficits. At the same time, excessive competition in the financial sector—particularly external competition—could pose considerable risks, especially given the vulnerabilities in the banking sector.

Policies toward foreign investment in India were significantly liberalized in the 1990s with a view to ensuring better access to modern technology and world markets and also to helping release the domestic resource constraint on investment. In a series of policy announcements more and more sectors were opened up to foreign direct investment, and the maximum cap allowed was raised for many sectors, ranging from 25 percent in some to 100 percent in many. More recently, in an attempt to simplify procedures for foreign investors, the government initiated a

---

21. Reserve Bank of India, *Annual Report of the Reserve Bank of India* (2003).

process of reviewing restrictions on FDI, especially in infrastructure sectors. An official committee of experts (the N.K. Singh Committee) recommended an increase in foreign investment caps in critical sectors such as insurance and telecommunications. However, no decision was taken on these recommendations and the new UPA government in its latest budget announced an increase in the FDI limit in insurance (from 26 percent to 49 percent), civil aviation (from 40 percent to 49 percent), and telecommunications (from 49 percent to 74 percent).

Agriculture

Considering that a quarter of the GDP in the Indian economy originates in agriculture and 60 percent of the population is dependent upon this sector, it should have been a major area for economic reforms. On the contrary, the agricultural sector has received relatively little attention, partly because the central government has not looked seriously beyond its traditional food grains–oriented strategy and also because the state governments, which are principally responsible for agricultural development, have failed to provide the incentives, institutions, and infrastructure for the development of diversified agriculture. Agricultural research and extension have also suffered from benign neglect. Delaying reforms in agriculture could have serious implications for growth as well as poverty alleviation.

One of the major problems in Indian agriculture has been the crowding out of public investment by agriculture-oriented subsidies. Public investment in agriculture declined from 17.7 percent of the total public investment in 1980–81 to 7.1 percent in 1990–91, and further to 5.3 percent in 2000–2001. In particular, a long-term decline in public investment in irrigation has cost the economy dearly. Agricultural growth in the 1990s showed no acceleration compared to the 1980s, while there has been a marked slowdown in the second half of the 1990s. After growing at about 3.3 percent per annum up to the mid-1990s, agricultural growth decelerated to around 2.3 percent in the subsequent period.

The substantial lowering of protection to Indian industry by the central government during the 1990s has helped level the field for Indian agriculture. The trade policy liberalization of agriculture undertaken in the wake of the Uruguay Round Agreement of 1994 has also exposed Indian agriculture to foreign competition by removing quantitative restrictions on imports, but the net effect was very limited because tariff bindings were set at very high rates. There has also been significant liberalization of agricultural exports.

The domestic policy regime for Indian agriculture, however, has not moved with the needs of a growing economy and a changing external environment dominated by the ongoing negotiations in the World Trade Organization (WTO). Policy has continued to subsidize inputs such as water, power, and fertilizers and provide price supports to food grain crops through a system of public procurement and distribution. These policies, associated with the Green Revolution and initiated during the 1960s, did serve their purpose in generating productivity increases in areas with assured irrigation. Such policies also contributed toward building food security by making food grains available at highly subsidized prices through the public distribution system. Contrary to several forecasts that predicted India as a large importer of grains in the 1990s, India actually exported a total of 33 million tons of food grains, primarily to liquidate its bulging stocks, which had reached 63 million tons in July 2002. The subsidy burden of this strategy has eaten into the scarce public resources, which could otherwise be used for investment in rural infrastructure. As mentioned earlier, the period from 1980–81 to 1991–92 saw a sharp increase in subsidies to agriculture and a decline in public investment in agriculture. In the early years of reform during the 1990s, some attempt was made to reverse these trends, but it could not be sustained, and the period after 1996–97 again saw a decline in public investment in agriculture, while subsidies resumed their upward climb. To the extent that public investment in rural infrastructure crowds in private investments in agriculture, this has had a dampening effect on private investment in agriculture, which has, however, shown some increase during the 1990s.

The "physical balance" approach to food security also has not worked because the problem seems to be inadequacy of purchasing power in the hands of the poor. To some extent this is also due to the fact that consumption patterns are changing toward high-value agricultural products such as fruits and vegetables, livestock products, and fish. But the policy regime has not adjusted to accommodate the change that is occurring in the production and consumption baskets of food. The policy-induced distortions within the agricultural sector continue to distort the production patterns in favor of food grains and against the more risky and perishable crops (e.g., fruits and vegetables).

At present, agricultural produce can only be sold in regulated markets (*mandis*) established by Mandi Boards, which are effectively controlled

Figure 2   **Public Investment and Subsidies in Indian Agriculture, 1980–81 to 2000–2001**

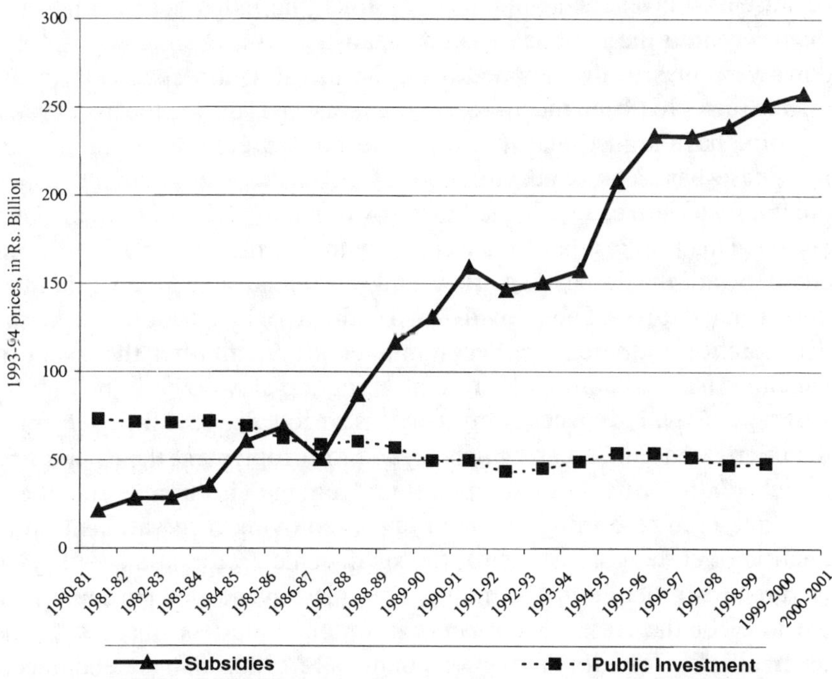

Source: Indian Agriculture: Strategic Issues and Reform Options, International Food Policy and Research Institute.

by the *arthias* (licensed brokers) and typically provide no facilities for grading or open, transparent auctions. There is a need to establish modern markets like the one (the only one of its kind) set up by the National Dairy Development Board in Bangalore in 2002, for which a special exemption was given by the state government of Karnataka. The requirement that produce be sold in *mandi* markets also militates against contract farming, which requires direct purchases from the farmer. (See Figure 2).

Private Investment

A principal assumption underlying the economic reforms of the 1990s was that the increased market orientation of the policy regime would generate a strong positive response from the private sector. Indeed, the private fixed investment response was very strong in the five-year period ending in 1996–97. Since then, the rate of private fixed investment has been sliding downward. There may well be a data reporting problem here, because new investments in the newly emerging industries may not find their way into the national accounts statistics. But even allowing for a downward bias in the reported data, the investment response from the private sector has been much weaker than was envisaged in the mid-1990s.

Some have argued that industrial capacities were created in the earlier phase based on expectations of stronger domestic demand which did not materialize, and this led to a slowdown in investment in the later period. This implies that Indian industry in the mid-1990s was still oriented toward the domestic markets and was not targeting the world markets for exports. The slowdown in the world economy and the deterioration in the external economic environment after the Asian financial crisis had some role in reinforcing the slowdown in private investment in the Indian economy. But this period also saw little reform in the microeconomic areas, which needed to complement the earlier first generation reforms. For example, improvements in the investment climate required reforming the labor laws, removing reservations in production of certain industries for the small-scale sector, and simplifying the process of obtaining the multiple permissions needed particularly at the level of the state governments in order to start businesses. Some reversal in custom duty reductions in the late 1990s also created uncertainty for potential investors about the government's intention to continue to expose Indian industry to the competition of imports.

Notwithstanding the fact that the overall pace of private investment in recent years has not picked up, there is evidence to suggest that Indian industry has been working toward restructuring and reducing costs in a slow but steady manner since the mid-1990s. There are also some star performers on the global scale, and new knowledge-based industries are making their mark globally. The story of the Indian IT sector is all too well known and not covered here. Pharmaceuticals and automotive components are the two most conspicuous examples of manufacturing industries that have successfully developed a global vision and penetrated world markets. The global output of the Indian pharmaceutical industry ranks fourth in terms of volume and thirteenth in terms of value. Investment in different sectors of biotechnology industry, especially in biopharmaceutical and agricultural sectors, has also been driving the very rapid growth of this industry. Two leading Indian companies, Biocon India and Serum Group, are among the twenty globally ranked biotech companies based on their revenue in 2003–2004. The animation industry has also been growing very rapidly. Given the evidence of a pickup in capital goods production and capital goods imports in 2003–2004, an upturn in investment may well be around the corner.

Challenges Ahead

After thirteen years of economic reforms designed to create conditions for higher growth and better conditions of living, the Indian economy still falls far short of reaching the targets set by its own policy makers and has not been able to realize its potential—facts which are increasingly becoming obvious to all observers of the economy. The rising expectations and faltering institutions make the task of policy reform even more challenging within a democratic framework.

Macroeconomic Management

India's fiscal situation has been one of the major areas of weakness in the past twelve years of reforms. The combined deficit of the center and the states at 10 percent of GDP in 2002–2003 is a little higher than in 1990–91 at the time of the crisis and is among the highest in the developing world. Since it is combined with an unsustainable debt situation there is every reason for concern, and many observers have sounded a clear warning. To quote only one such warning: "Current trends suggest that India is on an unsustainable path and will eventually have to adjust, one way or the other, i.e., with or without a crisis."[22] Another study draws attention to a number of longer term policy issues which may weigh on Indian policy makers, such as the gradual aging of the population and the more rapid aging of the civil servants eligible for pensions, besides the more common problems arising from the potential fiscal costs associated with climate change, national security risks, intensified urbanization pressures, prospective epidemiological patterns (associated both with HIV/AIDS and the likely increased demands associated with noncommunicable diseases), and the imperatives of social insurance reform.[23] Addressing the high level of public debt is

---

22. Hausmann and Purfield, "The Challenge of Fiscal Adjustment in a Democracy."

23. Peter S. Heller, "India: Today's Fiscal Policy Imperatives Seen in the Context of Longer Term Challenges and Risks" (paper presented at the NIPFP-IMF Conference on Fiscal Policy in India, New Delhi, January 16–17, 2004).

critical in order to provide future policy makers with greater fiscal leeway to address the challenges arising from these concerns which are, of course, not unique to India.

The need for a fiscal corrective is recognized by the government and is reflected in the targets of the Fiscal Responsibility Act. The present government has embraced the objectives of the act, except that the targets have been shifted forward by one year—the revenue deficit will now be reduced to zero and the fiscal deficit to 3 percent in the year 2008–2009. The budget presented in July 2004 appears to make a start in this direction by aiming at a reduction in the fiscal deficit from 4.8 percent of GDP in 2003–2004 to 4.4 percent in 2004–2005 and in the revenue deficit from 3.6 percent to 2.5 percent over the same period, but the projections are fraught with uncertainties. The revenue targets were based on a projected growth of GDP of 6 to 6.5 percent, which now appears uncertain in view of the late arrival of the monsoon. This is also likely to lead to additional expenditure on account of drought relief. More importantly, even if slippage in the current year is accepted as an inevitable outcome of the unexpected drought, the question remains whether the medium term targets are achievable.

The only indication of government thinking on this issue is the recently issued Report of the Task Force on the Fiscal Responsibility Act (the Kelkar Report), which bases the achievements of the targets on a significant improvement in the ratio of tax revenue to GDP of around 13.2 percent of GDP by 2008–2009 and a relatively modest increase in the ratio of plan expenditure to GDP with a substantial decline in the ratio of non-plan expenditure to GDP from 11 percent in 2003–2004 to 9.2 percent in 2008–2009. The achievements of the targets depend upon the credibility of these projections. The tax reforms are well designed and in line with what has been recommended by other expert groups, carrying the direction significantly forward in some respects. It remains to be seen whether these tax reforms as projected in the report will be indeed implemented in the next budget and will have the expected impact.

The report also projects a modest increase in plan expenditures up to 2008–2009.[24] This is certainly a move in the right direction, given the need to expand public investment in social sectors and infrastruc-

---

24. Plan expenditure is defined as the expenditure on new and ongoing development programs. It is partly in the nature of capital expenditure but also includes a large amount of current expenditure.

ture. But the proposed increase is much smaller than would be expected if the promises in the Common Minimum Program are indeed to be implemented. Whether expectations raised on these counts can be tempered in the face of fiscal reality or alternatively accommodated through drastic cuts in other areas remains to be seen. The Planning Commission's midterm review of the Tenth Plan, which is expected to be completed in January 2005, should provide a suitable basis to judge what we can expect.

The fiscal outcome for the central government will also be affected by the award of the Twelfth Finance Commission, which determines the sharing of taxes between the center and the states. This award is expected by January 2005, and it can be safely assumed that the share of taxes accruing to the states will be increased, putting a corresponding strain on the central government. While the transfer does not affect the combined deficit of the center and the states taken together—which is what matters for macroeconomic balance—the shift of revenues to the states is likely to determine the composition of expenditure. The relevant question is whether the greater freedom of maneuver gained by the states will be used to improve the quality of expenditure. The fear—and it is a legitimate fear—is that the states will be more likely to take up populist schemes leading to a deterioration in the quality of expenditure. A concerted effort is needed to improve the quality of the fiscal deficit through expenditure reforms and reallocation. These considerations suggest that the fiscal challenge facing the government in the years ahead is formidable. As pointed out earlier, there are good reasons why the weak fiscal parameters and debt ratios have not led to a crisis as in other countries, but continued fiscal weakness will mean that the government will continue to absorb the bulk of the financial savings generated by the nongovernmental portion of the economy—and the much needed push for private investment which is essential to achieve the targeted growth rate of 7 to 8 percent will not materialize.

Infrastructure

If India is to achieve high growth rates in GDP with an increasing integration into the world economy, it needs a significant increase in capacity and an improvement in quality of supply in sectors such as electric power, telecommunications, roads, ports, railways, civil aviation, rural infrastructure (such as irrigation and water management systems and rural electrification), and urban infrastructure (including especially drinking water and sewage systems). Since resources with the public sector are limited, it is necessary to resort to a combination of expanded private investment and a much greater role for the public sector wherever private investment is not feasible. This has indeed been the strategy underlying the reforms in the infrastructure sectors during the 1990s. But in fact there has been inadequate public investment in all infrastructure sectors, and the position regarding private investment is mixed. Good results have been achieved in telecommunications after some initial false starts, and this sector appears well on the road to takeoff. There have also been good results in ports with significant new capacities in the private sector. In the other sectors the involvement of private investment has been negligible.

Some rethinking is clearly needed. Evidently in many areas—especially but not only in rural areas—the scope for private investment is limited. It will be necessary to rely on public investment, and the resources for such investment will have to be found. In many areas (e.g., irrigation and power), the ability of the public sector to invest is seriously hampered by the absence of rational user charges, and correcting this deficiency must receive top priority. This will present politically difficult choices. For example, water rates for irrigation are currently one-fifth of what is needed to recover maintenance costs—to say nothing of recovering capital costs. Similarly, electric power is supplied to farmers at a fraction of unit costs, and some states that had recently moved away from free power have once again introduced it. Urban drinking water is similarly heavily under priced, leaving the utilities with inadequate resources to maintain the system let alone expand it. Given the severe constraints of the availability of public resources, it is clear that unless these features are corrected no significant improvement is possible.

There are obviously many areas where a greater role could be defined for the private sector, as has successfully been done for telecommunications. Perhaps the most important area where private investment could be inducted is the power sector. The basic regulatory structure is now in place, with independent regulators in many states and the possibility of opening up distribution of electricity to private investment. But all the elements needed are yet to be in place. For example, the Electricity Act 2003 provides for open access to encourage power producers to invest in generation capacity and sell directly to high volume consumers while paying a distribution charge to the distributor. However, the regulators have yet to specify the date when open access would become mandatory, and they also have yet to indicate the basis on which the distribution charge will be determined.

It is worth noting that private investment in regulated industries can only take place if the regulatory regime is transparent and independent and is perceived as being fair to both consumers and producers, and the society is willing to transit to a regime of reasonable tariffs with explicit subsidies where they are socially needed. These principles are increasingly recognized, but the political system has been very reluctant to push for their acceptance in practice. And yet until that is done India's infrastructure will continue to lag behind other countries in East Asia with a corresponding impact on India's ability to compete. In this context, the setting up of the Infrastructure Task Force under the chairmanship of the prime minister is a very welcome move to address the issue of infrastructure development in a holistic manner.

Agriculture

In order to help Indian agriculture face the challenge of external competition and exploit the new opportunities for exports, the domestic policy regime has to strive toward building a strong rural infrastructure which facilitates the development of a diversified agricultural sector with emphasis on high value added crops and linkages with agro-based industries. As mentioned earlier, this also requires a revitalization of the agricultural research and extension service system to address the current needs of Indian agriculture, as well as institutional reforms including especially liberalization of marketing restrictions in agriculture.

Studies undertaken by the International Food Policy Research Institute (IFPRI) show that investment in research and development accelerates agricultural growth the most. India has had a successful record of having imported the high yielding variety of seeds and adapting them to local conditions during the Green Revolution in wheat and rice. Although there is still ample scope for increasing the yields of rice and wheat, especially in the eastern belt with its abundance of water, the Green Revolution has been stagnating in the northwest states of Punjab, Haryana, and western Uttar Pradesh, as well as in the southern states of Andhra Pradesh and Tamil Nadu. If India has to keep pushing the production frontier outward, it must invest in rural infrastructure to facilitate the development of high value added agriculture.

It must invest in new technologies, for example, biotechnology that provides new crops favorable to India's climatic conditions and suitable for use by farmers in rural communities. It would also require effective reform of the regulatory structure and process, taking note of the local, national, and international debate on biotechnology, particularly genetically modified crops.

Social Development

The challenge of social development requires providing immediate attention to the long overdue task of meeting the basic needs of education and health. A larger role for the public sector will have to be combined with reforms in their delivery mechanisms for the social sectors and increasing reliance on public-private partnership. Stronger performance on the social development front would be an important instrument for attaining higher economic growth, particularly in the present phase of the demographic transition for India, with an increasing presence of youth in the workforce. At the same time, policies to accelerate economic growth would provide a stronger base on which social development can be built.

Concluding Thoughts

India's economic performance in the next ten years will depend critically upon its underlying institutional strengths and government policy. Today there is increasing recognition of India's institutional strengths. For example, a long tradition of vigorous entrepreneurship, an increasingly skilled workforce, and a judicial system which, although dilatory and time consuming, is much closer to what is needed for modern commerce than in many other countries. The high savings rate in the household sector can also serve the purpose of accelerating growth if further reforms can ensure that a modern financial system effectively channels these savings into productive investments. As the process of financial integration with the world markets moves forward, this should attract increasing flows of foreign investment. These are clearly positive factors, which with the right policy mix can generate a further acceleration of growth from the 6 percent or so currently observed to something close to 8 percent. The policies needed to achieve this transition have been discussed in this paper. Agriculture, infrastructure, and social sectors are being singled out for more focused attention in the new government. Should the fact of a coalition government cause concern about the prospect of continuing economic reform? Coalitions do pose problems, but this is not the first time India has had a coalition government. Past experience suggests that coalition governments in India do manage to move the agenda of reform forward.

As the benefits of the economic reforms become visible, a potential constituency for reform gets established. For this to happen, politicians from both the Left and the Right must respond to this constituency, even as they insist on product differentiation of the policies they emphasize in public. A good reason to believe that this might happen is that the West Bengal state government, under the Left parties, is setting a good example in encouraging private investment and growth, with an open effort to attract foreign direct investment even as the Left parties at the center question foreign direct investment in the telecom sector in New Delhi. The UPA government's emphasis on social development and poverty alleviation requires the government to spend more. But the government has also shown awareness that the results will crucially depend on the effectiveness of the spending and strengthening of the delivery mechanisms. The needs of infrastructure development are huge and the government has rightly emphasized encouraging public-private partnerships in the area. The enormity of the overall task requires that a growing volume of resources is generated so that the government can keep at least some of the major promises made in the Common Minimum Program. Economic reforms to generate 7–8 percent per annum growth are crucial for this purpose.

India's International Relations: The Search for Stability, Space, and Strength

Amitabh Mattoo

The defining moment in India's international relations occurred not on September 11, 2001, but on May 11, 1998, when—defying traditional assumptions, analytical predictions, and international opinion—New Delhi began to conduct a series of nuclear tests. The tests mark the inception of what has been widely described as a new phase of realism in India's foreign policy. But the terrorist attacks of 9/11 and their aftermath did impact India's foreign policy in less fundamental ways. By 2004 India's stark realism had graduated to a more nuanced view of the complexities of international politics.

This was most obvious in India's relationships with three critical players: the United States, China, and Pakistan. For instance, while New Delhi recognized the value of a sustained engagement with the United States, simple realpolitik equations that forecast bonding between New Delhi and Washington on the basis of long-term strategic convergence did not sufficiently provide for the complexity of U.S. tactical interests in the "war on terrorism." After 9/11 the United States focused more on the immediate advantages of a relationship with Pakistan, causing New Delhi to realize that it must factor in a diversity of variables, even while constructing a de-ideologized and pragmatic foreign policy.

Similarly, even though India continued to view China as a potential strategic rival—and the principal rationale for constructing a nuclear deterrent—New Delhi began simultaneously, and more assertively than in the previous two decades, to pursue a policy of expanding cooperation with Beijing. The New Delhi–Washington axis to "contain" a rising China, an idea that had found favor among a section of the Indian strategic community after George W. Bush was elected president of the United

States in 2000, had lost most of its audience. Even with Pakistan—unarguably India's most trying relationship—New Delhi seemed to be realizing that the zero-sum pattern of relations was proving counterproductive and Indian policy had not been sufficiently sensitive to the heterogeneity of interests and views within Pakistan's state and society. By summer 2004 the realism in India's foreign policy finally came of age.

India's fundamental foreign policy goals, however, had changed very little. These objectives formed the bedrock of India's engagement with the outside world. India's search for security and stability in South Asia, and quest to influence international politics beyond the immediate neighborhood through its growing "hard" and "soft" power, formed the mainstay of New Delhi's foreign policy. Faced with the necessity of an accelerated and multifaceted engagement with the outside world, India also sought to retain the autonomy to make decisions on key issues of national interest without capitulating to international pressure or being crushed by the juggernaut of globalization. This was most strikingly evident in India's position in multilateral trade talks as well as in New Delhi's willingness to neither support the U.S.-led war against Iraq nor deploy Indian soldiers as part of the multinational force in that country.

The search for stability, space, and strength is not new to India's foreign policy. These objectives, at least philosophically, have defined India's foreign policy since Independence in 1947. It is the aggressive recent pursuit of these goals—clinically, amorally, and nonideologically—that is remarkable and unprecedented. And of late, as suggested earlier, the pursuit of these goals with surgical precision is being matched with a sensitivity and greater appreciation for the range of parameters that need to be analyzed to achieve targets with optimum effort and least pain. While there may be a shift in emphasis, and certainly a change of style, it is unlikely that the Congress-led government, which took office in May 2004, will dramatically move away from the pursuit of these goals. As will become obvious later in the chapter, unlike in domestic politics, a new consensus exists within India's strategic elite on the broad contours of New Delhi's foreign policy.

This chapter analyzes India's recent international relations through the dominant views of its strategic elite and reveals the principal debates related to the country's external ties. The first section briefly draws out the dominant recent trends in India's foreign policy. The second section discusses India's evolving relationships with the United States,

China, and Pakistan. The final section examines the prospect for resolving the Kashmir issue, which has often put India on the defensive in multilateral forums, especially in recent years.

Where Is India Headed?

How does India's policy-making elite view the world?[1] What are its fears and hopes? What kind of threats and opportunities does it recognize in the international system? Who does it view as its potential partners and allies? What kind of a role does it want to play in international relations? And what are the strategies that it is likely to employ in the pursuit of its goals? This section presents the findings of a survey, based on a series of conversations with nearly 120 key decision makers or potential decision makers.[2]

India's policy-making elite is consciously and systematically thinking about India's international relations and its place in the world. For those who have suggested that the Indian elite rarely thinks about strategic issues, the findings of this chapter should be enlightening.[3] The new awareness and activism on strategic issues seem to have been most recently provoked by 9/11, the May 1998 nuclear tests, and the 1999 "war" in Kargil, but they are more deeply rooted in developments dating to the early 1990s, including the end of the cold war and the disintegration of the Soviet Union. Only the dominant perceptions are brought out in this chapter. The description and the analysis presented below should not suggest that a homogeneity of opinion exists on key issues affecting

---

1. For the purposes of this paper, policy-making elite is defined as key decision makers in the political, military, business, and scientific fields or those likely to occupy important decision-making positions in the next five years.

2. These conversations, including formally structured interviews and free-ranging discussions, were carried out by the author from August 1998 to August 2002. The respondents included key functionaries of the major national political parties and the important regional parties; senior civil servants in the ministries of commerce, defense, external affairs, home, and finance; senior executives of some of India's largest corporations; heads of major scientific establishments; and senior officers from the armed forces. Respondents are not identified, and all interviews and conversations were off the record. Many of these interactions were possible because of my own professional engagement with foreign policy thinking and making. I have attempted to be as objective as possible and not let my own biases impact on the study. The interviews were supplemented with data obtained from opinion polls carried out by professional polling agencies.

3. See, for instance, George Tanham's essays in *Securing India: Strategic Thought and Practice in an Emerging Power,* ed. Kanti Bajpai and Amitabh Mattoo (New Delhi: Manohar, 1996).

India's relationship with the outside world, but that strong trends indicate the directions that this engagement could take in the future.

There is, however, a convergence of views on key foreign policy issues within what could be described as the core of the strategic elite. This core, located primarily in Delhi with a sprinkling in other metropolitan centers, is quite remarkable in character. Less than 100 strong, it includes prominent journalists; retired civil servants; former admirals, generals, and air marshals; academics and scientists; and a few politicians and businessmen. New entrants to the core group are socialized through regular seminars and workshops. This core group is often the main source of advice on foreign policy issues to even the major political parties like the Congress and the Bharatiya Janata Party (BJP), which continue to have only a few members actively interested in foreign policy issues. Most members of the core know each other, and they interact in forums such as the influential Saturday discussion group of the India International Centre. Members of the Saturday discussion group include a former prime minister, several former ministers, and diplomats. The group follows Chatham House rules, and membership is only by invitation. The group meets weekly to discuss a topical issue over lunch. A member or an invited speaker makes a presentation, which is followed by a discussion. In my experience, the presentations and the discussions are almost always very informative and candid. Over the years, a close bonding has developed among members of the group.

India and the International System

According to the policy-making elite, the emphasis of India's strategic worldview has clearly shifted from "moralspeak" to realpolitik, with a view toward acquiring and exercising military and economic power. Since 9/11 this shift has been modulated by a realization that securing strategic advantage within the complexity of international politics requires more than merely a commitment to the calculus of power. But there has been a clear transition in evidence from the Nehruvian view of the world, associated with the country's first prime minister, Jawaharlal Nehru, that continued to dominate the form and much of the content of India's foreign policy until the mid-1990s. The Nehruvian worldview is often seen as having given importance to norms and values and is generally perceived as having a principled and often idealistic view of international affairs. Indian interests, it is now felt, have often been compromised because of woolly-headed policies that did not reflect the realities of international politics. India's decision to take the Kashmir issue to the United Nations in 1948, as well as the "restraint" exhibited in not weaponizing after the first nuclear test in 1974, are viewed as one long saga of weak and often "spineless policies," to use the words of a prominent journalist.

India's strategic elite considers the international system to be anarchic, without any legitimate supranational authority, and based on the cardinal principle of self-help. Nation-states are here to stay and the possibility of a world government—often stressed by Nehru—seems negligible. It is unlikely that the new Congress-led government will differ significantly from its BJP predecessor in the articulation of its foreign policy. For instance, while the Congress was initially ambivalent about the nuclear tests of 1998, its electoral campaign in 2004 claimed the credit for making India a nuclear power since the country's first nuclear test was carried out during a Congress government. Indeed, Manmohan Singh, in his first address to the nation after becoming prime minister, stated that his government was committed to maintaining a minimum nuclear deterrent capability for India. Moreover, the Congress-led government seems to be following most of its predecessor's policies vis-à-vis the United States, Pakistan, and China.

As indicated earlier, India's primary quest seems to be to acquire the strength and strategic autonomy that will allow it to stabilize an "unfriendly neighborhood," give it the capability to make independent, even unpopular, choices in the international system, and be able to influence the course of international relations. Deterrence and balance of power are seen as vital instruments for promoting national and international security, as are economics and the softer elements of power. Engagement with multilateral regimes is seen as vital, but these are widely perceived to reflect great power interests rather than shared norms. Despite domestic challenges, India's strategic elite is confident that India will emerge as a key economic and military player by the end of the second decade of the twenty-first century and will be recognized as such by other great powers. In this view, order and stability in global relations will be a product of a concert of five or six democratic powers, including India, which would share responsibility for the management of the international system.

Most Indian elite would identify the following as essential internal elements of an Indian grand strategy to become a great power by 2020.

First, India must ensure a sustained economic growth of at least 8 percent for the next ten to fifteen years. India has the third largest economy in Asia, behind Japan and China, and it ranks twelfth in the world. Second, India must strengthen and build a capacity for rapid technological innovation and absorption. Third, India must generate political stability in an era of coalition politics, promote social cohesion in societies that continue to be deeply divided, and manage internal conflicts—especially in the north and northeast of the country.

The external elements of such a strategy include: First, India must strengthen diplomacy and improve negotiating strategies to ensure the protection of its interests in multilateral forums and in the wider process of globalization. Second, India must manage conflicts and relations within the region through a strategy of economic and cultural integration. Third, India must sustain a multifaceted engagement with the United States. Fourth, India must increase its military strength (including through the nuclear deterrent) and project its power from the Persian Gulf to the Straits of Malacca. Fifth, India must creatively use the softer aspects of its power—including culture, literature, and human resources—among those living in India and abroad. And, finally, India must forge economic and cultural links with its extended neighborhood, from Southeast Asia to Central Asia, particularly to ensure the fulfillment of India's energy needs.

India and the United States and China

Loving and Hating the United States

India's strategic elite holds a paradoxical view of the United States. On the one hand, the elite continues to be suspicious of American policies toward South Asia. Some of this tension, of course, is a legacy of the cold war, but the United States' relationship with Pakistan and, more generally, Washington's perceived behavior in international politics keep the tension alive. Resentment over the manner in which the United States continues to reward Pakistan—despite its support for terrorism within India—is palpable, as is the widespread perception that the United States has double standards in dealing with terrorism. Washington's post-9/11 support of the regime of Pakistan's president, General Pervez Musharraf, in exchange for the backing of military operations in Afghanistan against Al Qaeda, generated bitterness within India. It may be recalled that India had offered its full cooperation to the United States, including (it is widely believed) the use of its airfields for operations in Afghanistan, just a few days after 9/11. This offer was quietly, but firmly, declined by the United States. Washington's decision to declare Pakistan a major non-NATO ally in March 2004—within weeks of the confirmation of news reports that scientists in Pakistan had leaked nuclear technology to Iran, Libya, and North Korea—brought home to Indians the more cynical aspects of U.S. short-term interests. Similarly, it is widely held that Washington lacks sensitivity to Indian security concerns and its aspirations of being a great power. The Indian elite is clearly uncomfortable with U.S. "hyperpower," a term popularized by the French that has gained intellectual currency within India. This found expression, most recently, in India's quiet disapproval of Washington's military intervention in Iraq.

The controversy in the United States over business process outsourcing to India has generated anxiety within India. Similarly, the sparring between Indian and American negotiators in various multilateral trade-related forums over the pace of liberalization in agriculture and services continues to demonstrate to New Delhi's educated and influential elite the current limits of a relationship with Washington. It is clear that American self-interest will in no way be compromised in the process of building a relationship with the world's largest democracy.

On the other hand, despite such apprehensions about the United States, few Indians want a confrontation. Instead, there is strong support for engaging the only superpower in a meaningful relationship and for building a strong, pragmatic partnership. The terms "natural allies" and "strategic partners," often used to describe India and the United States, resonate deeply with India's elite, who perceive long-term strategic convergence between the two countries. Economic and technological ties, educational and societal links, shared concern over China's future, and the common battle against *jihadi* terrorism are key factors that bind the United States and India. A shared commitment to pluralism, democracy, and the free market, as well as the successful Indian diaspora in the United States, are strong foundations for the growth of the relationship. Washington's support for India's position during the 1999 Kargil conflict, and the hugely successful visit of President Clinton in 2000, dramatically increased U.S. appeal—even within the traditionally anti-American sections. Economically, the United States is India's largest trading partner and, despite the growing economic influence of China, vital to its recognition as a global player. A modus vivendi with the United States is necessary for India to translate aspirations into reality.

In fact, India's relations with the United States have grown tremendously in virtually every field in the last five years. Even in the once taboo military field, cold war estrangement has changed to engagement of a high order. For example, by 2002 the Indian and American navies had agreed to, and are carrying forward, a three-year program of cooperation that includes substantive exercises, combined operations, and port visits. The two armies have drawn up plans for a joint program that includes high altitude training and disaster management, while the two air forces were working out plans to participate in joint search and rescue missions. In addition, Washington and Delhi have been quietly cooperating on various aspects of national missile defense, sharing information on terrorists and terrorist organizations, and slowly developing a common approach to deal with the proliferation of weapons of mass destruction. The political relationship between India and the United States benefited from the 1998-99 dialogue between Jaswant Singh, India's foreign minister, and Strobe Talbott, President Clinton's deputy secretary of state, and later by the close contact between the two national security advisers, Brajesh Mishra and Condoleezza Rice, from 2001 to early 2004. The presence of President Bush's first ambassador to India, Robert Blackwill, proved to be invaluable during the difficult days immediately following 9/11.[4] It was Blackwill who limited the damage after Washington's new engagement with Islamabad through his contacts with the top political leadership in both countries.

Not unexpectedly, therefore, in January 2004 President Bush announced the "Next Steps in the Strategic Partnership" between India and the United States. The next steps included an agreement to expand cooperation in three specific areas: civilian nuclear activities, civilian space programs, and high-technology trade. In other words, there was a commitment to "expanded engagement on nuclear regulatory and safety issues and missile defense, ways to enhance cooperation in peaceful uses of space technology, and steps to create the appropriate environment for successful high technology commerce."[5] The text of the "Next Steps" declared that the relationship between the United States and India is based increasingly on common values and common interests.

---

4. Blackwill was one of the "Vulcans," a group of close advisers to President Bush during his electoral campaign.

5. Sridhar Krishnaswami, "Bush Announces Steps to Build Strategic Ties with India," *The Hindu,* January 14, 2004.

In sum, despite many irritants—and not all are trivial—India's relationship with the United States seemed more secure in 2004 than it had been in the last fifty years. Not only is there greater connectivity at the senior level of the political leadership, but the bandwidth has also greatly expanded. India seems to have found a place on the bookmarks of Washington's policy community. As the 2003 report of an independent task force on South Asia points out: "Democratic India, with its political stability and a decade of steady economic advance, has the potential for a long-term political and security partnership and substantially expanded trade and economic relations with the United States. Unlike during the Cold War years, U.S. and Indian interests broadly coincide. The medium-term political challenge is to complete the transition from past estrangement through constructive engagement on to a genuine partnership."[6]

China

China is still identified by many of India's educated and influential as the most likely source of insecurity to New Delhi and the greatest potential threat to Indian interests in the long-term future. The principal strategic rationale for constructing a credible and effective Indian nuclear weapon posture is to provide a hedge—an insurance policy—against the possibility of a belligerent China in an uncertain, anarchic world. Many, even within the Left, admit that a future clash of interests between India and China over trade and influence in Asia could happen, but few take the idea of U.S.-China collusion against India seriously. Likewise, few support an Indian role in any U.S.-led containment of China, although many predict that the United States will begin to rely upon India as a key source of balance in Asia. Multiple constructions of China inform public debate in India. Indeed, Indians hold at least three views of China: ancient friend and contemporary ally, role model, and unpredictable adversary and dangerous rival. These "images" need some expansion.

Ancient Friend and Contemporary Ally

The view of India and China as ancient civilizations with strong historical links in partnership in the modern world continues to be articulated

---

6. *New Priorities in South Asia: U.S. Policy Toward India, Pakistan, and Afghanistan* (chairmen's report of an independent task force cosponsored by the Council on Foreign Relations and the Asia Society), chaired by Frank G.Wisner II, Nicholas Platt, and Marshall M. Bouton and directed by Dennis Kux and Mahnaz Ispahani, 2003.

even in 2004. It is essentially a normative and idealized view, rooted in the hope of seeing India and China emerge as strong allies in the contemporary international system. This image often exaggerates the strength of past ties as well as the space for contemporary cooperation. Not surprisingly, critics find this view of China distinctly antediluvian.

There are three strands to this image. First, it is a view that is rooted principally in an anti-colonial and anti-Western discourse. It sees China and India, having been subject to years of western humiliation and re-entering the world stage more or less at the same time as independent actors, challenging the status quo and helping to create a more humane and just world order. The fight against colonialism and the desire for Afro-Asian unity were policy expressions of this view in the 1950s. In its current avatar, issues such as the struggle against American hegemony and the western discourse on human rights and in support of a multipolar world foster this image. Second, this image takes a rather benign view of China's future role, within both the international system and the neighborhood. According to this view, there is no real threat to India from China. Not only because China is satisfied with the status quo with respect to the Sino-Indian border, but also because India does not figure in China's "threat cosmology." Finally, China's future role in Asia and in the international system is also seen as stabilizing and largely defensive rather than subversive and offensive. China's foreign policy, it is argued, has increasingly become deradicalized. Ideology—it is suggested—no longer plays, if it ever did, a decisive role in China's policy toward the outside world. China is no longer seeking to export a revolution, nor are its relations with other countries determined by the nature of their political systems.

In this view, China has accepted the basic parameters of the international system as it operates today. China has gradually become a shareholder in the world economic system. It has a stake in global economic stability, and the prudent, responsible manner in which Beijing responded to the late-1990s economic crisis in East Asia is seen as an important example of China's maturity. China is one of the largest oil importers in the world and one of the largest investors in oil exploration. In short, China is seen as being well integrated into the international economic system. It is also argued that there are increasing external constraints on China's behavior. Beijing has willingly accepted these limits by signing up for the Nuclear Non-Proliferation Treaty and accepted, by and large, the tenets of the Missile Technology Control Regime and is actively associating with regional Asia-Pacific institutions.

Role Model

Closely related to the image of China as both an ancient friend and a contemporary ally is the view of China as a role model. Again, three aspects of this image merit attention. First is the image of China as the near ideal communist state and society. This image of China, although much eroded, inspired a whole generation of communists as well as activists of the Naxalite movement and even middle-class radicals in Delhi colleges. As the Tibetan scholar Dawa Norbu recollects: "When in 1969 I joined the St. Stephen's college (Delhi), to my surprise, I found the very people from whom we had escaped a decade ago right next door. In fact my college proved to be the center of the Naxalite activities. They used the same jargon, had the same convictions, and they held identical views to the Chinese communists. One of their popular slogans was 'China's way is our way; and China's Chairman Mao our Chairman.'"[7] While revelations about the excesses of the Cultural Revolution, the Tiananmen Square massacre, and Beijing's drift toward capitalism have done much to erode this image, it continues to find takers within sections of the Left. Second, China's ability to make hard internal decisions as well as to face up to pressure from the West have been lionized by sections throughout the spectrum of public opinion in India. "Why can India not do a Tibet in Kashmir? Would China have capitulated before the hijackers in Kandahar? Would China sign the Comprehensive Test Ban Treaty under pressure?" These are a few of the questions that are being rhetorically posed in public debates in India. Third, China's emergence as a significant economic and military power and its ability to reform its economy without compromising its security posture are viewed with awe and admiration.

Unpredictable Adversary and Dangerous Rival?

Despite its magnetism, China is consistently identified as the most likely source of insecurity to India and the greatest potential threat to Indian interests. From this perspective, there are many warning signs already. By far the most serious concern is the help provided by Beijing to Pakistan's nuclear program. It is argued that the true extent of Beijing-Islamabad nuclear collusion may never be revealed, but it is clear that

---

7. See Dawa Norbu, *Tibet: The Road Ahead* (London: Trafalgar Square Publishing, 1999).

Pakistan's nuclear weapons program has relied enormously on China's help and Chinese nuclear engineers may have designed Islamabad's nuclear weapons. Nuclear cooperation of this kind is unprecedented in the history of international relations since 1945; indeed, not even the United States and Britain shared such a relationship. Why would China want to help Pakistan become a nuclear weapon state? India's elite feels that Beijing has consistently regarded a nuclear-armed Pakistan as a crucial regional ally and a vital counterweight to India's growing capabilities. The unwillingness, until recently, on China's part to settle any of the bilateral irritants to which India attaches importance reinforced this perception. Beijing has still not recognized the northeast border state of Arunachal Pradesh as part of India, and it was only recently that it signaled that it might be willing to formally accept Sikkim's accession to India. For a dominant section of the Indian elite, Chinese inroads into Myanmar, including the reported construction of a Chinese naval facility on the Coco islands, should be of deep strategic concern to India. Additionally, the presence of thousands of Tibetan refugees is an irritant that is likely to worsen, as a new generation of Tibetans becomes increasingly radicalized. China has deployed nuclear missiles in Tibet that clearly have one target: India. Admittedly, it is argued, Chinese intercontinental ballistic missiles elsewhere could also target India, but the potential political and psychological impact of these missiles—literally a few miles from India's border—during a future conflict cannot be underestimated.

Which View Predominates?

Which view is prevailing? It seems that a combination of factors has led to the construction of a three-track policy toward China. First, cooperation with China is being accelerated at all levels. Trade has substantially increased, and India's foreign direct investment in China is not insignificant.

The process of introducing confidence-building measures, which began in the early 1990s, has also been consolidated. Although there are continued reports of incursions by the Chinese across the disputed boundary, these seem to have reduced in the last year or so. In 2003, after Prime Minister Vajpayee's visit to China, it was decided to set up a dedicated channel for negotiations on the boundary dispute. A joint working group had tried to resolve the differences for several years without much success. India's position changed remarkably from the 1960s, when senior leaders declared that not an inch of Indian territory would be allowed to be taken by China. In contrast, in 2004 New Delhi believed that India's negotiations should be dictated by "interest bargaining" instead of "position bargaining." It was within this framework that the third round of talks on the boundary dispute by India's national security adviser, J.N. Dixit, and China's vice foreign minister, Dai Bingguo, were held in July 2004. Although the talks lacked a dramatic breakthrough, progress had been made. India seemed finally prepared for a grand compromise on the boundary issue.

India was also cooperating with China on issues such as human rights in multilateral forums. Both Beijing and New Delhi seemed convinced that a multipolar world was essential for global stability.

The second element of India's strategy toward China included expanding cooperation with many of China's neighbors. This included, for instance, naval exercises in the South China Sea with the Vietnamese, improved military ties with Singapore, and greater activism in Asian multilateral forums. The strategy was not to position New Delhi explicitly as a counterweight to China, but to slowly and surely enlarge the space of Indian interests, from the Strait of Malacca to the Persian Gulf, in order to emerge as a key balance to China. Finally, India was seeking to build an effective minimum nuclear deterrent, through a triad of sea, land, and air forces. The "minimum" was clearly defined as the possession of an Indian second-strike capability against China.

India's Neighborhood

Pakistan continues to be India's most challenging relationship, yet Nepal, Bangladesh, and Sri Lanka also pose security concerns. India's chief concern with Nepal is the Maoist insurgency there, as well as the issue of Pakistani intelligence using Nepal as a transit route to infiltrate militants into India. Bangladesh, over the years, has been taking an anti-India stance and is reportedly harboring anti-India terrorists apart from helping the Pakistani Inter-Services Intelligence in its operations against India. Of late, however, there are signs of improvement due to the commercial interests of both countries in the gas and oil sector.

Engaging Pakistan

Since 9/11, bilateral ties have been tumultuous. A terrorist attack on Indian Parliament on December 13, 2001, alleged to have been carried out by

Pakistan-sponsored terrorists, led to the largest mobilization of the Indian armed forces in recent years and preparations just short of war. Relations between Islamabad and New Delhi dipped to a nadir as India decided to recall its high commissioner from Islamabad and terminate its transport links with Pakistan. Indeed, in January 2002, the Indian army chief, General S. Padmanabhan, declared that the Indian army was prepared for war. There were widespread fears internationally that the crisis could lead to a full-blown conventional war, which could potentially escalate into a nuclear one. Fortunately, by summer 2002 a combination of factors including pro-active western diplomacy, assurances by Pakistan's top leadership on cross-border terrorism, and India's own strategic calculations helped diffuse one of the most severe crises in the history of India-Pakistan relations. While the fear of war ended, it took more than a year before India and Pakistan had once again established normal diplomatic relations.

The promise of a substantive dialogue was generated after a meeting between Prime Minister Vajpayee and President Musharraf in early 2004 alongside the summit of the South Asian Association for Regional Co-operation (SAARC) in Islamabad. The real challenge of addressing the number of bilateral irritants, including Kashmir, was left to the new government of Prime Minister Singh, which seemed inclined, at least initially, to carry forward the policies of its predecessor. Pakistan, not surprisingly, invites the most passionate debates within India's elite. Opinion is divided almost equally between those who want to aggressively counter Pakistan; those who want to ignore and benignly neglect Islamabad; and those who want New Delhi to proactively promote peace, even to the extent of making unilateral concessions. But even those who seek to make unilateral concessions consider the *jihadi* threat to be the most serious threat that India faces and one likely to pose even greater problems in the future. The more hard-line sections believe that India, despite persistent efforts, has been unable to inject a modicum of civility and stability in bilateral relations. For them Pakistan presents perhaps the most intriguing example in the history of state-to-state relations. They look to the military defeat in 1971, constructive engagement, unilateral gestures, passive disregard, and international pressure as proof that nothing seems to be able to reduce the pathological hostility that the Pakistani state bears toward India, which goes much beyond the problems in Kashmir. They view the Pakistani state, and its most important institution, the Pakistan army, as needing hostility toward India for its survival, and consequently believe that only a dramatic reconstruction of the Pakistani state would create the possibility of peace in South Asia. They point toward the recent history of India-Pakistan relations and the manner in which the whole spectrum of policies adopted by New Delhi toward Islamabad has floundered.

Thrice since 1998 New Delhi has publicly engaged Pakistan. The Lahore summit of February 1999 raised expectations that a new détente in the subcontinent was in the offing, and indeed the summit documents included an imaginative set of cooperative measures, particularly on the nuclear issue. Even prudent analysts seemed to have been convinced that the overt nuclearization of the subcontinent would help Pakistan acquire the confidence and maturity to normalize its relations with India without being burdened by existentialist fears that had plagued it since 1947, but particularly since the 1971 war against India (that led to the establishment of Bangladesh). Rather than seek to project itself as a responsible nuclear power, Pakistan then sought to use the cover of nuclear weapons to escalate the conflict in Kashmir. Similarly, in the eyes of India's hardliners the Agra summit in 2001 failed—primarily because Pakistan was unwilling to concede that no normalization of relations is possible while Islamabad continues to sponsor violence and terror across the border. Indeed, it is argued that India was much more willing to concede at Agra than it had been during the last decade—to the extent that it was even willing to set up a high-level bilateral group to discuss only Kashmir. But whatever was left of the spirit of Agra evaporated after the terrorist attack in Srinagar on October 1, 2001, and the attacks on Indian Parliament on December 13, 2001.

According to the hardliners, unilateral gestures of goodwill and co-operation have made no difference in India-Pakistan relations. India's continued treatment of Pakistan as a most favored nation has not been reciprocated by Islamabad and the report of the SAARC Eminent Persons Group, which recommends imaginative time-bound steps to promote regional economic integration, has been given short shrift by Pakistan, despite the presence of one of its former foreign secretaries in the group. New Delhi's pre-Agra decision to unilaterally relax visa rules and its decision to open further crossing points on the border have failed or have had little effect in the absence of Pakistani reciprocity. The hope that there could be a détente from below, a genuine breakthrough because of greater human contact, has been dashed.

Surprising as it may seem, despite the Kargil conflict in 1999 and the terrorist attacks on Indian Parliament in 2001, a significant section of Indian opinion believes that India—more than ever before—has a stake in the future of Pakistan. Former Prime Minister Vajpayee unambiguously stated that Pakistan's stability was in India's national interest, and sizable sections of the population echo this sentiment. They argue that Vajpayee's statement is a harsh reality rather than a political slogan. True, Pakistan's demise may finally bury whatever is left of the two-nation theory, but that would be too heavy a price merely to prove that a mistake—huge as it may have been—was made fifty-seven years ago.

Pakistan needs to survive, not just for the sake of its own citizens, but also for the health of South Asia. Pervez Hoodbhoy, a nuclear physicist in Islamabad and an anti-nuclear activist, put it most graphically: "Pakistan's state is already fractured by multiple violent ethnic and religious conflicts. Disintegration into molecular civil war with fiefdoms and warlords is a terrible possibility. India will find, too late, that it has created a South Asian nuclear Somalia for a neighbor."[8] Hoodbhoy's sentiments have been echoed by a variety of respondents, who argue that a nuclear Pakistan, on the verge of economic and political disintegration, will endanger the whole region. Deterrence stability requires a modicum of political stability and control. In other words, political turmoil and economic chaos in Pakistan can create conditions in which nuclear stability in South Asia could be seriously threatened. The political and economic health of Pakistan is of concern to India's strategic elite for other reasons as well. Ethnic turmoil in Pakistan could easily spill over to India, and the country's balkanization could even lead to a huge refugee problem in India. Similarly, self-styled warlords could well expand their narcotics and gunrunning businesses into India. In broader terms, the crumbling of Pakistan's economy could extend to India's economy. South Asia would be viewed as a zone of turmoil and lead to erosion in investor confidence, as well as possible flight of capital, even from India. But, perhaps most crucially, the collapse of Pakistan would inevitably lead to a larger cultural demoralization. It would suggest that even after years of independence South Asian countries lack firm control over their citizens. It would suggest a failure to develop coherent systems of governance. South Asia, not just Pakistan, would become an

---

8. Pervez Hoodbhoy, "Surviving South Asia's Nuclear Whirlpool" (paper presented at the Regional Centre for Strategic Studies [RCSS] conference on the Future of Security Studies in South Asia, Ahungalla, Sri Lanka, July 14–16, 1998), p. 2.

international object of ridicule, and the whole project of nationhood in the region would become deeply suspect.

Predictably, many felt that the previous BJP-led government was uniquely positioned to help Pakistan. In this view, the BJP alone occupies the political space in which gestures of goodwill toward Pakistan will be interpreted as neither appeasement nor sellout. Nevertheless, the new Congress-led government is following the 2004 BJP-initiated policy toward Pakistan. The policy has five elements. First, the Indian government recognizes the importance of sustained engagement with Pakistan. Although there is continued suspicion of the Pakistan army and intelligence agencies and a strong belief that long-term peace and stability in South Asia will be impossible while armed forces continue to dominate the state, a comprehensive dialogue is seen as essential to reduce tensions and assuage international opinion. Second, there is a growing view that it may be possible to do business with President Musharraf. While President Musharraf is seen as the architect of the Kargil war and one who, with his fellow soldiers, shares a pathological hostility toward India, the interests of Pakistan's president and New Delhi may converge, especially in the fight against *jihadi* forces. Third, India has begun to recognize the importance of other actors and institutions within Pakistan, especially its civil society. New Delhi is willing to engage and strengthen Pakistan's civil society, through unilateral gestures if needed. Fourth, India may be willing to settle, through increased flexibility, many of the minor bilateral irritants that affect the relationship. These include the continued "war" over the Siachen glacier, often described as the highest battlefield in the world, the dispute over the Sir Creek maritime boundary, and the Tulbul Navigation Project.[9]

---

9. The dispute over the Siachen glacier stems from the demarcation of the Line of Control between India and Pakistan in Kashmir. The LOC is demarcated only up to map reference point NJ 9842. Siachen lies beyond this point, and because of competing claims has witnessed fierce fighting since 1984, when India—in a bid to preempt Pakistani intrusion—occupied the glacier.

Sir Creek is a sixty-mile-long estuary in the marshes of the Rann of Kutch in western India. The region lies between the Indian state of Gujarat and the Pakistani province of Sind. India claims that the boundary should lie in the middle of the estuary, basing its claim on pillars built down the middle of part of the channel during British colonial rule. Pakistan says the border should lie on the southeastern bank of the creek, showing a line given on a British era map.

As for the Tulbul Navigation Project (Pakistan describes it as Wullar Barrage), India wanted to build the barrage in 1984 on the Jhelum River, which is at the mouth of Wullar Lake near Sopore town in the Indian part of Kashmir. Pakistan considers it a violation of the Indus Water Treaty, signed in 1960. The barrage would make the river navigable in summer, but Pakistan thinks that it would give India the control of the flow of the river and, therefore, could be used as a geo-strategic weapon.

Finally, New Delhi is prepared to address the issue of Jammu and Kashmir with Pakistan. However, a compromise on the issue will be possible only when the atmosphere of hostility has lifted and relations have been normalized. This will require a speedy movement toward the economic integration of South Asia as well as the introduction of a range of confidence-building measures that allow for greater exchange of ideas, people, goods, and services. The Indian cricket team's recent visit to Pakistan and the welcome it received demonstrated the potential positive impact of greater popular contact between the two countries.

Strengthening Unilateral Ties

With India's smaller eastern neighbors, there is a virtual consensus that a healthy dose of unilateralism can help bind them into a stable integrative relationship with India. Nonreciprocity was the essence of the Gujral Doctrine, spelled out by the former prime minister of India, Inder Kumar Gujral. India would not impose a tit-for-tat policy toward its smaller neighbors; instead, unilateral gestures of goodwill would not demand immediate reciprocity.

Building free trade arrangements with all of India's neighbors is seen as a key to creating a stable Asia that will accommodate Indian interests. Indian dominance is a reality, but India recognizes that the road to being a global player also passes through Colombo, Dhaka, and Katmandu, and perhaps even Islamabad. Particularly great emphasis is being placed on building and strengthening India's presence in Central and Southeast Asia and within the Indian Ocean Rim. Evidence of this includes India's recent engagement with Afghanistan (including substantial aid provided for its post-Taliban reconstruction) and its growing ties with Iran (including an India-aided project for the construction of a port at Chabahar to facilitate India's transit through the "garland route" to Central Asia) and most of the Central Asian republics.

Resolving Jammu and Kashmir

Two central hurdles stand in the way of peace in Kashmir: the conflict between India and the people of Jammu and Kashmir (the conflict *in* Kashmir) and the problems between New Delhi and Islamabad (the conflict *over* Kashmir). Sustainable long-term peace would require resolution of both conflicts, but the situation on the ground would be greatly improved if New Delhi were able to arrive at a modus vivendi with representatives of the Kashmiri people, especially of that section which has been demanding secession from India. While for some *azadi* (loosely translated as "freedom") would be achieved only if full sovereignty was transferred to the people of Kashmir, many others believe that *azadi* and popular aspirations can be accommodated within the federal structure of India through an imaginative framework of devolution of powers.

The Conflict in Kashmir

Indeed, despite the apparently intractable nature of the conflict, several factors have coalesced to produce one of the most significant opportunities for peace in Kashmir's recent history. After the Kargil war of 1999 and the terrorist attacks of September 11, 2001, India perceived a shift in international public opinion as well as in the popular sentiment in Kashmir. These factors are, however, rooted in deeper changes within the Indian polity, including the growing consensus on economic and political decentralization and New Delhi's ambitions of increasing India's influence within the international system. India's top political leadership, including the new government of Prime Minister Singh, seems willing to commit itself to a more long term and imaginative course for its Kashmir policy.

In January 2001, Prime Minister Vajpayee declared: "In our search for a lasting solution to the Kashmir problem, both in its external and internal dimensions, we shall not traverse solely on the beaten track of the past. Rather, we shall be bold and innovative designers of a future architecture of peace and prosperity for the entire South Asian region. In this search, the sole light that will guide us is our commitment to peace, justice, and the vital interests of the nation."[10] Vajpayee's words reflected New Delhi's shift in policy toward Kashmir during the previous year, particularly since November 2000. Elements of the policy initiative included a move toward the isolation of forces perpetrating violence, a readiness to initiate unconditional negotiations with Kashmiri separatists, and a willingness to reengage Pakistan in a composite dialogue. The government of India has achieved varying degrees of success

---

10. Atal Bihari Vajpayee, "My Musings from Kumarakom," part 1, "Time to Resolve Problems of the Past; Time to Move on Towards a Better Future," January 3, 2001 (http:// pib.nic.in/focus/foyr2001/fojan2001/fo020120011.html, accessed September 12, 2004).

in these objectives, but clearly New Delhi's policy is part of a larger rethink on Kashmir, and not merely a tactical maneuver to secure short-term advantage. These efforts seem to be based on a broad framework of understanding that is spelled out in detail below.

Kashmir Is Unique, and Must Be Dealt with Specially

Jammu and Kashmir's uniqueness is obvious for a variety of historical reasons recognized even by the Indian Supreme Court. More significant, however, is Kashmir's singular importance to the very idea of India —which has often been forgotten and is now re-entering the consciousness of the political elite. A Muslim majority state that voluntarily acceded to India, Kashmir lent tremendous strength to the construction of India as a vibrant, secular, and pluralistic state. Maharajah Hari Singh's decision to accede to India in October 1947 was supported by the most powerful political party of the state, the National Conference, and the most popular Kashmiri Muslim leader, Sheikh Abdullah. The battle to recover the trust of the Kashmiri people is critical not just to regain the ideals that inspired Indian nationhood but also to strengthen the war against obscurantism and fundamentalism, especially of the Islamic variety. In other words, India has realized that Kashmir must no longer be treated with the kind of political ineptitude and bureaucratic inertia that has often characterized New Delhi's policies toward many other states in recent decades.

Autonomy Is Not a Dirty Word

There is a growing realization that granting autonomy to the province will not weaken its relationship with India. Today, autonomy is associated with empowerment, giving people a sense of belonging, and increasing the accountability of public institutions and services. Autonomy is synonymous with "decentralization" and "devolution of power," phrases on the charter of virtually every political party in India. In Jammu and Kashmir, autonomy resonates with people because puppet leaders from the state colluded, over time, with the central leadership and gradually eroded the autonomy promised by the constitution. There is no contradiction between India's desire for Kashmir to be part of the national mainstream and the state's desire for autonomous self-governance. If this balance is struck, Jammu and Kashmir could become a model of "cooperative federalism," a special model that could be gradually applied to other states in the union. Separatism grows when people feel disconnected from the structures of power and the process of policy formulation; in contrast, devolution ensures popular participation in the running of the polity. The aspirations for *azadi* could easily be accommodated through greater autonomy.

Restoration of autonomy in Kashmir requires neither elaborate reports nor reference to past agreements and accords—they obfuscate rather than clarify the issue of meaningful self-governance. Autonomy can be achieved through a simple plan.[11]

Admitting Mistakes: The First Step Toward Restoring Trust Between New Delhi and Kashmir

Over the years, the federal government has made a number of appalling mistakes in Kashmir. Several elections have been rigged, genuinely elected governments have been dismissed, puppet leaders have been installed, and—in the last decade—the ordinary Kashmiri has faced tremendous harassment from security forces. Some of these mistakes were avoidable, others inevitable given the complex situation on the ground. Admission of these mistakes will be construed not as an expression of guilt, but as a signal that fresh initiatives toward Kashmir will be based upon an awareness of past mistakes and a genuine desire to avoid their repetition.

Recovery of Kashmiriyat Is Vital to Sustained Peace

While there does seem to be a genuine, all-pervasive desire within Jammu and Kashmir to recover the social capital lost in the last decade and to restore Kashmir's traditional society based on ideas of peaceful coexistence, pluralism, and the common syncretic identity of Kashmiriyat, New Delhi seems to have realized that the recovery of this ethos must be central to its efforts to build peace in the state. Kashmiriyat, often described as the composite cultural identity of the Kashmiris, is rooted in a blend of Kashmir's three most important religions: Mahayana Buddhism, Sufi Islam, and Shaivite Hinduism.

---

11. In 1997, the Delhi Policy Group, an Indian think tank, set up an independent study group to recommend measures to restore normalcy in Jammu and Kashmir. See Kanti Bajpai et al., *Kashmir: An Agenda for the Future* (New Delhi: Delhi Policy Group, 1999).

Moreover, the return of the Kashmiri Pandit minority community, which left Kashmir en masse because of the insurgency, is crucial for the revitalization of the traditions of pluralism and communal harmony. The Kashmiri Pandits, although a tiny Hindu minority, have (because of a traditional commitment to education) occupied prominent positions of authority and influence within Kashmir and the rest of India. India's first prime minister belonged to the community. A dialogue between civil society leaders of Kashmiri Pandits and Kashmiri Muslims is now being promoted and facilitated. The return of Pandits continues to be a top priority of the state and central government.

Ensuring Greater Regional Balance Is Vital, but Dividing Indian Jammu and Kashmir Should Be Ruled Out

Powerful forces, including sections of the Rashtriya Swayamsevak Sangh, the Jammu-based Jammu Mukti Morcha, and the Ladakh Buddhist Association, are demanding a trifurcation of Jammu, Kashmir, and Ladakh into separate administrative units. Posing as an imaginative solution this demand, if conceded, could lead to violent social disruptions in the state and create a communal polarization that would irretrievably destroy the cultural and social fabric of the state, with perilous consequences for communal relations in the rest of India. In addition, trifurcation would forever end the possibilities of reviving the plural traditions of communal harmony in the state that once made it a symbol of the very idea of India. New Delhi seems to have realized that while it must help create greater regional balance, it must not divide the state.

The demand for a division of the state is not new. United Nations mediator Sir Owen Dixon recommended a partition in 1950, and elements within the Praja Parishad agitation of the early 1950s also held that Ladakh and Jammu should be detached from the valley if full integration of the state was not achieved quickly. But, in its new avatar, several factors have coalesced to produce a potentially explosive situation.

Most important is the widespread feeling within Jammu and Leh of deprivation, as well as political and economic discrimination, by politicians from Kashmir. While this sentiment may have some grounds, it is being exploited by sectarian political groups who are demanding separate statehood for Jammu and union territory status for Leh. They argue that not only would separation from Kashmir ensure better governance, more economic opportunities, and a greater share of political power, but it would also allow Jammu and Leh to distance themselves from the militancy. They claim that it is in the national interest to limit the "area of operations" of the security forces to the Kashmir valley, and that after the division only one-sixth of the state would remain troubled.

This logic is dangerous for at least three reasons. First, trifurcation would destroy the composite identity of the state, which has existed as one unit since 1846, and send a dangerous message to the whole nation. If Hindus, Muslims, and Buddhists cannot live together in one state, can they do so in a larger entity? Second, trifurcation would most probably lead to a transfer of Muslims from various parts of Jammu, including parts of the city but also Doda, Rajouri, and Poonch, assuming that the whole province becomes a separate state. Finally, trifurcation would lead to such deep communal polarization that riots would almost inevitably follow. It is no coincidence that the only group in the Kashmir valley that has supported the idea of trifurcation is the Jamat-e-Islami.

The Conflict Over Kashmir

While the conflict in Kashmir is showing signs of slowly moving toward a possible settlement, India and Pakistan are still deadlocked over the region. Until recently, Pakistan continued to aid, train, and arm militants who operate in Kashmir; these militants are increasingly non-Kashmiris, and many of them are threatening to wage *jihad* all over the Indian subcontinent. But there are indications that a small but increasingly influential constituency in Pakistan might be willing to accept a "solution" that the Kashmiris work out with India. This constituency needs to be strengthened. India, together with the international community and especially the United States, can provide economic and other incentives to Pakistan to prevent it from subverting the peace process in Kashmir. In addition, New Delhi can keep Islamabad informed of the progress of its dialogue with the Kashmiris.

If India can find a modus vivendi with the Kashmiris, a permanent division of Jammu and Kashmir between India and Pakistan along the present Line of Control (LOC), with minor adjustments if need be, is viewed as the only realistic, practical, and just settlement of the problem. Such a move would require that India forsake its commitment to the unanimous parliamentary resolution that calls for reclaiming the territory "under Pakistan's occupation" and that Pakistan relinquish its traditional claim to all of Kashmir. Yet a conversion of the present LOC into an international border would settle a problem that has defied solution for more than half a century.

The LOC corresponds, more or less, to the Cease-fire Line (CFL) created after armed hostilities between India and Pakistan were suspended on January 1, 1949. It was delineated on maps during the Karachi Agreement of July 27, 1949, formally known as the "Agreement Between Military Representatives of India and Pakistan Regarding the Establishment of a Cease-fire Line in the State of Jammu and Kashmir." By November 3, 1949, with the help of United Nations military observers, the borders on the map had been demarcated on the ground by the two sides. The CFL, however, was demarcated only from the west of the Chenab River up to map coordinate NJ 9842, and not beyond. The absence of any physical demarcation has led to competing claims over the Siachen glacier, but the legality of the CFL itself has never been questioned. The CFL, with minor changes, became the LOC after the Shimla Agreement of July 2, 1972. It was delineated on maps and demarcated by top military officers from both India and Pakistan. Until the Pakistani intrusion in Kargil, the sanctity of the LOC had been accepted and respected as such by the governments in Islamabad and New Delhi and their military commanders on the border. In short, the CFL/LOC has been the de facto border for more than fifty years.

There have been at least three occasions on which agreement was almost reached between top Indian and Pakistani leaders that Jammu and Kashmir be partitioned along the CFL/LOC, with some adjustments. In 1955, Prime Minister Jawaharlal Nehru and Pakistani Governor General Ghulam Mohammad supposedly agreed to a division along the CFL with minor adjustments. Between December 1962 and May 1963 Pakistan's foreign minister, Zulfiqar Ali Bhutto, and Sardar Swaran Singh, a senior Indian cabinet minister, discussed a plan for partitioning along the CFL, with India conceding an additional 3,000 square miles west and north of the Kashmir valley, including Tithwal and Handal forests and the river Kishanganga. In 1972, Prime Ministers Indira Gandhi and Zulfiqar Ali Bhutto arrived at an understanding that converting the LOC into the international border was the only way out of the Kashmir conundrum. Bhutto, however, did not want to put the agreement in black and white. Bhutto "wanted time" to prepare his people for the "deal" because they had been traumatized by the defeat in the 1971 war and the dismemberment of Pakistan. Bhutto reneged on this understanding within months. However, most of Indira Gandhi's advisers knew about the secret agreement.[12] Gandhi's secretary, P.N. Dhar, has written about it, and her closest adviser during that period, P.N. Haksar, was also aware of the understanding.

History aside, converting the LOC into the international border is still the most practical solution to the Kashmir issue, for at least four reasons. First, a solution cannot be based upon absolutes. Absolute victory is impossible for either India or Pakistan. It is unrealistic for either country to imagine that it can, through force or diplomacy, reunify the whole of Jammu and Kashmir. Similarly, Islamabad must realize that neither war, nor support for insurgencies, nor international pressure will force New Delhi to give up the provinces of Jammu, Kashmir, and Ladakh. Second, rewriting boundaries in South Asia would have disastrous consequences for the region. Apart from displacing huge populations, it could lead to communal clashes bloodier than those during the partition of India. Third, the present LOC corresponds, more or less, to a broad ethnic-linguistic division within the former princely state. Finally, the two regions have lived as a part of India and Pakistan for more than half a century. Although they have grievances against their respective leaderships, the cumulative process of integration will be extremely difficult to reverse. It is hard to imagine how the existing economic and communication links could be erased without causing a tremendous upheaval.

Conversion of the LOC does not mean continuation of hostilities. If India and Pakistan were to see the sense in such an idea, both New Delhi and Islamabad could work toward converting the territory around the LOC into a demilitarized zone. Gradually, there could be a resumption of trade, free passage of goods, and visa-less travel for Kashmiris across the divide, and Kashmiris would enjoy autonomy within India and Pakistan.

To conclude, in 2004 India was attempting to put together a set of pragmatic policies on a range of critical issues. These policies were rooted in realism but recognized the need for factoring in the number of variables that impact India's relationship with its neighbors and the rest of the world. Whether these policies will help India emerge as a power to reckon with in the years to come remains to be seen.

---

12. P.N. Dhar, *Indira Gandhi, the "Emergency," and Indian Democracy* (New York and New Delhi: Oxford University Press, 2000).

The Cultural Background of Hindutva

Richard H. Davis

Over the past two decades, one of the most significant and far-reaching developments in the subcontinent has been the rise of Hindutva as a cultural, religious, and political force in modern India. A watershed event in the emergence of Hindutva was the Ayodhya Ramjanmabhumi mobilization, which led to the destruction of the Babri Masjid, a Mughal era mosque, in December 1992. The mosque was destroyed to recover what promoters identified as the birthplace of the god Rama. On the heels of this movement, the Bharatiya Janata Party (BJP) rose to prominence as the political or electoral instrument of Hindutva and became the leading national alternative to the fading Congress Party. From 1998 to 2004 the BJP was the principal member of the governing coalition, the National Democratic Alliance.

No less important than the political rise of the BJP, however, have been the social, cultural, and religious effects of Hindutva, some of them tragic. In the wake of the Babri Masjid destruction, widespread riots erupted throughout northern India. Within two months, some three thousand lives had been lost and countless families dislocated as a result of social violence. Since then numerous other conflicts have led to extensive street violence. Most recently, in February 2002, a group of Muslims in Godhra, Gujarat, torched two train cars carrying Hindutva activists who were returning from Ayodhya, killing fifty-eight passengers. In a three-day spree of retaliatory violence, Hindu rioters looted and burned Muslim homes and shops, raped and mutilated Muslim women, and altogether caused between 850 and 2,000 deaths. Meanwhile, the BJP-led state government did little to quell the violence, and some have accused the chief minister, Narendra Modi, with actively abetting an anti-Muslim pogrom.[1] Beneath these public conflagrations are the countless unrecorded

---

1. Human Rights Watch, *"We Have No Orders to Save You": State Participation and Complicity in Communal Violence in Gujarat,* 2002 (www.hrw.org/reports/2002/india).

changes in everyday life—the mundane intimidations, humiliations, and fears of minorities—that are the amorphous consequences of the spread of Hindutva activism. And the shape of Hinduism itself may be changing as well. Observers have pointed to a homogenizing shift, by which certain upper-caste practices and values are extended to all classes, and some regional practices are consciously spread throughout India. Some have called this move toward unity a "semiticizing" of Hinduism, which has for centuries been a wonderfully diverse religious culture. It may be no exaggeration to suggest, as historian K.N. Panikkar puts it, that proponents of Hindutva have brought about a "molecular transformation" in contemporary India, as if the very grounds of public life have been altered.[2]

To understand these changes, it is necessary to look at the agency of the groups promoting Hindutva. It is undoubtedly true that many broad developments in India have laid the groundwork for the rise of Hindutva groups, such as the decline of the Congress Party, the economic consequences of globalization, separatist movements involving religious minorities in Punjab and Kashmir, and the rising aspirations and frustrations of the lower classes. However, Hindutva groups have successfully mobilized followers and disseminated their messages within these circumstances, and in the process they have altered the conditions as well.

This chapter sketches the cultural background for the rise of Hindutva within Indian public life. After a brief consideration of some of the terms associated with Hindutva (including that term), the ideological and organizational history of the Hindutva movement is outlined. The focus then narrows to two projects of the Hindutva groups over the past two decades in order to indicate how they draw upon, and also transform, the cultural and religious past of South Asia. Finally, the conclusion addresses the ways these projects may be changing the nature of Hinduism itself.

Terms

The preeminent theorist of Hindutva, Vinayak Damodar Savarkar, began his seminal essay, *Hindutva: Who Is a Hindu?* (1923), by taking issue with the lines Shakespeare gives to Romeo, "What's in a name? That which we call a rose by any other name would smell as sweet."

---

2. K.N. Panikkar, *An Agenda for Cultural Action and Other Essays* (New Delhi: Three Essays, 2002), ix.

Since the association of the word with the thing it signifies is strong and long lasting, counters Savarkar, words certainly do matter.[3] The Indian debates surrounding Hindutva have often centered around disputed words, and so it will be valuable to begin this inquiry by looking at a few of its primary terms.

"Hindutva" literally means "Hindu-ness" and has become, since Savarkar's coinage, widely accepted shorthand for referring to various groups and projects that aim at redefining India as a "Hindu Rashtra" or Hindu nation. These groups contend that, as a nation-state whose population is more than 80 percent Hindu, India should identify itself more closely with the cultural and religious values of Hindus. By privileging the values of one putative group (which is considered to be a unified entity), Hindutva or "Hindu nationalism" distinguishes itself from "Indian nationalism," the dominant form of national ideology in the independence movement and in post-Independence India through the 1970s. As one Hindutva theoretician framed it, the mainstream independence movement pursued "territorial nationalism" while Hindutva groups sought a form of "cultural nationalism." While many proponents see Hindutva as expressing primarily cultural values, other observers characterize it as a type of "religious nationalism."[4] The hazy dividing line between culture and religion within Hindutva will be addressed later in this chapter.

Groups espousing Hindutva depart from, and contrast themselves with, the dominant governing ideology of India since Independence, often labeled "secularism." The value of secularism was embedded in the preamble of the Indian Constitution and defined as "the neutrality of the state in relation to different religious communities."[5] This view of the limited place of religion in the Indian nation-state is so closely identified with India's first prime minister, Jawaharlal Nehru, that his name is often affixed as an adjective, "Nehruvian secularism." However, in the view of Hindutva proponents, this kind of secularism disadvantages the Hindu majority by "appeasing the minorities" and implicitly privileges

---

3. Vinayak Damodar Savarkar, *Hindutva: Who Is a Hindu?*, 6th ed. (New Delhi: Bharti Sahitya Sadan, 1989), 1–2.

4. Anthony D. Smith, *Theories of Nationalism* (New York: Harper & Row, 1971), usefully distinguishes between forms of nationalism based on territory and those based on ethnicity. For religious nationalism, see Peter Van der Veer, *Religious Nationalism: Hindus and Muslims in India* (Berkeley: University of California Press, 1994), 22–24.

5. T.N. Madan, *Modern Myths, Locked Minds: Secularism and Fundamentalism in India* (New Delhi: Oxford University Press, 1997), 31.

a cosmopolitan irreligiosity. Secularism is itself a foreign ideology, they contend, not one that grows directly out of the Indian experience. Therefore they prefer the term "pseudo-secularism," to suggest that Nehruvian secularism is not entirely without its own ideological preferences.

Critics often accuse Hindutva groups of instigating "communalism" or "communal conflict." In its distinctive Indian usage, communalism refers to the mobilization of collective antagonism of "communities" based on ethnic, linguistic, or religious identities. Some juxtapose "communal" and "secular" as antithetical terms—for example, in characterizing the 2004 election as a choice between a "communal" party, the BJP, and "secular" parties such as the Congress-I—usually to the detriment of the so-called communalists. According to this charge, proponents of Hindutva seek to organize Hindus and engender hostility toward other communities, notably Muslims. There is no question that a great deal of communal violence has accompanied the rise of Hindutva. However, Hindutva leaders regularly deny the charge of communalism. If India is in essence a Hindu nation, as they contend, they are not acting on behalf of one among several communities. Rather, they claim to represent "the real India struggling to become itself," as historian David Ludden puts it. For them, "communal conflict is an unintended by-product of Hindu national self-assertion that results from adverse reactions from minority communities and the Indian state."[6]

Hindutva has sometimes been identified by journalists, scholars, and critics as a form of "Hindu fundamentalism." This label implicitly assimilates Hindutva, often in a pejorative sense, to other varieties of religious fundamentalism better known to American readers, such as the Christian Coalition and the Moral Majority in the United States, the Muslim Brotherhood of Egypt, or the revolutionary Shi'a movement led by the Ayatollah Ruhollah Khomeini in Iran. Although the term is not indigenous to India, there is some basis for this comparison. Like fundamentalist religious groups elsewhere, Hindutva is not simply a conservative or defensive religious response to modernity, but rather an active and innovative response that embraces selective elements of the religious past and seeks to insert religious values more prominently into the public and political domain.[7] However, if one perceives "fundamental-

---

6. David Ludden, introduction to *Contesting the Nation: Religion, Community, and the Politics of Democracy in India* (Philadelphia: University of Pennsylvania Press, 1996), 16.

7. Martin E. Marty and R. Scott Appleby, *The Glory and the Power: The Fundamentalist Challenge to the Modern World* (Boston: Beacon Press, 1992).

ism" as indicating a return to religious "fundamentals"—such as biblical literalism or the implementation of the Shari'a—then the term fits less well. Hinduism does not offer to modern mobilizers the same core features, a single sacred text or a historical founder, that Christianity and Islam do. While Hindutva advocates often ascribe an eternal character to Hinduism by speaking of it as "Sanatana Dharma" (eternal faith), Hindutva draws on a more heterogeneous assembly of the Hindu past, as we will see, in constructing what may come to be a new and distinctive form of Hinduism.

In India, Hindutva groups are often referred to collectively as the "Sangh Parivar," the Sangh family or "brotherhood." This has more to do with the organizational shape of Hindutva than with its ideology. The key group in the promotion of Hindutva over several decades has been the Rashtriya Swayamsevak Sangh (National Volunteer Association), also referred to as the RSS or "Sangh." The RSS recruits and trains youth in small units or cadres. Other Hindutva groups, the most notable of which are the BJP and the Vishwa Hindu Parishad (World Hindu Council), are offsprings of this mother-organization, and these groups draw their leadership from among RSS initiates. Hence the Hindutva groups and their members form an extensive brotherhood. This family imagery suggests the ideal of consanguineal harmony and solidarity. However, as with most large and growing families, these brothers may not always share the same values and aims. Later in this chapter some of the lines of tension within the Sangh brotherhood will be discussed.

Ideological Formation

Persons and groups espousing Hindutva often portray their ideas as continuous with a rich cultural past. In their view, Hindus form a cohesive cultural community dating back several millennia to the time of the Vedas. As an often subjugated majority in its own homeland, they claim, this community has been seeking to recover its cultural and political dominance in South Asia from outside invaders for many centuries. In fact, Hindutva is a modern project. Its ideological roots lie in the specific historical ground of British colonial control in the late nineteenth and early twentieth centuries, and it took form principally in the 1920s. It has risen to prominence in Indian life more recently still, in the late 1980s and 1990s, under altogether different circumstances, through the successful mobilizations of several Hindutva organizations. To understand the formative ideas and values of Hindutva, it is necessary to look back to the colonial situation of the British Raj.

For many thoughtful Indians, the situation was a cultural and even psychological crisis instigated by political subordination. What qualities in Indian or Hindu culture, Indians asked themselves, had made it so easy for the British to conquer and rule them? Were there aspects of the Indian character that made it particularly susceptible to invasion and external control? What kinds of changes would be required to make Indians ready to rule themselves? The opposition of British colonizers and Indian colonized was often figured in morally loaded terms: masculine British versus feminine Hindu, adult West versus infant India. As the political movement for Indian independence took form, these introspective questions were mingled with ones of political strategy. On what basis could a mobilization to gain self-rule be based? By what means could leaders of this movement best mobilize Indian subjects toward the goal of independence?

Of course the responses of Indian leaders to these challenges were complex and varied. Ashis Nandy explores many of these in his studies of colonial psychology and highlights the unique response of Mohandas Gandhi.[8] For the purposes of this chapter, though, the genealogy of a Hindutva response can be traced through the lives and works of two primary figures: Narendranath Datta (1863–1902), who renamed himself "Swami Vivekananda," and Vinayak Damodar Savarkar (1883–1966), often called "Veer Savarkar."

Narendranath Datta received an excellent English-language education in Calcutta, but as he was studying law he came into contact with the famous Bengali mystic, Ramakrishna, and by 1885 Datta had abandoned law to become a disciple of the guru. Ramakrishna died the following year, and Datta was left with a sense of spiritual vocation but uncertainty about his mission. He traveled the country for several years, and took on his new religious name. In 1893 Swami Vivekananda heard of a "World's Parliament of Religions" that would take place in Chicago and decided to attend. He managed to raise the money, and the Parliament organizers were delighted to add a representative of Hinduism to the program. He was a great hit. As one newspaper proclaimed, Vivekananda was "an orator by divine right and undoubtedly the greatest figure at the Parliament."[9]

---

8. Ashis Nandy, *The Intimate Enemy: Loss and Recovery of Self under Colonialism* (New Delhi: Oxford University Press, 1983).

9. *Encyclopaedia Britannica, Micropedia*, 15th ed., s.v. "Vivekananda" (Chicago: Encyclopaedia Britannica Inc., 2002), 409.

His speech at the World Parliament is the central event in Vivekananda's career as a Hindu teacher. He had traveled to the United States not simply to represent Hindus in Parliament, but to gain from the West new ideas and resources with which to build a new kind of Hindu institution. After his extraordinary success in Chicago, Vivekananda traveled the lecture circuit, attracting numerous followers in the United States and Europe. Meanwhile, news of his Chicago triumph made him an absentee celebrity back home. Upon his return to India in 1897, he had the reputation and funds to begin organizing the Ramakrishna Mission. Modeled on Western social reform organizations, the mission embodied a new kind of "Hindu social gospel" by ministering to the poor and carrying out relief work.[10] By the time of Independence, the Ramakrishna Mission had grown to include ninety-one permanent centers, forty missions, and thirty-one monasteries in India, as well as numerous centers abroad. Swami Vivekananda, however, died in 1902, just a few years after establishing the mission.

Vivekananda's agenda was energetic and ambitious. Central to his thinking was a bifurcation between West and East. He identified the West with its scientific outlook, material progress, and social conscience. The East, by contrast, was preeminent in the spiritual realm. For Vivekananda, the spiritual superiority of the East, namely India, was to be found not in all aspects of Hinduism, but in the philosophical monism of Advaita Vedanta, derived from the ancient Upanishads, and in its austere traditions of spiritual practice such as renunciation and yoga. Like many other colonial-period Indian reformers, he was a vehement critic of many features of contemporary Hindu culture: caste divisions, purity practices, ritualism, and what he termed "superstitions" of various sorts. These, he believed (employing the gendered terms of the Victorian period), created a "feminine passivity" among Hindu Indians. Vivekananda looked toward an integration of East and West. As he had sought to bring Hindu spiritual teachings to Western audiences, he also attempted to incorporate Western features, such as an organizational ethos and social activism, which would make Hinduism a more energetic and "masculine" religious culture.

Modern Hindutva groups claim Vivekananda as part of their legacy. For them, he was an exemplary "militant Hindu" who traveled to the

---

10. Kenneth W. Jones, "Socio-religious Reform Movements in British India," in *New Cambridge History of India* vol. 3, pt. 1, (Cambridge: Cambridge University Press, 1989), 43–46.

West and successfully challenged the supposed superiority of Western religious formations. His goal of a more socially engaged Hinduism also strikes a chord with modern proponents of activist Hindutva. However, his critical stance toward modern Hindu practices and his conciliatory or collaborative attitude toward a foreign occupying power separate Vivekananda from modern Hindutva.

A more direct progenitor for Hindutva ideology can be found in the writings of V.D. Savarkar, a nonreligious Brahmin of Maharashtra.[11] Born in 1883, Savarkar became involved in the extremist wing of the anti-colonial movement as a student. His first major work, *Indian War of Independence, 1857*, published in 1908, offered both a historical account of the uprising against the British and a detailed assessment of insurrectionist tactics. The work was intended to draw lessons to guide Indian freedom fighters in a more effective revolutionary struggle. However, in 1909 Savarkar was implicated in a conspiracy to assassinate a British official, and the following year he was transported to the Cellular Jail in the Andaman Islands.

While in isolated confinement Savarkar began *Hindutva: Who Is a Hindu?*, an essay completed soon after his relocation to detention in India in 1922. As the title indicates, Savarkar's central question here was one of definition. Given the tremendous range of beliefs and the immense variety of practices included within the religious label Hinduism, how was it possible to locate its center or its boundaries? Many Indian teachers had sought to identify Hinduism with a fundamental corpus of texts or essential philosophical viewpoint, for example, Vivekananda's promotion of an Upanishad-based Advaita Vedanta perspective. Savarkar, on the other hand, adopted an etymological and historical strategy of definition. He traced the usage of terms like "Hindu" (from the *sapta-sindhu*, or seven rivers of the Indus river system) and asserted that they had consistently denoted a single continuing community of people occupying the Indian subcontinent, called Hindustan, from the earliest Vedic period right up to the present. In his sweeping historical vision, Hindutva was not primarily a matter of religion: "Hinduism is only a derivative, a fraction, a part of Hindutva." More fundamental to the identity of this putative national community were the three shared essentials of Hindutva: common territory

---

11. Lise McKean, *Divine Enterprise: Gurus and the Hindu Nationalist Movement* (Chicago: University of Chicago Press, 1996), 71–96.

(*rashtra*), common birth (*jati*), and common civilization (*sanskriti*). Savarkar answered the rhetorical question of his title with a Sanskrit verse: "A Hindu means a person who regards this land of Bharatvarsha, from the Indus to the Seas, as his Fatherland as well as his Holy-Land that is the cradle land of his religion."[12]

In this schematic articulation of a Hindu nation grounded in land, blood, and culture, issues of inclusion and exclusion are crucial. In several respects Savarkar's definition is broad and inclusive. He makes no effort to identify an essential Hindu set of beliefs and no suggestions for the reform of Hindu practices that others might have deemed degenerate. Rather, Hinduism consists in "all the religious beliefs that the different communities of the Hindu people hold." Savarkar accepts the full range of indigenous beliefs and practices adhered to by the people of the Hindu nation as part of a shared religious culture. His emphasis on Hindutva rather than Hinduism thereby accommodates many varieties of Hindus, as well as members of other homegrown Indic religions like the Jains, Buddhists, and Sikhs as equal sharers in Hinduness. However, in another direction, Savarkar's definition erects a formidable boundary. It pointedly excludes adherents of religious ideologies brought from outside the national territory, namely Muslims and Christians. If Vivekananda saw a fundamental difference between East and West and sought to integrate what he considered the primary virtues of each, Savarkar organized his thinking around a distinction between Hindus and Others, valued the continuation of an autochthonous cultural unity, and promoted the subordination of all that was foreign to Hinduness.

At a time when the mainstream of the Independence movement sought determinedly to unite Indians of all faiths in opposition to British colonial control, Savarkar's writings set out in another direction. Communal tensions and violence between Muslim and Hindu groups in Maharashtra had risen alarmingly during the 1920s. In Savarkar's next work, *Hindu Pad Padshahi* (1925), Muslims replaced the British as paradigmatic opponents of Hindu self-rule. He focused on the seventeenth-century Maharashtrian leader Shivaji, who led the Marathas in a series of struggles against the Mughals and other Muslim rulers in the subcontinent. This, argued Savarkar, was no less than a struggle for national sovereignty between foreign conquerors and a determined

---

12. Savarkar, *Hindutva*, 116.

indigenous resistance. In a later study completed after Indian Independence, *Six Glorious Epochs of Indian History* (1963), Savarkar continued to expound this broad historical narrative of foreign threat and Hindu struggle to regain freedom. Here, the entire history of India consists in recurrent Hindu struggles against the domination of foreign invaders, beginning with the resistance against Alexander's invasion in the fourth century B.C.E. and culminating with the successful attainment of Independence from British colonial control in 1947. Throughout his works Savarkar highlights not the passivity, but rather the military heroism of Hindus through the ages and creates, as John Zavos puts it, "a more brazen, aggressively triumphalist vision of the Hindu nation."[13]

V.D. Savarkar was a political activist and historical writer, not a religious teacher and reformer like Vivekananda. He was a "Veer" (hero), not a "Swami" (wise man). But his writings, more than any others, articulate the ideological foundations of Hindutva. He defines Hindutva, not in terms of a religious essence, but in terms of an inclusive territorial, racial, and cultural legacy, and he identifies this Hinduness in a broad sense as the moral principle of national unity. He projects Hindu nationhood into the deep past, to the time of the Vedas, and sees it as an unfolding continuity into the present, interrupted in its sovereignty but never fundamentally altered by foreign invasions and conquests. He reserves his greatest praise for those like Shivaji who fought against foreign domination on behalf of Hindu values and dominion. And, particularly in his later writings, he identifies Muslims as the paradigmatic Other, the most persistent and dangerous threat to Hindutva.

Organizational Formation

The various groups promoting Hindutva refer to themselves, and are often seen as, an extended family or brotherhood. The undisputed patriarch of this family is the Rashtriya Swayamsevak Sangh (RSS), the progenitor of many offspring organizations. By another metaphor, the RSS is the semi-secret "core" organization, from which other "front" groups extend its values and aims in the public domain.

The RSS was founded in 1925 by Dr. Keshav Baliram Hedgewar, a

---

13. John Zavos, *The Emergence of Hindu Nationalism in India* (New Delhi: Oxford University Press, 2000), 182.

Brahmin from Nagpur, then capital of the Central Provinces. As a medical student in the 1910s in Calcutta, Hedgewar joined a revolutionary group, then returned to Nagpur and involved himself in Gandhi's noncooperation campaign in the early 1920s. But by 1925, influenced by his reading of Savarkar's *Hindutva* and disturbed by communal conflicts between Hindu and Muslim communities in Nagpur, Hedgewar took a path differing from both revolution and Gandhian nonviolence. Hindus, he decided, suffered from a psychological problem, and "what was required was an inner transformation to rekindle a sense of national consciousness and social cohesion."[14] He determined to approach this need for transformation at the grassroots level and adapted the model of the *akhara*, or local gymnasium club, for his new organization. The basic unit of the RSS would be the *sakha* (branch), a small group of male volunteers, between fifty and a hundred divided into age groups, who would meet daily for fitness exercises, military training like marching and lathi practice, group singing, and ideological discussion. The volunteers, or *svayamsevaks*, would take an oath of loyalty and regularly salute the Bhagwa Dhvaj, a saffron flag associated with the Maratha hero Shivaji. Through this regular training, volunteers would gain the masculine, *kshatriya* (warrior class) virtues of physical strength, fortitude, resolve, and intellectual acumen. The young men, who were recruited into the organization and met daily with their cohort, would develop close lifelong personal bonds with one another and a common allegiance to shared symbols. Assisting the *swayamsevaks* would be full-time RSS workers, known as *pracharaks*, who would organize local RSS activities and maintain links between the local *shakhas* and the central organization. If the *swayamsevaks* formed a kind of committed laity, the *pracharaks* would constitute a monk-like leadership of unmarried full-time workers.

These cadre groups acted in various capacities. Hedgewar envisioned the RSS as a service organization that would work toward the broader vision of a Hindu nation, through the removal of foreign domination and the recovery of Hindu cultural traditions. The first appearance of the RSS in action came at a regional festival in Nagpur, where a cadre of volunteers showed up in uniforms of khaki shorts, white shirts, and caps and worked to discipline the unruly festival crowd. In situations of urban communal violence, such as the Nagpur riots of 1927, RSS volun-

---

14. Walter K. Andersen and Shridhar D. Damle, *The Brotherhood in Saffron: The Rashtriya Swayamsevak Sangh and Hindu Revivalism* (Boulder: Westview Press, 1987), 34.

teers acted collectively to "protect the Hindu society." During its first two decades, RSS members were also active in the anti-British struggle under the broad umbrella of the Indian National Congress. Like the Congress, the RSS sought to remove foreign rule, though it did not share Gandhi's commitment to nonviolence, and the nationhood it worked for differed significantly from that of the Congress leadership.

The RSS grew slowly, first in the Maharashtra region and then in parts of northern India, especially the Punjab and other regions most directly affected by partition violence in 1947. In 1948, Nathuram Godse, a former RSS member, assassinated Mahatma Gandhi. The government promptly banned the RSS and arrested as many as 20,000 RSS members. The ban was lifted in 1949, though at that time the ruling Congress party voted to exclude RSS members from its membership. RSS survived as an organization largely thanks to its grassroots structure and by the 1970s became an active participant, through its political front group, in the national movement against Prime Minister Indira Gandhi led by socialist Jaya Prakash Narayan. This was perhaps the first time the RSS played a visible and significant role in national affairs. RSS membership began to grow rapidly starting in the late 1970s, and for the first time it began to organize *shakhas* in southern India as well. This growth at the grassroots level, with the recruitment and training of much larger numbers of *swayamsevaks*, provided the base for the dramatic rise of Hindutva cultural and political activities at the national level in the late 1980s and 1990s.

Over its seventy years of existence, the RSS has engendered a proliferation of front groups, which have pursued the general aims of Hindutva among various constituencies. The earliest was a women's auxiliary, the Rashtra Sevika Samiti, which Lakshmi Bai Kolkar instigated in 1936 after Hedgewar insisted the RSS remain an exclusively male organization. Post-Independence initiatives have included a student organization (the Vidyarthi Parishad), a trade union affiliate (the Bharatiya Mazdoor Sangh), and a lay order of Hindu missionaries known as the Vivekananda Kendra, after the famous Swami. It has initiated regional groups, like the Hindu Munnani in Tamilnadu, or affiliated itself with regional groups that share its orientation, such as the Shiv Sena in Maharashtra. But the two groups that have made the greatest impact on Indian life are undoubtedly a political party, the Bharatiya Janata Party, and a religious affiliate, the Vishwa Hindu Parishad.

Political Hindutva

The question of political involvement in electoral politics is a long-standing topic of debate within the RSS. The two early leaders, Hedgewar and M.S. Golwalkar, generally preferred to keep the RSS, as a "cultural" organization, out of politics. During the pre-Independence period, RSS members were free to work as individuals within the Congress coalition, and a political party already existed that was pursuing the politics of Hindutva. The All-India Hindu Mahasabha was constituted in 1921 out of several previous Punjabi groups, with the aims of consolidating Hindus into a single community with a coherent voice. It enjoyed its period of greatest visibility in the late 1930s and early 1940s, when V.D. Savarkar, finally released from confinement, served as its president. However, the Hindu Mahasabha failed to build an effective party organization and remained a minor player in Indian political life throughout its history.[15] Perhaps its greatest legacy, as John Zavos suggests, was that it "created the space for the elaboration of Hindu organization as a significant ideology in Indian political discourse."[16] This space would later be filled, more effectively, by the BJP.

The RSS leadership reconsidered its role in Indian politics in the early years after Independence. In 1949 the working committee of the ruling Congress party excluded RSS members from the party, thereby removing one option for political engagement. The Hindu Mahasabha had done poorly in its electoral efforts, and its president, Savarkar, was antagonistic to the RSS leader, Golwalkar, so neither was supporting the Hindu Mahasabha an attractive option. Golwalkar was not willing to allow the RSS to enter directly into politics, nor would this have been feasible so soon after Gandhi's assassination. The solution was to spin off a new political affiliate, structurally distinct from the RSS but allied to it in orientation. Members of the RSS, led by a young *pracharak* named Atal Bihari Vajpayee, entered into talks with a Bengali politician, S.P. Mookerjee, who had resigned from a position in Nehru's cabinet, and together they formed the Bharatiya Jana Sangh (Indian People's Organization) in 1951. RSS members worked within the new party and provided much of the organizational structure. In fact, according to one survey covering the years 1968–71, 90 percent of Jana Sangh office

---

15. Christophe Jaffrelot, *The Hindu Nationalist Movement in India* (New York: Columbia University Press, 1996), 11–33.

16. Zavos, *Emergence*, 177.

bearers came from an RSS background. However, during the years of near-hegemony of the Congress party, the Jana Sangh fared about the same as the Hindu Mahasabha had. In 1952 it contested ninety-two seats in Parliament and won only three, with just over 3 percent of the vote, and in 1957 it won four seats. By 1967 the Jana Sangh had risen to thirty-five seats and 9 percent of the vote—its greatest national electoral success—but then it fell to twenty-two seats in the 1971–72 elections.

After the complex political reconfigurations of the Emergency of 1975–77, the Janata coalition rule, and Indira Gandhi's return to power in 1980, the Jana Sangh reconstituted itself—along with others disenchanted with the fractious Janata Party—as the Bharatiya Janata Party in 1980. The BJP maintained its close ties with the RSS, and the first president of the party was RSS *pracharak* Vajpayee. Yet it also sought a broader appeal. In its formative period, the BJP cited both the Hindutva ideology of Deendayal Upadhyaya and the populist and socialist ideals of J.P. Narayan as guiding principles. It chose a new flag, adding "secular" green to the RSS-style saffron flag employed by the Jana Sangh. This tension between a Hindutva-oriented base of RSS cadres and the electoral imperative to reach beyond this limited core constituency, already evident at its founding, characterizes much of the subsequent career of the BJP. The party emerged as the leading nationwide opposition party through an indisputably Hindutva campaign in the early 1990s, the Ayodhya Ramjanmabhumi mobilization. Yet after forming a ruling coalition in 1998 the BJP often had to pull its Hindutva punches, to moderate its positions to maintain amity among the coalition partners that did not necessarily share its commitments to Hindu nationalist values. This in turn posed the risk of backlash from other Hindutva groups less constrained by political civility, such as the Vishwa Hindu Parishad. The tension remains unresolved, and it will be interesting to observe how the various Hindu organizations respond to the BJP's loss in the 2004 elections.

Religious Hindutva

In 1964 M.S. Golwalkar convened a meeting of select Hindu religious leaders, and under the leadership of Swami Chinmayanand they formed the Vishwa Hindu Parishad (VHP). The initial aims of the group were to consolidate and strengthen Hindu society, to protect and spread Hindu values through various activities, and to establish and strengthen links among Hindus in different countries. In other words, this group would act as the RSS affiliate in the field of religion. However, it was not quite clear how best to accomplish these broad aims, and in its early years the VHP experimented with various projects and symbols to spread its mission. Initially, the group directed much of its effort toward northeastern India, where the VHP tried to counter the work of Christian missionaries. After a highly publicized case in 1981 where low-caste Hindus converted to Islam in southern India, the VHP began "reconversion" campaigns designed to bring Indian Christians and Muslims back into the Hindu fold.

In late 1983, in its most ambitious action to date, the group organized a month-long Ekatmata Yagna (Sacrifice for Unity), in which three processions traversed some 85,000 kilometers throughout India. In each procession, a truck carried a picture of Bharat Mata (Mother India) and large bronze pots filled with water from the Ganges River, sacred to many Hindus. The Ganges water was distributed in villages and towns along the way, for use in local worship, and the pots were refilled from local sources of holy water, such as temple tanks and pilgrimage sites, thereby creating a pan-Indian reservoir of holy water. In this campaign, for the first time the VHP found a resonant symbolic idiom for the "Hindu unity" they sought to create. This newfound mastery of religious and cultural symbolism was put to even more effective use in the VHP's next campaign, the mobilization to regain the site of Rama's birth, beginning in 1984.

Just as the RSS creates affiliates, its affiliate VHP has engendered its own sub-affiliate groups. In 1982 it first convened a new group of religious figures, known as the Dharma Sansad (Assembly of the Faith), to deliberate and formulate a unified Hindu perspective on the social and political issues of the day. The idea was to create a kind of ecclesiastical body that might claim to speak with Hindu religious authority. Throughout the twentieth century, some Hindu religious priests and renunciants had involved themselves energetically in political issues they saw as affecting Hindu interests, such as legislation bearing on the slaughter of cows and the Hindu Code Bill. In such cases they formed an effective though sporadic lobby on behalf of conservative Hindu values. By organizing the Dharma Sansad, the VHP aimed to give pandits and sadhus a more consistent organizational voice. Not incidentally, the VHP also sought to direct that voice toward issues of concern to the VHP, such as the Ramjanmabhumi mobilization.

In 1984 the VHP also spun off a youth group, the Bajrang Dal, named after the legendary "monkey army" that assisted Rama in his battle with the demon Ravana in the epic *Ramayana*. More than any other group in the Sangh brotherhood, the Bajrang Dal has been at the cutting edge, often quite literally so, in Hindutva mobilizations and street violence.

Perhaps the most significant VHP affiliate has been the VHP of America, established in 1970. Working with the growing and increasingly affluent community of Indian Hindus residing in the United States, the VHP of America has focused much of its work around a key concern of the Indian diaspora, the religious education of the second generation. The group has created summer camps for Hindu youth, instituted campus organizations for Hindu college students, and sponsored lecture tours for Hindutva spokespersons. It has also raised significant funds to support VHP and RSS activities in India, including the Ayodhya mobilization. Its success has given rise to other VHP groups in Canada, Germany, Malaysia, the Netherlands, the United Kingdom, and many other places where Indian Hindus have settled. And following the VHP's lead, the BJP created the Overseas Friends of the BJP. As Sadanand Dhume has pointed out, these overseas affiliates are consistent with an "ethnic" or religio-cultural concept of national citizenship, according to which Hindus living abroad remain (in the words of former Prime Minister Vajpayee) "all children of Mother India."[17] In power, the BJP supported the cause of dual citizenship, which would formalize the continuing connection of Indians living outside India, and worked assiduously to promote and strengthen ties with overseas Indians.

With so many Hindutva groups in the Sangh Parivar, unity of purpose remains an open question. Proponents of Hindutva often invoke the ideal of organizational brotherhood and familial harmony. Opponents of Hindutva often see a conspiratorial singleness of purpose behind the activities of all RSS-affiliated groups. But such a broad movement, with groups often representing distinct interests and pursuing divergent aims, can also breed tensions and the basis for internal conflict. This is particularly the case where Hindutva political parties assume governing control.

Sometimes differences in approach among Hindutva groups are complementary. In the 1990 Rath Yatra, the participation of both the

---

17. Sadanand Dhume, "From Bangalore to Silicon Valley and Back: How the Indian Diaspora in the United States Is Changing India," in *India Briefing: Quickening the Pace of Change*, ed. Alyssa Ayres and Philip Oldenburg (Armonk, NY: M.E. Sharpe, 2002), 110–11.

political BJP and the religious VHP (along with the VHP's more combative younger brother, the Bajrang Dal) in the same campaign led to a doubling of the campaign's message, as if the groups were broadcasting on two separate channels. The VHP took a hard line in this mobilization, enforcing religious, militant, masculine, and decidedly anti-Muslim aspects of the campaign. The BJP leaders attempted to articulate a more political, realistic, and ostensibly inclusive view.[18] This two-tiered approach was advantageous for both groups. The participation of the BJP enabled the VHP to project its message to a much wider audience, while the BJP, even while disavowing some of the more aggressive language and activities of the VHP and the Bajrang Dal, profited from the undoubted commitment of the VHP's *kar sevaks* (voluntary workers).

Since the destruction of the Babri Masjid in 1992 and the ascent of the BJP to power in Delhi, however, the agendas of these two groups have not always been so mutually beneficial. The VHP has continued to identify itself with the Ayodhya campaign and to push for construction of a vast new Rama temple atop the ruins of the mosque. Heading a coalition government, the BJP found its links to this divisive proposal problematic and sometimes tried to distance itself from the more committed Hindutva proponents on this issue.

Mobilizing the Gods

If Hindutva as an ideology and the RSS as an organizational locus for Hindu nationalism emerged in the particular colonial situation of the 1920s, the movement of Hindutva groups from the peripheries of Indian public life to the center in the late 1980s and 1990s must also be considered. Much has been written by social scientists about underlying conditions in India leading to this shift: the loss of legitimacy in the Congress Party and the economic failures of Nehruvian socialism, the erosion of caste hierarchies and the emergence of lower-caste pressure groups threatening the upper castes, the threats to national cohesion posed by several regional secessionist movements, the social disruptions brought about through economic liberalization and globalization, and the like. Yet it is crucial to recognize also, in the midst of these conditions, the agency of the Hindutva groups themselves. The VHP and the BJP have

---

18. Richard H. Davis, "The Iconography of Rama's Chariot," in *Contesting the Nation: Religion, Community, and the Politics of Democracy in India*, ed. David Ludden (Philadelphia: University of Pennsylvania Press, 1996), 42–43.

devised and successfully carried out far-reaching campaigns to bring their own vision of Hindu nationhood before the Indian public on an unprecedented scale.

Hindutva groups have reformulated and mobilized select religious and historical figures and narratives in order to promulgate their agenda. The following sections discuss two Hindutva campaigns. The first is the Ayodhya Ramjanmabhumi campaign, initiated by the VHP in 1984 and endorsed and later joined by the BJP for the 1990 Rath Yatra. More than any other, this campaign served as the catalyst for the movement of Hindutva into the Indian mainstream. The second is the more recent effort, with the BJP in power, to rewrite history textbooks. Critics have termed this the "saffronization of history." If the Ayodhya mobilization illuminates the rise of Hindutva, the history textbook controversy demonstrates how these groups seek to insinuate a Hindutva vision more deeply throughout Indian society.

In April 1984 the VHP convened a meeting of the Dharma Sansad, and the assembly of religious figures issued a unanimous resolution for the "liberation" of three North Indian temple sites "occupied" by mosques at Mathura, Varanasi, and Ayodhya. The group further resolved to focus initial efforts on the Ayodhya site they called the "Ramjanmabhumi," the birthplace of Rama. The campaign rested on three premises: that the god Rama, hero of the epic *Ramayana*, was physically born at that exact place; that an ancient Hindu temple had formerly stood at that location commemorating Rama's birth; and that the Mughal conqueror Babur had ordered the destruction of the temple and the construction of a mosque atop the ruins. Each of these premises was subjected to extensive criticism and historiographical debate during the ensuing campaign, but for the purposes of this chapter the factuality of the claims is less important than their symbolic resonance. The VHP campaign juxtaposed two primary figures, Rama and Babur, a Hindu deity and a Muslim ruler, who were made to stand for two religious formations in a highly unequal manner.

Rama is an incarnation of Vishnu, the god of preservation in the present-day Hindu trinity, who entered the world to preserve moral order, or *dharma*. In the stories of his worldly deeds, told and retold in South Asia over more than two millennia, Rama battles the paradigmatic demon Ravana, rescues his wife Sita, and returns from exile to establish a righteous regime in Ayodhya, the "Rama-rajya" (or utopia). As a this-worldly, interventionist, and morally energetic deity,

Rama served the rhetorical purposes of the VHP well, better in fact than other Hindu deities such as the lovable but morally ambiguous Krishna (born in Mathura) or the remote ascetic Siva (associated with Varanasi).

In the Hindutva campaign, Rama was singled out as more than just one god among a polytheistic pantheon. He was promoted as the primary deity and symbolic center of Hindu India. As the BJP's official statement put it, "Sri Rama is the unique symbol, the unequalled symbol of our oneness, or our integration, as well as of our aspiration to live the higher values. Maryada Purushottam Sri Rama has represented for thousands of years the ideal of conduct, just as Rama Rajya has always represented the ideal of governance."[19] There is an ambiguity in the use of the first person plural in this statement. When the BJP speaks here of "our" oneness, it could denote either the Hindu community or the Indian nation. In the Hindutva vision, these two ought to be the same. The campaign to liberate Rama's birthplace was, in a larger sense, a campaign to bring this about.

The choice of Rama was fortuitous in another sense, for in January 1987, just as the VHP Ayodhya campaign was getting under way, the government-run national television network Doordarshan began to air a lengthy serialized retelling of the story of Rama, directed by Ramanand Sagar. This turned out to be the most popular show ever aired on Indian television. Something like eighty to one hundred million people watched the weekly installments, roughly an eighth of the Indian population—especially impressive in light of the limited number of television sets in India at that time. In many homes the watching of "Ramayan" became a regular religious rite. Television sets were garlanded and conch shells blown before the show began, and viewers adopted attitudes of prayerful piety whenever Rama appeared on-screen, as if television offered a new medium for the mass realization of *darshan* (direct eye contact) with the deity. But it was not only a religious phenomenon. The directors also had a definite political aim. From the start, Sagar presented the televised "Ramayan" as "an All-India tradition, a symbol of national unity and integration."[20] In effect, the VHP's Ayodhya campaign and the

---

19. Bharatiya Janata Party, *White Paper on Ayodhya and the Rama Temple Movement* (1993), p. 1, quoted in Davis, "Iconography," 35.

20. Philip Lutgendorf, "Ramayan: The Video," *Drama Review* 34 (1990): 135. See also Arvind Rajagopal, *Politics After Television: Religious Nationalism and the Reshaping of the Indian Public* (Cambridge: Cambridge University Press, 2001).

state-sponsored "Ramayana" series colluded in promoting Rama as the central divinity for modern Hindu India.

As a result, the mobilization and the television series raised new debates over the identity of Rama. The Rama of Indian religious history is an enormously complex figure. Stories of his activities on earth have been related in many different ways in every Indian language, and they have been sung, danced, enacted, and represented visually in sculpture and painting countless times.[21] There can be no single or final image of Rama, and so in one way the new visions of Rama in the 1980s can be seen as part of an ongoing Rama tradition. The VHP disseminated two new visual images of Rama that reinforced their own agenda. In one, Rama appeared as a cherubic child with a plaintive expression imprisoned in a mosque, at the very place of his birth. The second portrayed him as a muscular young warrior prince, striding forward and holding weapons of bow and arrow, with a look of resolution and confidence on his face.[22] This depiction emphasized Rama's human qualities, rather than his divine Otherness, by giving him a "wheatish" (pale) complexion rather than his usual Vishnu-like blue, and by keeping his arms to an anthropomorphic two rather than the four more common to gods. If the first image evoked maternal devotion and the need to liberate the child-god from captivity, the second provided a model for the kind of militant and masculine Hindu action that, in the VHP view, could accomplish this liberation. Rama was the ideal RSS *svayamsevak.*

Others disputed these new claims on Rama. The editor of the feminist journal *Manushi*, Madhu Kishwar, for example, responded that the loving Rama she had learned about as a child bore no resemblance to this new militaristic Hindutva incarnation of Rama. But what was most troubling to many was the way these new visions threatened to control Rama's identity. Romila Thapar, a prominent historian at Jawaharlal Nehru University and an expert on the Rama tradition, wrote that the televised "Ramayana," in its powerful dissemination of a single and seemingly comprehensive version of the story, threatened to homogenize the pluralistic tradition of multiple Rama narratives.[23] Indeed,

---

21. Paula Richman, ed., *Many Ramayanas: The Diversity of a Narrative Tradition in South Asia* (Berkeley: University of California Press, 1991).

22. Anuradha Kapur, "Deity to Crusader: The Changing Iconography of Ram," in *Hindus and Others: The Question of Identity in India Today*, ed. Gyanendra Pandey (New Delhi: Penguin Books, 1993), 74–109.

23. Romila Thapar, "The Ramayana Syndrome," *Seminar* 353 (1989).

there were signs that Hindutva groups were exercising surveillance over Rama. When a touring cultural exhibition about Ayodhya featured a panel based on an early Buddhist version of the Rama story where Rama and Sita are brother and sister rather than husband and wife, BJP representatives in Parliament expressed strong objections to this "anti-Hindu" representation.

The second figure in the VHP's juxtaposition, Babur, was the founder of the Mughal dynasty, the most powerful of all Islamic regimes in India. Descended from both Timur and Genghis Khan, Babur was a Turko-Mongol conqueror who came from outside the subcontinent to defeat the ruling power in Delhi in the early sixteenth century and establish a new polity that would last over two centuries. Along with conquest, according to the VHP, came destruction. In the Ayodhya campaign, Babur was represented by "his" mosque, the Babri Masjid, allegedly built over the ruins of an obliterated Hindu temple. This action was portrayed not as a singular political act, but as an expression of principles, inherent in Islam itself, which were enacted by Muslim warriors over and over again throughout India. Forgotten were the successes in political integration and cultural synthesis that took place under the Mughal dynasty that he founded. Rather, Babur and the Babri Masjid were made to stand as symbols, for a purported legacy of Muslim conquest and iconoclastic destruction, the "fanatic religious statecraft" that had invaded a once-harmonious Hindu India.[24]

During the Ayodhya mobilization, Hindutva authors like Sita Ram Goel compiled lengthy lists of Hindu temples supposedly torn down by Muslim invaders. In *Hindu Temples: What Happened to Them*, Goel argues that some two thousand Muslim monuments occupy the sites of earlier Hindu temples and demonstrate what he calls an "Islamic theology of iconoclasm" directed at Hinduism.[25] Historians have rightly criticized the evidence used in constructing these lists, and the historical issue of Islamic iconoclasm in India became a matter of heated public debate.[26] However, the effect of works like those of Goel was signifi-

---

24. Sita Ram Goel, *Hindu Temples: What Happened to Them*, 2 vols. (New Delhi: Voice of India, 1990, 1993).

25. Bharatiya Janata Party, *White Paper on Ayodhya and the Rama Temple Movement* (1993), p. 15, quoted in Davis, "Iconography," 36.

26. Richard M. Eaton, "Temple Desecration and Indo-Muslim States," in *Beyond Turk and Hindu: Shaping Indo-Muslim Identity in Premodern India*, ed. David Gilmartin and Bruce B. Lawrence (Gainesville: University Press of Florida, 2000).

cant in reinforcing for many Hindutva sympathizers the key elements of Savarkar's historical meta-narrative of foreign invasion, with medieval Muslim invaders cast as the demons and indigenous resistance.

For the VHP and its allies, Rama was neither a legendary figure of literature or myth nor a distant deity. He was a divine figure who had taken real human birth, at a time and place that could be determined, and who had ruled a real kingdom. The Hindutva groups promoted him not just as an object of devotion, but more as a model and rallying point for Hindus in the modern world. Nor was Babur simply a figure from the distant historical past. Just as Rama was to be identified with the contemporary Hindu community, so Muslims in modern India were to be held responsible for the actions of Babur and other past Islamic conquerors. "Are you children of Babar or Ram?" asked one prominent Hindutva spokesman during the campaign. "Those who do not answer this question properly have no right to be in this country." Even though more than 90 percent of the Indian Muslim population is descended from indigenous converts to Islam, the identification of all Muslims as "children of Babur" effectively cast them out of the Hindu, and therefore Indian, family and relegated them to a marginalized status.

Prior to 1984 the dispute over the Ayodhya Babri Masjid had been a matter of largely local concern, but now the VHP sought to publicize it as a matter of national importance. The group tried various strategies, such as the distribution of Rama stickers and saffron banners. VHP organizers solicited Hindus all over India and beyond to make special bricks, inscribed with the words Shri Ram, to be used for constructing the planned temple at Rama's birthplace. These bricks were to be collected and transported to Ayodhya, where they would constitute an evergrowing physical demonstration of support for the temple. The brick campaign spread the VHP's agenda widely, but even more successful was the Rath Yatra of 1990, a meandering procession of some 10,000 kilometers that passed through ten states in northern India. The BJP became actively involved in the Ayodhya campaign during the Rath Yatra. In this dramatic staged event, one can see again the adept combination of old and new, the VHP's innovative selection and redeployment of traditional Hindu elements to serve novel ends.

For Indians, the term "Rath Yatra" (chariot procession) denotes first of all a Hindu temple procession. During religious festivals, temple deities in image form are placed in palanquins or atop large wooden vehicles, transported out of their temple sanctums, paraded through the surrounding streets of the town, and finally returned to the temple. Festival processions are designed to be public and inclusive. They allow participation by those who might otherwise not approach the god inside the shrine. Not simply religious in nature, temple processions employ royal imagery, and the processing deity is viewed as a sovereign touring his or her domain and enforcing dominion over it.

In the Rath Yatra organized by the VHP and BJP, no consecrated image of a deity was involved. Instead, the political leader of the BJP, L.K. Advani, rode atop a DCM-Toyota flatbed truck, addressing the crowd through loudspeakers. The Toyota was decorated to look like an ancient chariot, with cutouts and designs of lotuses, lions, and the ancient mantra, Om. Apparently, the design was based on the simulated chariots in the televised "Ramayana" and "Mahabharata." The chariot traveled not in a circle, but on a long winding route that began in Somnath, Gujarat (another famous contested temple site), and would eventually reach Ayodhya in eastern Uttar Pradesh.[27] As it traveled, Rama's chariot attracted large audiences and evoked all sorts of responses, from the purely devotional to the confrontational. Some along the route worshiped the decorated truck as if it were indeed a sacred chariot of the god Rama. Others saw the procession as a kind of extended political rally and attended to hear the speeches of Advani and other Hindutva spokespersons. For some, it was a communal provocation. When the Rath Yatra passed through "sensitive" areas (i.e., Muslim neighborhoods), members of the VHP's youth group, the Bajrang Dal, flourished tridents and swords, and street fighting frequently ensued.

The procession was undoubtedly a political event. Devi Lal, a prominent opponent of the Yatra, compared it to an ancient royal progress, such as the medieval *digvijaya* (conquest of the quarters), where a king and his armed forces would venture out from their capital on a tour in all directions, challenging to battle any who might oppose his rule. However, there was a difference: Advani was not an autonomous ruler, but rather a leader of a political party that was challenging the ruling government. The Yatra posed a difficult dilemma for the ruling National Front coalition. The street fighting and riots that followed in the wake of the procession created a significant problem of civil order. However,

---

27. On Somnath and its legacy, see Richard H. Davis, *Lives of Indian Images* (Princeton: Princeton University Press, 1997), chaps. 3 and 6. A more recent expansion of these themes is found in Romila Thapar, *Somanatha: The Many Voices of a History* (New Delhi: Penguin Books, 2004).

stopping the procession required acting against Rama—as well as one of the coalition partners—and might well instigate greater social unrest.

Finally, on October 23, 1990, shortly before the procession reached Ayodhya, police were ordered to stop the procession and arrest Advani and other leaders. Riots and mass arrests followed. The movement to liberate Rama's birthplace was temporarily halted, but the momentum created by the Rath Yatra did not dissipate. Two years later, on December 6, 1992, the BJP and VHP organized a mass rally in Ayodhya. Some 300,000 people gathered. By this time the BJP had come to power in the Uttar Pradesh state government, and the local police showed little interest in preventing the Hindutva groups from carrying out their publicly announced aim. Vanguard groups broke down police barricades, and then many others swarmed the Babri Masjid. By evening the old mosque had been leveled. The next step, leaders announced, was to construct a new temple on the site.

If the destruction of the Babri Masjid was a watershed event in recent Indian history, it carried different meanings for different groups. For the VHP and other dedicated proponents of Hindutva, the destruction represents a successful example of militant Hindu activism—but the campaign is only half completed. They continue efforts to build a Rama temple atop the Masjid ruins. For opponents, the act of Hindu iconoclasm and the ensuing riots illustrate the irresponsible and divisive exploitation of communal antagonisms, for which they hold Hindutva groups responsible. For the political leadership of the BJP, whose rise to power resulted in part from its association with the Ayodhya campaign, there is a more ambivalent legacy.

Mobilizing the Past

History, or more precisely a vision of the Indian past, is central to Hindutva. We have seen how Savarkar articulated his definition of Hindutva in terms of a historical narrative. Historical claims about Rama's birth and Muslim iconoclasm were central to the Ayodhya campaign. Hindu nationalist groups actively promote figures from India's past, such as Rana Pratap and Shivaji, as heroes who exemplify the virtues of Hindutva.[28] It is not surprising, therefore, that Hindu nationalists have

---

28. Christiane Brosius, "'I Am a National Artist': Popular Art in the Sphere of Hindutva," in *Iconographies and the Nation in India*, ed. Richard H. Davis (New Delhi: Orient Longman, forthcoming).

concerned themselves with how history is taught in India. While the BJP was in power, Hindutva proponents initiated controversial efforts to reorient the historical profession and revise school textbooks.

Savarkar's narrative of Indian history rests upon two crucial reifications. First, he postulates an ancient Hindu community that constitutes the earliest and autochthonous civilization of the subcontinent, and he claims that this cultural and ethnic group has persisted without any fundamental change up to the present. Second, he identifies Islam as a radically foreign ideology in fundamental conflict with the Hindu community. Among all the foreign forces that have threatened the Hindus, he views Islam as the most pernicious and dangerous. Muslim attacks on Hindu institutions, such as Babur's alleged destruction of a Rama temple in Ayodhya, reflect this essential antipathy. And because he and other Hindutva proponents see Indian Muslims also as a distinct, continuing, and bounded community, modern Muslims are held responsible for the acts of medieval Turk and Afghan warriors who adhered to Islam. In both cases, these postulations are fundamentally at odds with views held by the mainstream of professional historians of South Asia.

Since the late eighteenth century, when scholars like William Jones first observed the linguistic family resemblance between Sanskrit, Greek, and Latin, historians have postulated an earlier "Indo-European" cultural and linguistic forebear and have sought to locate the geographical origins of this seminal group. The corollary to this is that the "Indo-Aryan" tribes who brought proto-Sanskrit to the subcontinent and expressed their worldview in the Vedas originally came from outside India. The weight of linguistic and archeological evidence strongly supports this migration hypothesis, and a large majority of scholars in India and abroad accepts that the Indo-Aryans were not indigenous to India. However, Hindutva historiography is deeply invested in a distinction between indigenous Hindus and foreign Others, and so it strongly resists any notion that Indo-Aryans may have come from elsewhere. As Vinay Lal puts it, "any such concession, militant Hindus believe, renders the meaning of 'home' or homeland conceptually flexible and deflates the possibility of construing Indian civilization as a civilization that is Hindu in its most essential and fundamental aspects."[29] So the composition of the Vedas is projected far back into history, as far as 9000 B.C.E. and India is preserved not simply as the homeland of the Hindus but also of all Indo-

---

29. Vinay Lal, "History and Politics," in *India Briefing: A Transformative Fifty Years*, ed. Marshall Bouton and Philip Oldenburg (Armonk, NY: M.E. Sharpe, 1999), 223.

Europeans, and the earliest center of human civilization. If there was any Indo-European migration, it must have set out from India.

The Hindu nationalists' "communalist" view of permanent antipathy between Hindus and Muslims draws largely upon British colonial historiography. Pursuing a colonial policy of divide and rule, the British were eager to establish the separateness and the mutual animosity of their colonial subjects through historical sources. Great British-era compilations such as the eight volume *History of India as Told by Its Own Historians*, assembled by Henry Eliot and John Dowson and first published in 1849, seem to convey a story of continuous war and destruction between Muslim regimes and others in medieval India. Historians of the Hindutva persuasion, like Sita Ram Goel, draw heavily from this British well. The history of medieval India is complicated, however, and recent mainstream historians have argued for a strongly "syncretist" viewpoint.[30] The sources used by Eliot and Dowson, for example, are exaggerated, partial, and often simply mistranslated. Medieval wars did not as a rule follow religious affiliations, and iconoclastic destruction of religious sites was an infrequent strategic action, not a universal Muslim practice. Most importantly, the creation of genuinely syncretic cultural forms— at court, in religious institutions, and throughout society—appears to have been much more characteristic of this period than the state of perpetual religious conflict postulated by British and Hindutva historians.[31]

Recently these and other historiographical disputes have become matters of public debate and government policy. A key figure in the controversy over history is Murli Manohar Joshi, a BJP politician and a member of the RSS since 1944. In 1998, with the BJP leading the ruling National Democratic Alliance, Joshi was appointed head of the Union Human Resource Development Ministry. He quickly moved to insert Hindutva sympathizers into organizations like the University Grants Commission (UGC), the Indian Council of Historical Research (ICHR), and the Indian Council of Social Science Research. Soon, funding for research began to move in new directions. The UGC insisted on funding new university courses in Vedic astrology, Vedic mathematics, and other topics that emphasized the pertinence of traditional forms of Hindu

---

30. Vinay Lal discusses the "communalistic" and "syncretistic" views of history in "History and Politics," 217–18.

31. An important recent collection developing this viewpoint is Gilmartin and Lawrence, eds., *Beyond Turk and Hindu.*

knowledge. The ICHR, meanwhile, pulled the plug on two volumes of the important multivolume compilation of documentary sources, *Toward Freedom*, which provides primary materials pertaining to the independence movement between the years 1937 and 1947. Evidently the two volumes, which had already been approved and sent to Oxford University Press for publication, documented a period in which the RSS did not play a significant role in the struggle for Indian freedom, and the Hindutva members of the ICHR deemed this unacceptable.

The national government agency that supervises curriculum and arranges for textbook publication is the National Council for Educational Research and Training (NCERT). Until recently, NCERT has commissioned school textbooks in history by highly respected professors, many of them from Jawaharlal Nehru University, including R.S. Sharma, Romila Thapar, and Satish Chandra. However, the Joshi ministry appointed J.S. Rajput, an RSS member, as new chair of NCERT in 1999, and in 2000 Rajput issued a controversial new "National Curriculum Framework for School Education." Older textbooks were altered without consulting the authors, and then NCERT commissioned a new set of history books, which began to appear in autumn 2002. In response, the primary professional organization of Indian historians, the Indian Historical Congress, established a committee to evaluate the new textbooks, and in 2003 this group issued a highly critical report, "History in the New NCERT Textbooks: A Report and an Index of Errors." As with the site of Rama's birth, history itself became another terrain on which a battle between two competing visions of India, secularist and Hindutva, is being waged.

It is not possible to discuss here all the points of controversy, so two examples will have to suffice. In the earlier textbooks on *Ancient India* by R.S. Sharma, first published in 1977, the early Aryans had been described as beef eaters. There exists substantial historical evidence for this. However, it did not fit well with a Hindutva view of history. Hindu nationalists and religious activists promote the cow as a key symbol of Hinduism and have often sought legislation to protect cattle from slaughter. Over the past 150 years, "cow protection" has frequently been used as a slogan to mobilize against Muslims, who do not share the same bovine veneration. Since Hinduism is seen as a continuous tradition, it is not possible for Hindutva adherents to accept that their Hindu ancestors might not have shared this central value, and so the mention of ancient Aryan consumption of beef had to be deleted from Sharma's text.

Likewise, Sharma had the temerity to observe that archeological evidence did not support the postulation of an "epic age," dated to 2000 B.C.E. in which the events of the *Ramayana* and *Mahabharata* took place. This was particularly sensitive because it might impinge on the historicity of Rama as a human prince born in Ayodhya, a central tenet of the Ramjanmabhumi mobilization. Here too, NCERT officials removed the offending passage from Sharma's book that might have undercut the postulate of Rama's human life.

Joshi, along with Rajput and his fellow members of NCERT, engaged in a serious attempt to rewrite the way Indian children are taught their own history. Members of the Indian historical profession organized to oppose that effort. In the process, matters of ancient history became matters of broad public debate in the Indian media. It is not certain at this point whose vision of Indian history will prevail, though the BJP loss in the 2004 elections will certainly hamper the Hindutva effort to gain control over school textbooks in the immediate future.

Hinduism in an Age of Hindutva

One of the original purposes of the VHP, we have seen, was to consolidate Hindu society, to unite Hindus into the single community that Hindutva proponents postulate. Such an attempt to bring unity to Hinduism is not entirely novel. During the colonial period of the nineteenth and early twentieth centuries, reform organizations like the Brahmo Samaj and the Arya Samaj also envisioned and pursued a more cohesive Hindu faith, with limited success. Based in the Punjab, the Arya Samaj pioneered many of the organizational practices later adapted by the RSS. However, the Hindutva attempt, in its use of new technologies of dissemination and in its proximity to political power, may represent something new and efficacious in the modern period.

The theorist Savarkar attempted to define Hindutva around a shared cultural ethos that accepted the great variety of existing Hindu religious belief and practice. When it came to religion, Savarkar adopted a laissez faire attitude. The VHP and its relatives have a more ambitious, hegemonizing religious agenda. The VHP formed the Dharma Sansad as a new ecclesiastical order to pronounce with religious authority on social and political issues of the day. The VHP and related groups have promoted Rama as the integrating god of Hinduism, and they have launched nationwide campaigns like the Ekatmata Yagna and the Ayodhya mobilization to broadcast their message throughout India. Their activities go still further, with attempts to extend select regional practices throughout India and to promote upper-caste or brahminical rites for all strata of society. Observers such as political scientist Rajni Kothari have charged that this amounts to an attempt to "semiticize" Hinduism: to transform a diverse and pluralistic Hindu religion into a more centrally organized, monotheistic, monolithic faith on the model of the Abrahamic religions of Judaism, Christianity, and Islam.

It is unclear just how successful these Hindutva efforts are, or how far they reach. While much has been written about the political rise of the Sangh groups and the social upheavals that have accompanied this rise, there has been comparatively little scholarly study of changes in Hindu religious practices instigated by Hindutva. This concluding section will consider two examples described by anthropologists working in Tamilnadu, in the deep south, farthest from the main centers of Hindutva organization. One looks at the successful inculcation of a new ritual practice from Maharashtra, and the other describes how the VHP brick campaign entered into the local culture of a Tamil village.

When I lived in Tamilnadu in the early 1980s, Hindu nationalism was virtually invisible to me. But during this time, the Sangh brotherhood was beginning to organize a new affiliate, the Hindu Munnani (Hindu Front), which would cooperate with the RSS and BJP and play a role in Tamilnadu similar to that of the VHP elsewhere in India.[32] The group also developed close ties with the Tamilnadu Brahmins Association, which defends the interests of brahmins in the state.

One of the first activities of the Hindu Munnani was to begin promoting and transforming the Vinayaka Chaturthi, a fall festival devoted to the god Ganesha. Prior to this, most Hindus in Tamilnadu had celebrated quietly with domestic rites or by making special offerings at a local Ganesha temple. In Maharashtra the Vinayaka Chaturthi was an entirely different matter. In the late nineteenth century, the festival was transformed by the anti-colonial activist B.G. Tilak into the primary public festival of the year, with large decorated pavilions, public image processions, and dramatic final immersions of the images in the sea or another body of water. Another crucial aspect of the Maharashtrian celebrations introduced by Tilak was the dissemination

---

32. C.J. Fuller, *Renewal of the Priesthood: Modernity and Traditionalism in a South Indian Temple* (Princeton: Princeton University Press, 2003), 132–37.

of political messages through public speeches. For Tilak the religious festival was a convenient cover for anti-British agitation, and the political dimension of the festival has continued in Maharashtra in the form of politicized *mandapa* displays.[33]

The Hindu Munnani set out to replicate the Maharashtrian model in Tamilnadu. In 1983 the Munnani initiated the public celebration of Vinayaka Chaturthi in a suburb of Chennai with a procession and an immersion of a Ganesha image in a nearby temple tank. The next year the group held several public celebrations around Chennai, and by 1990, the year of the Rath Yatra in northern India, the public celebrations of Vinayaka Chaturthi were expanding to other cities and towns in Tamilnadu. Of course, this spread was never entirely innocent. Also in 1990, a provocative procession of Ganesha past a mosque in downtown Chennai instigated a bloody riot. In the mid-1990s, Chris Fuller reports, the Vinayaka Chaturthi had become a common public festival throughout the state. At the same time, it had lost some of the overt anti-Muslim and anti-Christian rhetoric that was characteristic of the initial celebrations. Other groups beside the Hindu Munnani were organizing their own versions of the festival, so the Munnani no longer enjoyed complete control over the festival. This transplanted regional festival from Maharashtra was now a part of the Tamilnadu religious calendar.

In promoting this ritual innovation, the Hindu Munnani saw Vinayaka Chaturthi as "a means to unite Hindus by overcoming internal divisions among them." They intended the festival for all Hindu castes and classes, including *Dalits*. It also had the effect of linking Hindu religious practice in Tamilnadu to that of another region, and thereby of promoting the sense of Hinduism's national breadth. As Fuller puts it, "Hindu unity is primarily a political and ideological project to persuade people to become conscious of themselves as Hindus belonging to a single, assertive, majority 'community' on which a strong Hindu nation can be built."[34] The Hindu Munnani's transposing of a new public festival into Tamilnadu offers one example, within the sphere of religious practice, of how that persuasion may be effected. Yet it also suggests how its specific political agenda may recede as new groups adopt their own versions of the festival.

The case of the Vinayaka Chaturthi in Tamilnadu highlights the agency of a Hindutva group in instigating new religious practices that help broad-

---

33. Raminder Kaur, "Spectacles of Nationalism in the Ganapati *Utsava* of Maharashtra," in *Iconographies and the Nation in India*, ed. Davis.

34. Fuller, *Renewal*, 133.

cast the values of Hindu nationalism. However, acceptance of new practices and new values is a matter of choice, of countless decisions that are local and personal. What are the conditions within which a local group chooses to embrace elements of a Hindu nationalist campaign? Diane Mines's anthropological fieldwork in a southern Tamilnadu village in the late 1980s provides one example.[35]

Yanaimangalam is a small, predominantly Hindu village of about 1,700 people. Three caste groups predominate, and among these three the Thevars were attempting to establish dominance in the village during Mines's stay. A group of brahmins also resided in the village, and they recalled a time when their residential neighborhood was the center of village activities. Brahmins formerly owned much of the land, they claimed, and ran elaborate festivals in the now-dilapidated Shiva temple. Once the center of the dharmic order of the village, the brahmins viewed the village itself as degenerating. The VHP campaign to liberate that other dharmic center, Rama's birthplace, must have appealed to them, and the brahmins of Yanaimangalam decided to send a consecrated brick to Ayodhya in October 1989.

The brick had the name of the village stamped on one side, and the name of the god Rama on the other. A brahmin schoolmaster conducted a small ritual to consecrate the brick in his home and then led a procession of the brahmins and several other members of high-status castes, chanting "Ram! Ram!" and ringing cymbals. At the border of the village, they gave the brick to a teenage priest who took it, got on his bicycle, and rode off toward the next village, accompanied by two policemen. The idea was that this brick would join with others, and gradually make its way by train to the district seat Tirunelveli, then to the state capital Chennai, on to the national capital Delhi, and from there to Ayodhya, where it would take its place in the new Rama temple the VHP proposed to build there.

Mines cites the psychoanalyst Sudhir Kakar's observation that it is "a sense of loss that propels people, individually and in groups, to identify with larger cultural and revivalist movements, such as Hindu nationalism."[36] The loss of a golden age echoes through the rhetoric of Hindutva, just as the brahmins of Yanaimangalam speak of the loss of their own centrality to the village. But so too does a project for the future: building

---

35. Diane P. Mines, "Hindu Nationalism, Untouchable Reform, and the Ritual Production of a South Indian Village," *American Ethnologist* 29, no.1 (2002): 58–85.
36. Sudhir Kakar, *Colors of Violence*, 148–49, quoted in Mines, "Hindu Nationalism," 76.

a temple, restoring a remembered way of life, reconstituting a unitary national community of Hindus that (in the Hindutva vision) has always been present. The participation by the brahmins of Yanaimangalam in the VHP's brick campaign links them to a national, and even transnational, network of Hindus. Just as important, though, it has to do with the village order. Yanaimangalam's modest brick ceremony was, as Mines puts it, "an effort to redefine and expand this brahmin community's sense of belonging-in-the-world by also finding new ways to define their place in the village."[37]

Other village groups, meanwhile, were pursuing their own agendas. Attempts by the Thevar groups to claim village precedence led to disruptions in the annual festival processions. Members of the Pallar caste, a Scheduled Caste or Dalit group, tried to assert their own place in the village pecking order by identifying themselves with Ambedkar, the Maharashtrian Dalit leader of the 1940s who articulated an egalitarian critique of caste privileges. As with the village brahmins, the Pallars sought to enhance local status through a national marker of identity. All are strategies that, together, remake the village on an ongoing basis. The brahmins' singular act of assertion through brick consecration does not appear to have altered their local situation.

From the perspective of this village, then, the seeming juggernaut of Hindutva appears attenuated. (The English term "juggernaut" derives, appropriately, from the great temple chariot festival at the temple of Jagannatha, in Puri, Orissa.) While the powerful imagery of the VHP's Ayodhya mobilization penetrates even to this distant village, the brick the local brahmins fabricated and sent may never have reached its destination. The new temple, embodying the new order of Ramrajya, remains unbuilt.

In spring 2004 I visited Madurai, in southern Tamilnadu, to observe the annual Chittrai festival, twenty-two years after I had first seen it in 1982. National elections were under way, and the newspapers and daily conversations were filled with the battle between the BJP and Congress, as well as the statewide and local contests. The Chittrai festival is one of the largest temple celebrations in India, and on the culminating day of the festival, the gods Shiva and Minakshi come forth from the temple riding on massive wooden chariots, pulled by hundreds of excited young devotees. A crowd of half a million watches the parade, and tens of

---

37. Mines, "Hindu Nationalism," 74.

thousands spill into the streets to march along with it. This time I no-ticed a new feature in the great procession. Situated somewhere between the temple elephants and camels that led the train and the great chariots of the gods was a small coterie of young men wearing saffron bandanas surrounding a bicycle-and-wagon, with a sign identifying it as the float of the VHP. As the parade moved on, I noticed that many onlookers also wore the saffron headscarves, inscribed with the Hindu symbol Om. The VHP cadres were busily distributing the free scarves, and as the sun heated up on this May morning many gratefully accepted them. Though dwarfed by the massive chariots of Madurai's long-standing divine sov-ereigns, the local representatives of Hindutva had managed to find a small niche for themselves in the procession, and were doing their best to disseminate their message.

The future of Hindutva in India will rest in part on the electoral for-tunes of the BJP. Hindutva concerns like the Ayodhya temple and the status of the Muslim minority in India were definitely issues in the 2004 campaign, but the Tamil voters with whom I spoke had other things—like water, a scarce commodity in drought-stricken Tamilnadu—on their minds when they cast their ballots. Court decisions about the future of the Masjid site in Ayodhya, and the way the next editions of history textbooks are written, will no doubt play an important part. But Hindutva's future will also rest on the roles that groups like the VHP and the Hindu Munnani are able to play in the everyday religious life of Hindus, and on the impact of their activities on the varied ways Hindus practice their faith. Will they transform Hinduism, or will Hinduism find a way to incorporate and subordinate Hindutva? Panikkar's "mo-lecular transformation," evident no doubt from the perspective of Delhi, may grow weaker as one travels toward the peripheries like Tamilnadu.

Work and Wealth

Renana Jhabvala

India is undergoing rapid changes in communication and technology, as well as in the opening up of trade, the import of products from other countries, and the out-migration of people. The economic growth rate has been higher than in most other countries, and the rapid growth of infrastructure—highways and rural roads, electricity and water resources—is a visible sign of India's prosperity. India's wealth is increasing.

There is no doubt that this growth has led to new opportunities, a higher standard of living for a large number of people, and a burgeoning middle class. But what is the relation of this growing wealth to the majority of India's people? Who is creating this newfound wealth—a small section of the economy or large numbers of people? Who benefits from this wealth—the small but growing middle class or a larger section of people? Who is excluded from the creation and benefits of India's new wealth?

There has been a great deal of debate in India on the effect of the economic reforms of the 1990s on the poor. Some analysts claim that the poor have become poorer, while others claim that poverty has rapidly declined. Many feel strongly that employment is stagnant and the economic growth benefits only a minority, while the majority—dependent for their living on agriculture and more traditional forms of work—has been neglected.

More than 846 million people in India live in rural areas and depend for their living on agriculture. Although the urban population has a wider variety of work opportunities in manufacturing, services, and other sectors, only a small minority works in the modern growth sectors such as information technology or call centers. The majority of the workforce in both urban and rural areas works in the informal economy, where work is insecure and unprotected, social safety nets are unavailable, and access to social security such as paid health care and maternity or old age benefits is nonexistent. Nevertheless, the work of the 370 million people in the informal economy is one of the main reasons for the sustained economic growth of the country.

In many ways these workers live unseen and unheard. Their view of society and the economy is very different from what we read in the newspapers, see on television, study in our schools, or read in policy documents, and few people get to see both sides. I have been fortunate to work for more than twenty-five years with the Self-Employed Women's Association (SEWA), a trade union in the informal economy, which has enabled me to hear and see firsthand how poor women live and work, to experience their struggles, to understand their needs and their dreams, and, above all, to see the strength and courage with which they face a hard world. SEWA works to give a voice to the reality and needs of its members, to articulate their problems and to show the world how important they are to society and how they deserve a much better deal. We work together to build organizations and institutions to move our members toward full employment and self-reliance, toward economic security and self-help.

With more than 700,000 members, SEWA is the largest trade union of informal workers in India. However, it is more than a trade union. SEWA is a confluence of three movements—the labor movement, cooperative movement, and women's movement—based on a Gandhian philosophy. Through this movement, self-employed women become strong and visible and their tremendous economic and social contributions are recognized. SEWA's main strength lies in building the capacity of illiterate and barely literate women to manage their own activities. Its cadre of "barefoot professionals"—such as managers, lawyers, engineers, doctors, and researchers—become "barefoot professionals" by virtue of the practical experience they gain and the focused capacity-building input provided by SEWA. These members and grassroots organizers constitute the spearhead teams which are formed for each activity and which take the lead in providing direct assistance to members at the village level. They also play a key role in promoting activities in new villages and mobilizing and organizing women to participate. Through this mechanism, sustainability and capacity for replication are built into the SEWA organizational structure. SEWA's philosophy embraces a holistic approach to development: multiple inputs and interventions are essential for women to emerge from poverty, vulnerability, and years of deprivation. SEWA's integrated approach to poverty alleviation comprises organizing for collective strength, capital formation through access to financial services, capacity building, and social security (essentially health care, child care, shelter, and insurance) to enhance women's productivity and to ensure that sudden crises do not drain their fragile household economies. SEWA has two main goals: full employment (employment that ensures work security, income security, food security, and social security) and self-reliance (individual and collective autonomy in terms of both economics and decision-making ability).

SEWA's activities are driven by the needs and demands of its members. Its wide range of activities includes savings and credit groups, micro-insurance, watershed development, dairy cooperatives and fodder security, agricultural development, forest plantation, drinking water, craft production, salt production, gum collection, health care, child care, functional literacy, mobile ration vans, training, and research. Education in the philosophy of SEWA and basic leadership is provided to all members.

Members implement SEWA activities through a number of different SEWA institutions, including a total of ninety-six cooperatives (dairy, fodder, grain banks, plantation, ration shops, and so forth), of which the largest is SEWA Bank; village committees for integrated watershed development; water users groups for management and operation of village tanks and ponds and piped water supply schemes; handicraft associations; urban community slum organizations; and health care workers and child care workers cooperatives.

This chapter combines my experience with SEWA, studies done by researchers, and figures collected by statistical agencies in order to present a comprehensive picture of the lives of workers in the informal economy. The contributions of these workers to India's economic growth are examined alongside the effects on their lives of that growth and the country's economic reforms. The chapter also discusses this vast number of workers in terms of what would improve their lives and which reforms would extend to them the benefits of national wealth.

Work and the Creation of Wealth

Who creates India's wealth? Who produces most of India's gross domestic product? The information technology sector has been identified as a major growth force in the Indian economy, and it is true that information technology has brought a new dynamism to the Indian economy, not only by creating wealth but by providing employment opportunities

Table 1

Gross Domestic Product by Economic Activity

Industry	Percent of gross domestic product
Agriculture, forestry, fishing	23.9
Manufacturing	16.8
Trade, hotels, and restaurants	15.1
Community, social, and personal services	13.5
Financing, insurance, real estate, and business services	12.5
Transport, storage, and communications	8.4
Construction	5.1
Electricity, gas, and water	2.5
Mining and quarrying	2.2
Total	100

Source: National Accounts Statistics, Central Statistical Organisation, Ministry of Statistics and Programme Implementation (New Delhi: Government of India, 2003).

to the growing number of young, educated people. Other visible growth sectors include communications and certain services.

However, if wealth is measured in terms of gross domestic product (GDP) we get a different picture. Agriculture contributes the maximum GDP of 24 percent. Over 60 percent of the GDP comes from the traditional sectors of agriculture, manufacturing, mining, construction, and trade. The communication and business services sector, which includes the growth sectors of media and information technology, contributes less than 14 percent. (See Table 1.)

Agriculture

Agriculture sustains the majority of India's population and creates much of its wealth. Yet most of the 235 million people working in agriculture barely make ends meet.[1] India's wealthy farmers constitute only a small percentage of the total number of cultivators. Over 65 percent of landowners are small farmers (owning 2.5 to 5.0 acres) or marginal farmers (owning less than 2.5 acres), and 45 percent of those dependent on agriculture are agricultural laborers.[2]

---

1. See Government of India, *Census of India Newsletter—Census 2001.* Statement 2, "Total Workers (Main + Marginal) and Their Categories (India, 2001)" (http://www.censusindia.net/results/eci6_page3.html).

2. National Sample Survey Organisation, *Land and Livestock Holding Survey,* 48th round, 1991–92; Government of India, *Census of India Newsletter—Census 2001.*

Agricultural laborers own practically nothing and work on the land of others. Their employment depends upon the availability of work, and in the more prosperous and irrigated areas such as Punjab, the western parts of Uttar Pradesh, the Godavari delta in Andhra Pradesh, and the tobacco-growing districts of Gujarat, work is available year-round and agricultural laborers can make ends meet, even when wages are low. In these areas commercial crops and food grains are grown in large quantities, often using modern methods, and farming has brought prosperity, especially to owners of large tracts of land. In contrast, in many areas of India agriculture is poor, crops depend upon the monsoons, and irrigation is practically nonexistent. The farmers in these areas can grow just one crop. This is especially true, for example, in many of the tribal areas of Madhya Pradesh and Orissa, and the dry and desert areas of Rajasthan and Gujarat. Most other areas fall in between, with a means of irrigation—wells, canals, rivers, ponds, or pumps—that is insufficient, inadequate, and often expensive. The growth of agriculture has caused a growing need for water and electricity for irrigation, as well as a growing dependence upon ground water, mainly through bore-wells. This has led to falling ground-water levels, making irrigation more and more costly. In these areas, farmers are careful about the number of times and the amount of land they cultivate, relying primarily on the monsoons for irrigation and supplementing with man-made irrigation sources. In these areas, work for agricultural laborers remains uncertain. A good monsoon creates plenty of work, but without it options are limited—a laborer might work only six months during the year.

In rural areas, those who depend upon agricultural labor as their major source of income are also poor and low in the social hierarchies. Traditionally, landowners were the higher castes of the village, whereas the poorer castes owned no land but earned a living through labor, artisan work such as pottery or weaving, and service-oriented jobs such as a washerman or barber. Artisans have lost most of their livelihood to competition from factory-made goods, and the ranks of the landless laborer have swelled.

Workers who rely only upon agricultural labor may be the poorest workers in the country. Nearly 36 percent of agricultural workers live below the poverty line. In general, agricultural daily wages are low, although they vary by task (plowing, sowing, weeding, harvesting, and so forth), by the prosperity of the state or region, and by gender. Tasks such as plowing are performed only by men, whereas others such as weeding are women-intensive. For example, in the prosperous state of Haryana, the daily rate for weeding is Rs. 80 ($1.78) for men and Rs. 75 ($1.67) for women, while both men and women are paid Rs. 91 ($2.02) for harvesting. In the middle-level state of Andhra Pradesh, the rates are much lower: the daily rate for weeding is Rs. 43 for men and Rs. 37 for women, and for harvesting men receive Rs. 42 and women receive Rs. 37. The all-India averages for weeding are Rs. 55 ($1.22) for men and Rs. 45 ($1.00) for women, and the all-India averages for harvesting are Rs. 60 ($1.33) for men and Rs. 48 ($1.07) for women.[3]

On average, agricultural laborers earn well below the "floor-level" minimum wage for India, which the government declared to be Rs. 66 for 2003. A family that lives on agricultural wages will earn below a poverty line of Rs. 45 ($1.00) per day per capita. Although the picture is quite bleak, conditions have improved somewhat over the years. Real agricultural wages were growing at about 5 percent per year in the 1980s and 2.5 percent per year in the 1990s.

Because they own land, small and marginal farmers fare somewhat better than agricultural workers. Nevertheless, marginal farmers usually cannot make ends meet with their small plots of land and work as agricultural laborers for part of the year. Small farmers usually struggle to make a profit but depend heavily on the monsoons; they incur debt when they cannot obtain irrigation. Both small and marginal farmers tend to mortgage their lands when they need funds for large lump-sum expenditures such as marriage or illness, and often they are unable to redeem their mortgages. This has led to a considerable decrease in the number of small and marginal farmers and a growing number of agricultural laborers.

Census figures show that between 1991 and 2001 the proportion of cultivators—all farmers—decreased from 59 percent to 54 percent, while the proportion of agricultural laborers increased from 41 percent to 46 percent. The number of women agricultural laborers has risen even more sharply in the last decade, leaving them subject to another trend, the shift toward employing workers on a casual rather than permanent basis.

The trend toward "casualization" is a rural rather than urban phenomenon. And while the number of both male and female casual labor-

---

3. *Indian Labour Journal* 45, no. 2 (February 2004): 188, 190. One dollar equals approximately 45 rupees.

ers has increased phenomenally, a larger proportion of the female workforce is employed on a casual basis. This means that a large number of women agricultural workers have no permanent jobs; their work is seasonal and they are not employed on all days of the month. Similarly, the large proportion of small and marginal farmers who work as casual wage laborers and the increase in landless households and precariously small holdings put pressure on the casual labor wage market. While men in landless households can find other kinds of work, women in such households are confined to wage work.[4]

Agriculture is often seen as a "backward" sector of the economy, and it is expected that, as in the "developed" counties of the North, more and more workers will leave agriculture for other sectors of the economy. This is already happening, as evidenced by the number of workers moving from rural to urban areas: between 1971 and 2001 the percentage of the Indian population in urban areas grew from 19.9 to 27.8. But perhaps more importantly, nonagricultural work in the rural areas is expanding. Most rural workers supplement their earnings from agriculture by working in construction, building roads and dams, or working in the small factories that have sprung up in most small towns. They also supplement with home-based work such as tailoring or leatherwork or offer services such as mechanics, painting, or midwifery.

In spite of this diversification, agriculture remains the mainstay of the Indian economy. From the point of view of those dependent upon agriculture, it provides food as well as income. In the poorer areas many families practice only subsistence agriculture, that is, they produce only enough for their own needs, but most farmers earn an income from crop sales. Nevertheless, most farmers produce at least a part of their own nutritional needs, and so they are assured of getting enough food. Furthermore, most farms support not only agriculture but a number of by-products such as livestock and fuel.

Agriculture is changing fast. Chemical fertilizer and pesticide usage has increased exponentially, and not only the large farmers but also the small and marginal farmers are using them. Mechanization in agriculture is also spreading rapidly, and mechanized threshers, crushers, and weeders are now replacing manual labor in many parts of the

---

4. Jeemol Unni, "Women Workers in Agriculture: Some Recent Trends," in *Gender and Employment in India*, ed. T.S. Papola and Alakh N. Sharma (New Delhi: Vikas Publishing House, 1999), 99–120.

country. Irrigation in India is also increasing, making agriculture somewhat less risky. New types of seeds are entering the markets and providing farmers with a rather bewildering array of choices, and India is rapidly linking in with the international markets, especially in milk, horticulture, and spices.

The case of one farmer illustrates these changes in agriculture. Rewabhai Purushottambhai Patel, of Boral village of Bayad taluka in Sabarkantha district, supports his family of fifteen with his earnings from fifteen *bigha*[5] of agricultural land and twelve cattle (six cows, four buffalo, and two oxen). In the last seven to eight years, he has made an enormous change in his agriculture pattern based on market demands, soil conditions, and availability of water, hybrid seeds, fertilizer, and pesticides, to produce better results from his agricultural field. Rewabhai says that the market changes of the last ten years mean that:

- Chemical fertilizer, pesticides, and hybrid seeds are available within accessible areas, whereas earlier they were not.
- Legumes and cash crops like cotton and peanut oil produce better returns in comparison with cereals like rice, millet, and maize. In the last ten years prices for legumes, cotton, and peanuts have increased by 300 to 525 percent, whereas prices for cereals have increased by 100 to 275 percent.
- Lack of storage facility for small farmers coupled with overproduction has created major fluctuation in the market prices of crops.

Rewabhai has also been affected by the following changes:

- Capital investment is now needed to get a better yield: for Rewabhai's fifteen *bigha* of land, hybrid seeds and thirty bags of chemical fertilizer are required to grow a crop in any season.
- Production has increased with the use of hybrid seeds and fertilizers.
- The water level in his well has dropped from 40 to 800 feet below ground in the last ten years.
- Hybrid seeds increase agricultural risk, as lack of adequate water results in complete crop failure, whereas local seeds yield some results (about 50 percent) even with less water.

---

5. A *bigha* is a traditional unit of land measurement in South Asia. Its exact size can range from one-third to one full acre.

- Storing produce is possible only if the crop is grown with local seeds. Produce from hybrid seeds needs special chemical preservatives if stored longer than three months. Moreover, the government has banned most of the chemicals needed to store hybrid crops, as they are poisonous and have been used by farmers to commit suicide.
- Lack of water and increasing mechanization have resulted in lack of work in the field, which has changed the total working hours in a day. Farmers used to work sixteen hours in a field, now Rewabhai works only eight.[6]

The challenge before policy makers is to ensure that the new developments in agriculture strengthen existing farmers, making them more productive so they will not end up as casual laborers. Agricultural laborers also need protection. They must increase their productivity so they will not be displaced by machines.

Construction

The construction sector in India is traditionally a major employer. With a growth rate of about 10 percent per annum, the construction sector is also driving the Indian economy forward. This growth is due to government investment in infrastructure, especially roads, bridges, and dams, as well as a growth of housing stock throughout the country. The construction industry itself contributes an estimated 5 percent of the GDP and 78 percent of the capital formation in the country.[7]

The construction industry employs around 31 million workers in India today, but to a very large extent this employment is casual and contractual. More than 95 percent of India's construction workers are employed on a temporary basis. Of the many seasonal workers, a large proportion are women.

Construction industry operations are based on a system of contracting, subcontracting, and labor contracting. The labor contracting system continues to be the main mechanism for recruiting construction workers. As a result, there is no direct relationship between the em-

---

6. Rewabhai's and all subsequent statements in this chapter are drawn from interviews carried out by the Self-Employed Women's Association.

7. Ashok Raj and Rakesh Kapoor, "Relocating Space for Women Workers in the Construction Industry," in *Globalization and Its Impact on Women Workers in the Informal Economy*, ed. Renana Jhabvala and Shalini Sinha (New Delhi: Sage Publications, forthcoming).

ployer and the worker. In fact, workers are virtually invisible to the principal and the prime contractor.

Construction workers' wages become reduced along this chain of subcontractors, and on top of that the contractual or casual nature of the employment results in a substantial difference in wage rates. Unskilled workers earn far less than skilled workers.

In the post-liberalization period, the Indian construction industry is witnessing many structural changes that will radically transform the business as well as the construction labor market. Under the prevailing World Trade Organization (WTO) regime, the essential requirement of global tendering has facilitated the entry of many multinational corporations in the Indian construction industry. With increased mechanization, labor would be displaced in nearly all construction operations. It is estimated that the overall deployment of labor will become one-fiftieth to one-fifth of the earlier numbers, depending on the particular operation. The introduction of ready-mix concrete plants, for example, would reduce the workforce by 80 percent. Women laborers would be the main victims of mechanized soil digging and carrying, concrete mixing and curing, and brick carrying. Obviously, manual labor, and especially women workers, would be increasingly eliminated from construction sites.

This is what Madhuben, a construction worker in Ahmedabad, had to say:

> I started at the age of fifteen and first carried loads of concrete on my head. Then I learnt to carry twelve bricks at a time. Later, I learnt to lay concrete and then do plastering. When I first started working we were attached to a contractor and would get work every day. We only had one holiday on *amavas* [no-moon day]. However, in the last ten to twelve years, the numbers of workers increased with the closure of the textile mills and the printing factories. Then workers started competing with each other, and we no longer had regular work. We all had to stand at the *kadiya naka* [roadside site for construction workers] and contractors came and hired us by the day. Still, I used to get about twenty days of work a month. However, over the last five years things have become especially bad. I hardly get six to seven days of work a month. This is the situation with all of us who stand at the *kadiya naka*. Why? I don't know why. The work seems to have decreased overall. Some say it is due to recession. Others say it is due to new machines. In some of the bigger sites now, I have seen that all digging is done by machines, and even carrying bricks is now done by machines, and in some sites whole walls are made elsewhere and brought to the site.

This decrease in the demand for unskilled labor has been accompanied by a rapid increase in the demand for skilled labor. A recent study found that the real wages of skilled workers have risen 30 to 50 percent, and in spite of the expansion and growth of the construction industry, the real wages of unskilled laborers have dropped 2 to 15 percent.[8]

As the construction industry expands and mechanizes, policy makers must ensure that the workers who will be displaced by machines receive training to develop their skills. The Construction Industry Development Council, established by the government of India in collaboration with industry, is in the process of setting up schools to train skilled workers. Given the fact that India has more than 30 million construction workers, the need for such training is enormous.

Manufacturing

India's manufacturing sector also generates a great deal of wealth. In fact, after agriculture, manufacturing has the largest number of workers and the greatest added value. India is unique in that cutting-edge manufacturing techniques operate alongside centuries-old manufacturing traditions. So while modern weaving and spinning factories in India are equipped with the latest Japanese machines, other weaving factories use machines discarded from European companies, and still other factories use machines discarded from Indian factories, some of which date from the 1920s. Many of these machines can be found in the homes of weavers and are tended by the family. Traditional hand weaving without power is also widespread. Hand-weaving worksheds abound in many parts of the country, many of them equipped with new inventions like the hand jacquard (a loom that weaves intricate designs with many threads). At the same time more than 7 million part-time and full-time hand weavers produce cloth on their own looms at home. In India, this range of operations —from large factories with the latest machines to home-based manual labor—produces almost every consumer good, from food to paper, brass ware to furniture.

A large, capital-intensive capital goods sector in India manufactures iron and steel, oil and gas products, and heavy machinery. These huge factories employ thousands of workers and rely upon modern technology. However, a large percentage of India's manufactured goods comes

---

8. SEWA Academy, unpublished internal study on women construction workers (2004).

Table 2

Organized and Unorganized Manufacturing Sectors (percentages)

	1994–1995		2000–2001	
	Organized sector	Unorganized sector	Organized sector	Unorganized sector
Number of units	0.8	99.2	0.7	99.3
Number of workers	15.4	84.6	14.3	85.7
Fixed capital	83.5	16.5	79.9	20.1
Gross value added	77.6	22.4	76.1	23.9

Source: Government of India, National Sample Survey Report No. 363/1, June 1989 and R 433, September 1997 and household level data (for 2000–2001), National Sample Survey Organisation and Government of India, ASO, 1999–2000, vol. 1, Central Statistical Organisation, February 2002. As quoted in G.K. Chadha and P.P. Sahu, "Employment in Unorganized Manufacturing in India" (paper, National Seminar on National Sample Survey 56th Round Survey Results, New Delhi, March 21, 2003).

from the "unorganized sector": the small enterprises with a few workers or own-account enterprises where the home of the owner is often his or her workplace. These "unorganized" enterprises far outnumber the organized ones, and the sector continues to grow.

From 1994–95 to 2000–2001, the number of manufacturing units has grown from 14.6 million to 17.1 million; the number of workers, from 39.2 million to 43.2 million; the fixed capital from Rs. 850.8 billion to Rs. 1,488 billion; and the gross value added from Rs. 535.6 billion to Rs. 731.6 billion. Table 2 shows a small increase in the share of the unorganized sector in all the measures of these two sectors of manufacturing. Ninety-nine percent of the units and 86 percent of the workers are working in the unorganized sector (i.e., in small or household enterprises). But that 99 percent owns only 20 percent of the fixed capital, and that 86 percent adds only 24 percent of the value. This means that the bulk of the workers and enterprises have little access to capital and technology and receive very low returns for their work.

Employment in the organized sector has been shrinking for a variety of reasons. First, mechanization has caused many firms to downsize. Second, many firms split themselves up or outsource work to avoid labor laws. Third, some of the older industries such as textiles and jute have either disappeared or completely changed their methods of production. This major change in the structure of the manufacturing sector has created immense hardships for the families of former employees, who had achieved a certain minimum level of security. Perhaps the most dramatic case is the organized textile industry.

Cotton textile production began at the turn of the twentieth century in India. By the 1920s cotton textile mills were widespread in India, with more than 150 mills in the main centers of Bombay and Ahmedabad in the west. The south (Coimbatore) and north (Gwalior, Indore, and Kanpur) also had a large number of textile mills. The industry flourished until the 1980s, when it began to decline. Almost all of the cotton textile mills had closed by the end of the 1990s, leaving more than 500,000 workers unemployed.

These workers had attained a certain minimum level of security— their wages were above the minimum, and more important, they had a steady income. They had access to health care through the Employees Social Security program, and old age security through the Employees Provident Fund Scheme. They sent their children to school, acquired small homes, and were reaching middle-class status.

Each city that experienced the process of closure faced convulsions as a result. In Ahmedabad, for example, the process lasted ten years. During that time nearly 80,000 permanent workers and more than 50,000 nonpermanent workers lost their jobs and were driven into the informal sector. The city experienced an economic recession as well as public disturbances—especially communal riots. A whole class of workers was thrown into poverty. Alcoholism and suicide were widespread. Children were withdrawn from school and sent to work.

The Informal Economy in India

The "unorganized sector" is by far the largest employer of workers in India, but internationally, too, this type of work is growing. In 2002 the International Labour Organization (ILO) took special note of this trend at the International Labour Conference by passing a "Resolution on the Informal Economy."[9] "Informal economy" is the term the ILO used to describe what in India we have been calling the unorganized sector. Since informal economy is a more internationally recognized term, it will be used hereafter.

---

9. International Labour Organization, "Resolution on Decent Work and the Informal Economy," General Conference of the International Labour Organization, 90th Session (2002) (http://www.ilo.org/public/english/standards/relm/ilc/ilc90/pdf/pr-25res.pdf).

The informal economy is where the bulk of the "working poor," those who earn less than enough to generate a family income of US$1.00 per day per capita, are concentrated. There is no simple relationship between working informally and being poor—or working formally and escaping poverty—yet a much higher percentage of informal economy workers are poor.

The informal economy accounts for some 93 percent of the total workforce in India, encompassing a wide range of activities, from street vending, domestic services, rag picking, and *bidi* rolling (a traditional hand-rolled filterless cigarette) to small enterprises and home-based manufacturing.[10] Workers in the informal economy are largely "invisible" and "unprotected." To the extent that they are unregistered or unrecorded under the legislation, regulations, and statistics of national and local governments many workers lack fundamental rights. Working conditions are poor, hours are irregular and often very long, and earnings are low. Workers are exposed to various forms of insecurity and occupational safety and health hazards. Their access to credit, markets, information, and technology is limited, and their entrepreneurship and creative potential is constrained. Informal economy workers lack social security and legal protection as well as organization and representation, whether for bargaining with employers or lobbying politicians and bureaucrats.

The informal economy employs 83 percent of India's nonagricultural workers, nearly 99 percent of agricultural workers (including forestry, fishing, plantation, and allied activities), and 90 percent of manufacturing and construction workers. Within manufacturing, informal economy workers predominate in industries such as garments, textiles, food, and electronics. (See Table 3.) Workers in the informal economy are subject to a range of exploitative practices and remain the most vulnerable and the poorest in the country, yet their contribution to the national economy must not be underestimated.

Contribution of the Informal Sector

It is generally believed that the poor are consumers, not savers, and that not only do they consume what they produce but they consume from the

---

10. Computed from National Sample Survey, Directorate General of Employment and Training, and Census 2001, and published in *Women and Men in the Informal Economy: A Statistical Picture* (Geneva: International Labour Organization, 2002) (http://www.ilo.org/public/english/employment/gems/download/women.pdf).

Table 3

Workforce in the Informal Economy: Percent of Total Workforce

	All	Male	Female
All informal workers	93	91.6	95.9
Agriculture	99.4	99.4	99.4
Nonagriculture	83.4	82.9	85.6
Community, social, and personal services	65.9	60.6	78.4
Construction	93.5	93.9	90.3
Electricity, gas, and water	6	6.2	0
Financial services	66	69	53
Manufacturing	86.3	84.7	90.8
Mining and quarrying	55.7	55.8	55
Trade, hotels, and restaurants	98.7	98.7	98.3
Transport and storage	78.7	81	5.2

Source: Jeemol Unni, "Size, Contribution and Characteristics of Informal Employment in India" (background paper written for ILO, *Women and Men in the Informal Economy: A Statistical Picture*).

national budget in the form of subsidies—especially for food and other necessities. However, the figures show that this sector's contribution to the Indian economy is often grossly underrated. Even according to the National Accounts Statistics, their contribution to the economy is high. According to one estimate, the informal sector contributed more than 59 percent of the net domestic product (NDP).[11] According to another, the sector also contributed nearly 60 percent of the total household savings.[12] The informal sector also contributed 39.3 percent (Rs. 46,000 crore) of India's total exports.[13]

The Central Statistical Organisation has been calculating the informal sector's share of the NDP for the last twenty-five years. In 1993–94 the informal sector's contribution was 62 percent of NDP; in 2000–2001 it had become 59 percent.[14] Although more workers continue to enter

---

11. National Accounts Statistics (NAS), 2000, Statement 76.1.

12. B.K. Pradhan, P.K. Roy, and M.R. Saluja, *Informal Sector in India: A Study of Household Saving Behaviour* (National Council for Applied Economic Research, 1999), subsequently published as "Savings from Informal Economy," in *Informal Economy Centrestage: New Structures of Employment*, ed. Renana Jhabvala, Ratna M. Sudarshan, and Jeemol Unni (New Delhi and Thousand Oaks, CA: Sage Publications, 2003), 189.

13. Vinayak Ghatate, "Informal Sector's Contribution to India's Exports: A Quantitative Evaluation" (New Delhi: Indian Institute of Foreign Trade, 1999), 6.

14. CSO, Ministry of Statistics and Programme Implementation, Government of India, 2003, New Delhi.

the informal economy, both capital investment and value added remain stagnant—while the shares of investment in the formal sector continually increase.

SEWA Bank: A Firsthand Experience in Wealth Creation

SEWA Bank was created in 1974 by a group of women street vendors, head-loaders,[15] and tailors. The women had nowhere to invest their small savings, and when they needed capital they had to borrow from moneylenders at interest rates of 5–10 percent per month, occasionally even 10 percent per day. When SEWA tried to link them with the large banks, it discovered that the women were unwelcome. The women were illiterate and, therefore, unable to transact with these banks.

During a SEWA annual meeting the women proposed their own bank. "If the big banks don't want us, why don't we start our own bank?" they said. "We may be poor but we are so many; if we all put in some money, we would have enough capital to start our own bank." SEWA Bank began with Rs. 60,000 (approximately $1,333) and has grown to more than 200,000 depositors with a working capital of nearly Rs. 1 billion (over $22 million). The bank has always been financially viable, its capital coming only from the small savings of its members.

SEWA Bank is a cooperative owned by the shareholders—the low-income women. They manage the money as they manage their household finances or small businesses, with thrift and wise business sense. Another example of wealth generation by the poor is illustrated by the following story:

> Nanuben started life as an agricultural laborer in the Mehsana district of Gujarat. Due to a lack of work in the village, her family decided to migrate to Ahmedabad city. Nanuben joined her mother in the "old clothes" business, going from house to house with a basket of new utensils in exchange for old clothes from housewives.
>
> Nanuben took a loan of Rs. 500 in 1978, out of which she bought a basket for Rs. 125 to store clothes, some aluminum utensils worth Rs. 125 to exchange for old clothes, and some food grains and oil for the family's consumption.
>
> She earned a profit of Rs. 400 out of this small investment which she

---

15. Head-loaders are laborers, largely women, who carry materials for construction work on their heads.

reinvested in the business, along with a second loan of Rs. 1,500. Thereafter, she kept repaying one loan and taking another loan, using the loan money and profit from the business to buy a house, household furniture, gold and silver, her daughter's wedding, and still contribute to a bank savings account.

"We were living in a hut and were eating only once a day, sleeping on the floor, when we came to Ahmedabad. . . . Now we have a real house, with a bed and a fan, stock for food-grains, peanut oil, spices, soaps, and match boxes. Earlier I was washing and repairing all the clothes by myself. Now we have employed one tailor who repairs clothes and a washerman comes daily to my house to collect clothes for washing."

Creation of Wealth: Who Contributes, Who Benefits

Wealth is necessary for the growth of the country, for removing poverty, for raising the quality of life for all. We have seen that the majority of the working population is contributing to the creation of wealth, gross domestic product, national savings, and exports. But we have also seen that most of these workers are in the informal economy—self-employed, casual, or home-based workers—and that although this economy is contributing 60 percent of the wealth, it does so without the benefit of investment of capital and technology. In other words, the workers and the enterprises in the informal sector have gained much less from the new growth opportunities than the workers and the enterprises in the formal sector. Since the investment in skills, technology, and capital is so much less, the gain in terms of income is also much less.

Wealth and Poverty

Economic reform began in earnest in the 1990s, resulting in economic changes which evoked varied, often rather extreme, reactions. Some believed that the reforms would create wealth and opportunities for all sections of the population, creating rapid growth and eradicating poverty. They pointed to Asian countries like Korea, Malaysia, and China where free trade had created unprecedented levels of income and lifestyle. Others felt that the reforms would benefit only one section of the population, creating wider inequalities and impoverishing large sets of people, especially the more vulnerable. They pointed to African countries where free trade had weakened the economy to the point of collapse and caused a decline in human development.

Following the international debates, the debates on globalization and the effects of economic liberalization policies in India have centered on poverty. The main question is: Have the number and percentage of the poor in India increased or decreased since the reforms began? The answer to this question would be revealing and useful if poverty were considered in all of its many dimensions.

The evidence suggests that poverty is a multidimensional social phenomenon. Definitions of poverty and its causes vary by gender, age, culture, and other social and economic contexts. For example, men associate poverty with a lack of material assets, whereas women define poverty as food insecurity. Generational differences emerge as well: younger men consider the ability to generate an income as their most important asset, whereas older men cite the status connected to a traditional agricultural lifestyle as key. A person's location also affects perceived causes of poverty. For example, farmers link poverty to drought, the urban poor link poverty to rising prices and fewer employment opportunities. Poverty never results from the lack of one thing, but from a cluster of interlocking factors.[16]

In India, the debates on poverty have focused around the "poverty line" and how many people are below or above it, avoiding entirely the question of multidimensionality. The poverty line is based on consumption figures as collected by the National Sample Survey Organisation. Separate rural and urban poverty lines have been defined. It is assumed that a person at the poverty line spends 80 percent of his or her income on food and 20 percent on the remainder of life's necessities. It is also assumed that a person will cross above the poverty line if he or she is able to consume 2,400 calories in the rural areas and 2,100 calories in the urban areas. Both of these assumptions have been questioned. There has been a great deal of debate around the issue of caloric intake: some argue that a caloric intake of 2,100 calories is not enough to sustain a person doing hard labor. It is accepted that people do survive on 2,100 calories a day, but that these people are malnourished and anemic, especially the women.

The opposite view is that the intake of 2,400—and even 2,100—calories greatly exceeds caloric requirements for modern living. Economic columnist Swaminathan Anklesaria Aiyar has argued that an intake

---

16. Deepa Narayan et al., *Can Anyone Hear Us?* (New York: Oxford University Press for the World Bank, 2000), 32.

of 1,600 calories is enough to sustain a person, partly because people today consume higher quality food and so need to consume less, and partly because mechanization has lessened the need for hard labor.[17] This is supported by the fact that caloric consumption has been declining in Indian consumers, from an average of 2,268 calories per day in 1972–73 to 2,030 calories per day in 1999–2000.

The other assumption—that the poor spend at least 80 percent of their income on food—is also wrong. In 1972, the lowest 30 percent of the population in India did indeed spend 81 percent of their income on food. However, by 1999–2000 they were spending only 63 percent on food.[18] What this indicates is also controversial. Some observers feel that this means that the poor are able to satisfy their basic need for food and are able to spend their income on other things such as clothing, education, and better housing. Others feel that, unlike thirty years ago, it is now necessary to spend income on nonfood items such as transportation and health care in order to earn an income. Also, certain basics such as water, which were available free and more plentifully, today must be bought by the poor. Furthermore, much of the nonfood expenditure also reflects payments for debts incurred during crises.

In spite of its inadequacies, the poverty line remains the touchstone by which policy makers measure their successes or failures. It is the sign that indicates whether poverty is increasing or decreasing in India. Therefore, a great deal of acrimonious debate surrounds the collection and interpretation of the poverty line figures, which are collected every five years by the statistical agency known as the National Sample Survey Organisation. India's consumption-expenditure survey is perhaps the largest sample survey in the world.

The most recent consumption-expenditure survey was conducted in 1999–2000, and its results were used by the government to declare that the economic liberalization policies had been successful in reducing poverty. The Planning Commission declared that the success of the anti-poverty programs was reflected in the decline in the combined (urban and rural) poverty ratio from 54.9 percent in 1972–73 to

---

17. Swaminathan S. Anklesaria Aiyar, "It's Not Just Calories, Stupid," *The Economic Times* (New Delhi), December 10, 2003 (http://www.economictimes.indiatimes.com/articleshow/348675.cms).

18. S. Mahendra Dev and Robert E. Evenson, "Rural Development in India: Agriculture, Non-Farm, and Migration" (paper presented at Conference on Indian Policy Reform, Stanford University Center for Research on Economic Development and Policy Reform, June 5–7, 2003) (http://www.credpr.stanford.edu/events/India2003/Rural_Development.pdf).

36.0 percent in 1993–94. The commission went on to say that the poverty ratio declined by nearly ten percentage points in the period that began in 1993–94 to reach 21.6 percent in 1999–2000. In absolute terms, the commission said that the number of poor declined to 260 million in 1999–2000, with about 75 percent of these being in the rural areas.[19]

The government's claims were challenged by economic reform opponents, who said that because the National Sample Survey (NSS) had changed its methodology the decline in persons under the poverty line was not real. This debate generated so much controversy in academic and policy circles—and so much confusion—that a number of academics sought a more objective understanding of the emerging numbers. The best known of these efforts is a study by Angus Deaton and Jean Drèze who reexamined the NSS data and presented a new series of internally consistent poverty indexes for the last three five-year periods. Deaton and Drèze found that "the broad picture emerging from these revised estimates is one of sustained poverty decline in most states (and also in India as a whole) during the reference period."[20]

The Deaton-Drèze study considered related evidence from three additional sources: the national accounts statistics (NAS) estimated by the Central Statistical Organisation (CSO), the employment-unemployment surveys of the NSS, and data on agricultural wages. According to the CSO data, the per capita expenditure has grown at about 3.5 percent per year, and the employment-unemployment surveys show a similar trend. Further, agricultural wages, which reflect the earnings of the poorest workers, show a growth of about 2.5 percent per year. The independent data from several sources show an overall decline in poverty.

An important point to note here is that although the number of people who crossed the poverty line is large—more than 10 percent in the rural areas and about 9 percent in the urban areas—in fact the increase in per capita expenditure associated with this decline in poverty is quite modest—about 10 percent in five years. That is, people are increasing

---

19. Government of India (Planning Commission), *Tenth Five Year Plan 2002–2007*, 2 vols. (New Delhi: Government of India, 2002) (http://planningcommission.nic.in/plans/planrel/fiveyr/welcome.html). See especially vol. 2, chap. 3, p. 293 and passim (http://planningcommission.nic.in/plans/planrel/fiveyr/10th/volume2/v2_ch3_2.pdf).

20. Angus Deaton and Jean Drèze, "Poverty and Inequality in India: A Reexamination," in *Economic and Political Weekly* (Mumbai), September 7, 2002, p. 3729 (http://www.cdedse.org/pdf/work107.pdf).

their expenditures at about 2 percent per year, as compared to the growth rate, which has exceeded 3.5 percent per year.

Another important finding of the Deaton-Drèze study was that in the five years between surveys, there was an increase in inequality:

> First, there has been a strong 'divergence' of per capita expenditure across states, with the already better-off states (particularly in the southern and western regions) growing more rapidly than the poorer states. Second, rural-urban disparities of per capita expenditure have risen. Third, inequality has increased within urban areas in most states. . . . In the rural areas of some of the poorest states there has been virtually no increase in per capita expenditure between 1993–1994 and 1999–2000. Meanwhile the urban populations of most of the better-off states have enjoyed increases of per capita expenditure of 20–30 percent, with even larger increases for high income groups within these populations.[21]

The Distribution of Wealth

There is no doubt that there has been a great deal of wealth created in India, leading to a strong growth rate. Large majorities of people, through their work, have contributed to this growth, and to some extent these workers have seen some improvements in their income. However, there is still the question of whether this growth rate has translated into a better quality of life for Indians.

Today there is a broad-based consensus to view human development in terms of three critical dimensions of well-being: longevity (the ability to live a long and healthy life), education (the ability to read, write, and acquire knowledge), and command over resources (the ability to enjoy a decent standard of living and have a socially meaningful life). Although these are all complicated and interdependent variables, the international community has attempted to reduce them to composite indicators. The main international indicator that measures the quality of life is the human development index brought out each year by the Human Development Reports of the United Nations Development Programme (UNDP). The index is divided into three categories of human development: high, medium, and low. India has been ranked 127 out of 174 countries, which is the lower end of the medium human development group. China, which has a growth rate comparable to India, ranks 94. Of course, this one

---

21. Deaton and Drèze, "Poverty and Inequality."

figure hides vast differences within the various Indian states. Kerala and Tamil Nadu have a high human development index comparable to countries in Southeast Asia, whereas Bihar and Orissa have a very low index, comparable to sub-Saharan countries.[22]

In some ways there has been a definite improvement in the quality of life of the average Indian. The life expectancy at birth, for example, has doubled in the last fifty years. An average Indian born today can expect to live sixty-one years. His grandfather, born at the time of Independence, could expect to live only thirty years.[23] But again, these averages hide very large differences among states: a girl born in Kerala could expect to live seventy-six years, whereas her sister in Assam would live only fifty-five years. This dramatic gap reflects better access to health care and nutrition in certain states.

Unfortunately, India's higher growth rates have not translated into equivalent improvements in the quality of life. The improvements that have occurred in income have not been matched by investments in health, education, provision of nutrition, and other basic necessities, so that although there is improvement in quality of life due to higher incomes and aspirations, the majority of the people are still poor in terms of their access to basic necessities.

Food

Access to food is an emotive issue in India—and an issue upon which political parties have won or lost elections. The following stories are quite typical:

> We do not have any food stored in the house, so we work every day and buy our provisions every day. I try to save a little money and buy enough grain for a week. If we have earned enough that day, we buy oil, vegetables, some spice, tea, sugar. If not, then we just do with chilies. If there is no work, the shopkeeper does let me buy on credit. No, I hardly use the ration card, we migrate a lot out of our village for work, and anyway, I have mortgaged it to the shopkeeper. Sometimes . . . yes, we do go hungry. My mother taught me to cook using a lot of water and a lot of chilies, it makes us feel less hungry.

---

22. United Nations Development Programme, *Human Development Report 2004* (New York: Oxford University Press, 2004) (http://hdr.undp.org/reports/global/2004/).

23. Government of India (Planning Commission), *India, National Human Development Report, 2001* (New Delhi and New York: Oxford University Press, 2002) (http:// planningcommission.nic.in/reports/genrep/nhdrep/nhdreportf.htm).

> We have a small plot of land, so we are able to grow and store rice enough for at least six months for our family. We also have two cows so we have some milk for tea. We buy vegetables, when we have money, but not every day. Oil, tea, sugar we get from the ration shop, but nowadays it is not available like before, so we have to buy from the shopkeeper. When we need grain we also buy it from the ration shop, but the quality is very poor. At the harvest time, when we sell the crop we do have income and we try to get eggs and other things for our children. But during the summer, we generally make do with rice and some curry.

The "mid-day meal" scheme for school children in Tamil Nadu and the "cheap rice scheme" in Andhra Pradesh have swept parties into power and kept them there. Conversely, a rise in the price of onions defeated the government in the 1998 Delhi elections.

The main instrument of distributing food at reasonable prices has been the government-controlled Public Distribution System (PDS). The system was established mainly to ensure price stabilization of food grains, and until the late 1970s it was restricted to urban areas. In the 1980s the system gained recognition as a welfare and anti-poverty measure, and PDS shops were extended to rural areas. However, in recent years more and more problems have surfaced in the system, and it is declining as a means to provide inexpensive food to people. At the same time, food production (especially grains, which are a dietary staple) has been increasing and food is being purchased by the government of India. The Food Corporation of India has stockpiled surplus grain in sheds, and in recent years the surplus has exceeded 65 million tons, with the food subsidy reaching Rs. 3 trillion (nearly $7 billion).

This stockpiled food, along with lack of distribution, has created "hunger amidst plenty." Various micro studies have documented hunger and starvation deaths in many parts of the country, and recently a "right to food" movement has been building. For example, a public hearing on hunger and the right to food held in Manatu block of Palamau district of Jharkhand following starvation deaths revealed gross irregularities in food-related programs and a disastrous level of public services. A fact-finding committee investigating three starvation deaths found that the entire village lived in a condition of permanent semi-starvation.[24] At the

---

24. S. Mahendra Dev, "Right to Food in India" (Working Paper 50, Centre for Economic and Social Studies, Hyderabad, 2003), 28 (http://www.cess.ac.in/cesshome/wp/wp_50.pdf).

national level, the Supreme Court, approached by the People's Union of Civil Liberties (*PUCL v Union of India* and others), ordered that all state and union territories introduce mid-day meals in all government primary schools. Many states are still resisting this order.

Commentators such as Swaminathan Aiyar deny that there is widespread hunger in the country and point to the National Sample Survey figures from 1999–2000, in which only 3 percent of those surveyed said that they went hungry sometime during the year.[25] Aiyar and others interpret this to mean that although pockets of hunger exist, most people have enough food.

In certain areas of the country extreme hunger and deprivation lead to death. Parts of Bihar, Jharkhand, and Orissa have made the news for "starvation deaths," and during periods of drought some parts of Rajasthan reported such deaths. However, on the whole, during times of drought or scarcity, the central and state governments manage huge relief and food-for-work programs that ensure at least a minimum level of food in the area.

If not active hunger, certainly malnutrition seems to be widespread in India. The National Family Health Surveys regularly find signs of poor nutrition throughout the population. Recently, 52 percent of women and 74 percent of children were found to be anemic, with the poorer states such as Bihar and Rajasthan showing even higher rates. The brunt of lack of food or poor quality food is usually borne by women and even more by children, especially girls. Perhaps the most telling figure is that over 47 percent of children under five years were found to be moderately to severely malnourished. According to United Nations Children's Fund (UNICEF), this is the highest rate of malnourishment in the world.[26]

Education

One of the strongest achievements in India over the past decades has been in the area of education. At Independence only 18 percent of the population was literate, whereas the most recent census found that this

---

25. Aiyar, "It's Not Just Calories, Stupid."
26. United Nations Children's Fund (UNICEF), *The State of the World's Children 2004: Girls, Education, and Development* (New York: UNICEF, 2003), 15 (http://www.unicef.org/publications/Eng_text.pdf).

percentage had increased to 65 percent. In particular, over the last twenty years the literacy rate has increased more than 50 percent.

As with all other indicators, the average hides vast differences among states. Nearly the entire population of Kerala is literate, whereas less than half of Bihar is literate. Nevertheless, many of the less literate states like Rajasthan and Madhya Pradesh have made major efforts to provide schooling for their children, starting new programs such as the Right to Education in Madhya Pradesh.

Perhaps the biggest change that has occurred has been a change in the attitude toward education. Families used to resist educating their children, as they felt that it brought little economic benefit and kept children from helping in the family. In particular, it was thought that girls did not need to be educated, as their main function was to look after their husband's families and their younger siblings. Sending girls to school might expose them to too many influences and make them less "obedient." Today, most families recognize that education is necessary for survival, and although education cannot ensure a job, lack of education makes a worker less competitive. As a paper picker in Ahmedabad said: "I have not been to school at all, but I want my daughter-in-law to be educated. She will be a better companion for my son and a better mother for my grandchildren. She will also be better able to earn something. After all, with so many expenses today we have to bring all possible income into the house."

Health Care

Are the people of India healthier than before? As we have seen, life expectancy has risen considerably and people are less susceptible to life-threatening diseases. On the other hand, the infant mortality rate is still high at ninety-three per thousand (children under five) as compared to China's thirty-eight and Indonesia's forty-five per thousand.

Health care is certainly a priority for most people. For the large majority—the workers in the informal economy—illness means not only an additional expense, but lost work days and lost income. For workers whose bodies are also their means to livelihood, it is vital to fall ill as little as possible. When a major illness comes along, manual laborers sink into debt and the vicious cycle of poverty. Studies have shown that illness is the major source of debt for most poor families, and that it is often the reason that families fall below the poverty line.

Jaswanti, a head-loader in the wholesale clothes market of Ahmedabad city, suffered from tuberculosis. She was prescribed costly medicine and nutritious food that she could not afford. She pawned her gold ornaments with a moneylender and the burden of repaying the loan created a food scarcity that caused the women of the house to eat less. This had an adverse effect on Jaswanti's health. There was no money to purchase a cup of tea, much less Jaswanti's medicine. If Jaswanti was a member of SEWA, she would have been entitled to at least some health education, referred to TB hospitals, and received insurance to cover some of her medical expenses and a bank loan at terms softer than those of the private moneylender.[27]

Adequate health care requires adequate financing, and certainly Indians spend a great deal on health care. Six percent of GDP is spent on health care every year, which is much higher than many countries with much better health attainments. The East Asian countries such as South Korea and Malaysia, for example, spend much less on health care and have much better health indicators for their populations.

The paradox of high expenditures and low health outcomes is explained by the fact that much of the health expenditure is in the private sector. The level of private sector expenditure in India was over 4 percent of GDP, whereas in a country like Sri Lanka, with much better health than India, the level was just 1.7 percent.[28] In India, the private sector is almost completely unregulated, with doctors of all kinds charging whatever the market can bear. The market for generic drugs is small, because most doctors tend to recommend the far more expensive brand names. In many states, the public health systems have declined or become partially privatized.[29]

The Planning Commission has listed some of the problems of India's public health care services as follows:

- Persistent gaps in manpower and infrastructure, with wide inter-state differences, especially at the primary health care level.

---

27. Ela Bhatt, *Women's Health Security, Strengthening Women's Economy* (Ahmedabad: SEWA, 1996).

28. As quoted in Seeta Prabhu and D.V. Selvaraju, "Public Financing for Health Security in India: Issues and Trends" (paper prepared for the National Consultation on Health Security, organized by the Institute for Human Development, New Delhi, July 26–27, 2001).

29. For more on the health and health care transformations in India, see Mark Nichter and David van Sickle, "India's Health and Health Care Transformations," in *India Briefing: Quickening the Pace of Change*, ed. Alyssa Ayres and Philip Oldenburg (Armonk, NY: M.E. Sharpe, 2002), 159–96.

- Suboptimal functioning of the existing infrastructure, poor referral services.
- Increased dependence of people on private health care services, often leading to indebtedness in rural areas.

Continuation of a universally free public health system—preventive as well as curative—is unsustainable in its present form. Moreover, there is inadequate policy movement on creating an alternative, accessible, viable, and dependable health care system for the majority of the people.[30]

Perhaps the two areas where the Indian government has succeeded in improving health has been in controlling communicable diseases and moving toward universal immunization. The pulse polio campaign of 2001–2002 was the single largest immunization project in the world. Certain diseases such as smallpox and leprosy have been totally eradicated, and others like *Kala Azar* (leishmaniasis) have been controlled. Malaria and tuberculosis are still widespread, but there are major programs to deal with them in areas of outbreak. To address the rising threat of AIDS in the country, government and voluntary agencies have taken up an anti-AIDS campaign to try and control its spread.

A unique feature of the Indian health care system is its large informal sector. In villages and poorer areas in the towns, medical care is provided not only by formally qualified doctors, but by a variety of informal health care providers such as midwives, *ayurveda* or *unani* medicine practitioners, and homeopathic practitioners.[31] This informal sector is estimated as more than twice the size of the formal sector.

Growth with a "Human Face"

Extending the benefits of economic growth to the working poor is not just a matter of creating a few more programs—it calls for a deeper understanding of the importance of people to the process of growth.

Perhaps the most fruitful way is for the people to participate more effectively in the process of growth. At present they participate at a very low level of productivity, so the results are incommensurate with their hard work. As we have seen, low levels of productivity result

---

30. Government of India, *National Human Development Report*, 85.

31. *Ayurveda* is a traditional Indian system of medicine based on Sanskrit texts. *Unani*, which means "Greek," is a traditionally Islamic system of medicine with a strong presence in South Asia.

from a variety of reasons, and so raising productivity requires a range of initiatives.

First, better skills, more skills, and widespread skills training are necessary. Given the changes that are happening to the economy, people need new skills—but very few institutions in the country are teaching them. A widespread, flexible, and effective system is necessary to help people in each sector develop the skills they need to increase their productivity and output. Linked to skills training is technology. New technologies exist and are being developed in each sector of the economy. Many of the technologies can be developed and disseminated to enhance worker productivity rather than displace manual labor.

Madhuben, quoted earlier to illustrate the displacement of unskilled workers in the construction industry, told a different story a few years later:

> One day I met Ramilaben from SEWA at the *kadiyanaka*. She advised me to join SEWA. Soon, I started attending SEWA meetings on the no-moon day and came to know all about Mahila Housing Trust [MHT, the housing organization promoted by SEWA] and its activities.
>
> While working with private contractors I took the initiative and learned how to lay a gutter line, tub, RCC [roller-compacted concrete] slab, and stone glazing. Now I am a master mason and train other women like me. Having trained women, I started taking labor contracts on my own.
>
> I have been working in the Parivartan—slum upgrading areas that MHT is doing work in under the labor contractors. In addition I also took a contract to build twelve toilets. My work under Parivartan has helped me earn Rs. 9,000 in two months.
>
> When Mr. Mataliya, an official from the West Zone office, came to inspect the work in Jadibanagar, a Parivartan area, he remarked that, "The work of Madhuben is better than that of the male workers."
>
> A resident of Jadibanagar, Ms. Nandaben Jaswantsingh, was so impressed with my work during the construction of her toilet that she requested me to build a bathroom for her home during my days off from the infrastructure construction with MHT. Nandaben bought new material for the bathroom at her own expense and I began the construction of the bathroom on the days that I was free.
>
> My life has really improved after upgrading my skills through the trainings by MHT. I earn enough to support my family and ensure that my three children get a good education. My eldest son has just finished his B.Com [bachelor's of commerce] and my daughter has studied till the twelfth standard.
>
> Now I also want to learn electrification, plumbing, and carpentry, as this will open up more work opportunities for me.

In India, about 50 percent of the workers are self-employed, own some small assets, and enter the markets on their own. Their productivity is often lower than it should be, due to the high costs of credit or other required inputs such as irrigation or seeds for farmers. Often their reach into the market is also restricted because of their small size. Many institutions have been developed in India to deliver credit and inputs to small producers and enable them to reach the market. My own experience in SEWA has shown that given such resources poor people, especially women, develop their own capacities and entrepreneurial skills to increase their own productivity.

During its 1998 annual general meeting, SEWA conducted a small survey of basic needs to see what the members deemed most important. We were surprised to learn that the most important basic need was "capacity building" and in particular, "research" or gaining knowledge. Of course, the women surveyed had been active in SEWA for some time and were local level leaders. Another important indicator of the need for greater capacity building and knowledge is the fact that many surveys of SEWA members have shown that the most important thing they gained from being part of an organization was the opening of a new world, of knowing more, of interacting outside their little circle. As one woman said: "A sun has opened in my mind."

Malnutrition and ill health are widespread in India, lowering the productivity of most workers, physically and mentally, in terms of their capacity to learn new skills. India has the means, the resources, and the know-how to make food universally available, and it must do so. Similarly, a system of universal health care that combines public, informal, and private sectors needs to be developed out of the systems that already exist.

India has a vibrant political system where democracy enables its citizens to be heard at the highest political level. This voice extends from local village government through district, state, and national levels. However, the economic issues of workers are not similarly reflected in any form of "economic voice." Economic policies are influenced by those with economic strength, who make their voices heard through organizations, such as the various chambers of commerce. India needs an economic system that would give voice to the millions of workers and producers who are the informal economy. They need to be organized, but they must be given the forums to represent themselves.

The Business of Bollywood

Manjeet Kripalani

Bombay Dreams, Andrew Lloyd Webber's musical about the Indian film industry, was a hit in London and ran for two years. The New York adaptation has been playing to packed houses on Broadway since early 2004. In Japan, girls are so crazy about south Indian star Rajnikant that a Tamil-Japanese film production is now under way. In the Middle East and Pakistan, the most watched films are those made in Mumbai.[1] In the recent Indo-Pakistan political détente, one of the first cultural exchanges to take place was between Lollywood (Pakistan's Lahore-based film industry) and Bollywood. Indians are surprised to find that films of the late actor-director Raj Kapoor are so well remembered in Russia that the pre-perestroika generation still hums along with their songs. And in war-torn Afghanistan, the most watched and pirated films are from Bollywood. The first movie to show in Kabul after the Taliban fled Afghanistan's capital in November 2002 was a Bollywood epic. Posters of Aishwarya Rai, India's most popular actress, can be seen all across Afghanistan and Pakistan. In August 2004, seven truck drivers of a Kuwait company, including three Indians, who were plying supplies in war-torn Iraq, were kidnapped by a renegade group of Iraqis. The crisis took a bizarre turn when Sheikh Hisham al-Dulaimi, a local tribal chieftain and negotiator between the kidnappers and the Kuwaitis, reportedly said the Indians would be released if Bollywood megastar Amitabh Bachchan and old-time heroine Asha Parekh appealed to Dulaimi on their behalf by telephone. Such is the appeal of Bollywood.

A third of the planet—the poorer third—has long swooned over the colorful conventions of Bollywood: The movie stars are gorgeous, the fashions trendy, the music toe-tapping, the story lines impossible and

---

1. In 1995, the local state government changed the name of Bombay to Mumbai. Since the nickname "Bollywood" obviously plays off of the city's older name and could hardly be used without reference to Bombay, both names are used in this chapter.

fantastic and escapist. These musical films have held audiences from Delhi to Durban in their thrall. In huge swathes of the world, when people think "film" they think Bollywood. The Indian film industry's influence in India—not to mention Asia, Africa, the Middle East, and the countries of the former Soviet Union—runs deep. It dominates and reflects—and has done so for decades—the rapidly transforming subcontinental culture from a traditional society to a modern one with all its complexities. It gives the Indian diaspora—an estimated twenty million Indians live overseas—a connection with the home left behind and updates on changing traditions. Conservative societies relate to Bollywood's no-kissing, family-friendly content—overseas sales bring an estimated $40 million to Bollywood. And this does not include the pirated material that brings in twice as much in sales overseas. Bollywood's only competition for Indian hearts and minds is the game of cricket.

Bollywood overwhelmingly determines popular music in India, too. Bombay cinema has evolved as a musical genre in which the songs are as important as the plot, and a hit film's musical numbers can take on a life of their own. Bollywood films routinely sell their music to companies like Sony, as well as to Indian music labels like Saregama and Tips, two to six months before a film's release; music sales constitute 15 percent of a film's revenues, and Bollywood music accounts for 45 percent of Indian music industry sales. Taking cues from Bollywood, "Indipop," or Indian pop music, has exploded as an industry in the last decade. Amalgamating the beat and romance of film songs with the dance moves of Western pop stars like Christina Aguilera and Jennifer Lopez, Indipop is a dramatic, infectious combination that swings listeners from New York to Vietnam. Cover bands from the Philippines—immortalized in Pico Iyer's travel book *Video Night in Kathmandu*—belt out not just American pop songs, but Indi and Bollywood pop too. Bars in Saigon often play Hindi. Hindi soundtracks are sold on the streets of Jakarta, and Bollywood's music has even inspired a Southeast Asian popular form. Indonesian "dangdut" music, a sort of dance hall genre popular in Java, is not just informed by Bollywood but sometimes covers *filmi* songs outright.

New global media have had to adapt to Bollywood's cultural mandate. When Viacom's MTV and Rupert Murdoch's Channel V first began broadcasting in India a decade ago, their business plans called for sticking to an international format of Western pop. But Indians would have none of the "global" Americanized fare, and three years after going on the air both channels had to rapidly "Indianize" to accommodate local tastes. Today, 80 percent of their programming in India, South Asia, and the Middle East is Bollywood music. According to Alex Kuruvilla, managing director of MTV Networks India, the only real global rival to Hollywood is Bollywood, and the only competition to American popular culture is Indian popular culture: "Indian music defies what music means to youth everywhere in the world. In the West, music is about rebellion and self-expression, in India it's about chants, and rhythm, and escapism. It's more mainstream, inclusive family fare. The era of the big American musicals of the 50s and 60s lives eternally on in India—fresh and reinventing itself all the time."[2] Slowly, the world is cottoning on to that sound—Indian melodies are invading Western music, creating hybrids in hip-hop and even mainstream pop.

That's the enduring success of India's film industry, whose annual output of nearly 1,000 films—the largest, about 300, Hindi films made in the studios of Mumbai and the rest in other languages, largely south Indian—far outstrips even the productivity of Hollywood. But now Bollywood is entering the consciousness of Western audiences and producers. *Lagaan* (Land Tax), a Bollywood blockbuster, was nominated for Best Foreign Language Film at the 2002 Academy Awards. *Moulin Rouge* was modeled after Bollywood's glitzy formula—which to some appears to be MTV on a $100 million budget. The Andrew Lloyd Webber musical *Bombay Dreams*—with all the songs, sparkles, and soft-shoe that are Bollywood's trademarks—was a hit in London's West End and, despite being panned by New York theater critics as trite, is running to packed halls on Broadway. Trite too was *The Guru*, a Peter Sellers–type takeoff about an Indian actor in New York who finds success as a yogic guru to Park Avenue society—but its producers had clearly caught the Bollywood bug, backed up by the increasing popularity of yoga and Indian mysticism in the West. In 2005 production starts on *Marigold*, a musical comedy about a C-grade Hollywood actress who finds love on a Bollywood set. Directed by former Disney executive Willard Carroll for Hyperion Pictures, an independent Hollywood studio, *Marigold* represents the first full-fledged joint venture between Hollywood and Bollywood. "Bollywood has had half the world as its audience forever,"

---

2. This and all further quotes are from interviews conducted by the author from 2002 to 2004. Some of the research for this chapter appeared earlier in two *BusinessWeek* stories: "Bollywood: Can New Money Create a World-Class Film Industry in India?" December 2, 2002; and "Bollywood: Invasion of the Young Turks," March 8, 2004.

says Mira Nair, director of the wildly successful *Monsoon Wedding*. "Western audiences have now woken up and joined the rest of the world."

The business of Bollywood is starting to look attractive to Hollywood, too. While not actually making Indian films, large studios like Sony, Warner Brothers, and Fox, which spent fifty or more years distributing only their own Hollywood productions in India, are now dubbing Hollywood action films like *Spider-Man* and *Jurassic Park* in Hindi and distributing Hindi films and music domestically, with some success. Smaller boutiques are bolder. The Hyperion production *Marigold* will be a $10 million musical complete with flamboyant song-and-dance sequences in Hindi and English and a mix of stars from both continents. Of late, overseas filmmakers are shooting in Indian locales like Goa and Kerala to take advantage of 60 percent lower costs—call it entertainment industry outsourcing with a dash of Bombay spice.

Bollywood Starts to Professionalize

If Bollywood the cultural icon is a winner, Bollywood the business is a mess. Despite a nearly century-old pedigree—the first Hindi feature film, *Raja Harishchandra*, was made in 1913—and a larger than life global footprint, Indian cinema is a puny economic success. Revenues in 2003 were a meager $900 million compared to India's twenty-five-year-old software services industry, which earned $15 billion last year. Compared to Hollywood's $52 billion, the Bollywood economy is small change. Studios are small, and the industry is highly fragmented. Few writers, directors, or actors ever see a written contract, and lax intellectual property laws make plagiarism rampant. Physical conditions are primitive: an air-conditioned studio or theater is a luxury, and in rural areas most theaters are no more than ramshackle sheds. That, along with rampant piracy, lopsided financing, and star-driven schedules, has led to time and money overruns that cause 90 percent of Bollywood movies to flop. The Federation of Indian Chambers of Commerce and Industry (FICCI) estimates that Bollywood loses $100 million a year to piracy, mostly in the form of home videos.[3] In the United States, home video sales and rentals are twice those of theater revenues collections.

Of course, there is plenty of potential. The huge popularity of Indian

---

3. "The Indian Entertainment Sector: In the Spotlight" (New Delhi: KPMG and Federation of Indian Chambers of Commerce and Industry, 2003).

films in emerging markets and, increasingly, in developed markets with large Indian populations, for example the United Kingdom and the United States, has fueled an annual revenue growth rate of 15 percent for the past six years—more than twice that of the Indian economy's stellar 8 percent economic growth rate last year.[4] In a good year, hits can deliver returns of 25 percent or more.[5] In India, moviegoers bought a staggering 3.6 million tickets last year—compared with Hollywood's 2.6 billion—not to mention the additional $115 million in revenues from overseas rights (2002 figure). New forms of distribution are also boosting profits: nearly 16 percent of Bollywood film earnings came from DVD, video, and satellite TV sales in 2002, up from 5 percent in 1999.[6] And the burgeoning Indian middle class wants more than simplistic musical fare—it wants sophisticated scripts with universal themes—a demand which will make Indian films more appealing to global audiences.

Change is gradual. Indian policy makers are finally recognizing the economic and cultural promise of Bollywood, which the government long relegated to second-class status. In 2000, after long decades of lobbying from the film community, New Delhi gave movie-making the official status of an industry. In India's oddly regulated economy, that designation gave producers access to legitimate bank loans, completion bonds, and insurance. It also ended an era of underworld financing, to which Bollywood resorted for lack of official financing options and which left many Bollywood producers dead—from noncompliance to the mob. In April 2001, the Industrial Development Bank of India (IDBI) became the first financial institution to enter the film financing business. So far, the IDBI has lent $33 million for twenty-seven Bollywood productions; despite high returns of 14 to 16 percent, the bank has not taken any losses so far. "Bank financing has helped bring discipline into the industry," according to Viney Kumar, general manager of IDBI in Mumbai.

A lot more discipline is needed before Bollywood can be held to U.S. standards and claim world-class status. Despite bank-approved lending, few state-run or private banks have loaned money to Bollywood because the banks, accustomed to tangible loan collateral, place little value on film reels as security for their loans. According to Sunir Kheterpal,

---

4. Despite Bollywood's recent surge in popularity, just a handful of films turned a profit last year.

5. That figure notably does not include the industries that surround Bollywood, like the hugely profitable live shows performed by Bollywood stars for Indian audiences overseas.

6. "The Indian Entertainment Sector: In the Spotlight."

the head of media and entertainment for Yes Bank Ltd. in Mumbai, bankers in India are seldom knowledgeable about how movies are made, and the disorganization and fragmentation of the film industry, from direction to distribution, hurt its chances of securing loans.

Bankers and consultants say Bollywood must restructure itself completely. Hollywood studios finance entire films, from script to distribution and exhibition. The big studios raise funding from banks, insure the films, and give everyone a contract. Most are listed on the stock exchanges, and shareholders and investors peer closely at their financials. In contrast, Bollywood is still a cottage industry and works in reverse order. Distributors finance films up to a point. They pay the costs of filming upfront to the producer, and the day the film is released, they get their money back—from the theater owners across India who buy the film. Ultimately, the theater owners bear the burden of a film's success or failure.

The plight of the film industry gets worse. Theater tickets are subjected to an "entertainment tax" of up to 100 percent, which makes theater tickets expensive in a poor country like India. So, to keep tickets affordable and to escape penalization by the revenue department, theater owners keep two sets of books: one accurately reports ticket sales, the other does not. This practice results in poor data collection, making film distribution planning difficult.

All of these factors make owning a theater unprofitable, and theaters are in chronic short supply: India has one screen per million people, compared to one screen per thousand people in the United States. Add to this the many Bollywood flops, and the losses keep totting up for hapless theater owners. Although the number of tickets sold in India is huge, ticket prices are also the lowest in the world—20 cents on average—making exhibition an unprofitable business. With little money left for maintenance and renovation, the majority of the 12,000 theaters across India have fallen into disrepair. (India has only fifty multiplexes, so better to use "theater" instead of "screens.") The public watches the latest releases, albeit in shabby surroundings: with scratched prints, under the noisy whirr of ancient fans, and swarmed by mosquitoes.

This sort of lopsided financing and loopy structure has made Bollywood a less than stellar public investment. Just five major Indian film firms are publicly listed—Adlabs, Mukta Arts, Padmalaya Films, Pritish Nandy Communications (PNC), and Tips Films—and only two mirrored the stunning 100 percent rise of the Bombay Stock Exchange index during 2003. According to Yes Bank's Kheterpal the film business is insular, showing little correlation to stock market movements. This in turn discourages other film production houses from going public. There are billions of takers for Bollywood movie tickets but few for Bollywood stocks.

Married to the Mob

Blame Bollywood's business problems on lack of legitimate finance. For decades Indian films were financed by wealthy individuals, who saw a decent 50 percent return on their investment. Bollywood producers in the 1950s and 1960s were typically immigrants from Punjab and Sindh who had fled their homes in Pakistan after 1947, when India and Pakistan were partitioned. Much like the Jews who left Europe during the Second World War and were unable to get jobs in established industries helped finance the growth of Hollywood, so too did these entrepreneurs build Bollywood. They were enterprising and hardworking individuals, making films that reflected the evolution of the newly independent India. It wasn't hard to find financing then, and for the most part it worked, even though producers paid usurious rates of interest—up to 40 percent—on loans.

Then, in the 1980s, television began eating into movie audiences. As film budgets grew ever larger, producers found ready cash from the underworld. Mumbai's mob, it seems, was drawn to the industry's glamour and found Bollywood a good place to invest its ill-gotten gains. Until 2003, 40 percent of the industry's finances came from the underworld, police say. "It's a seduction process," said Shridhar Vagal, former joint commissioner of crime for the Mumbai police. "The mob offers money, gets friendly, then all sorts of things happen."

The underworld dons often dictated story lines and stars, further eroding the appeal of films. Then the mob started losing money and extorting funds from successful producers. During the seven years ending in 2003, dozens of producers and directors of blockbusters were threatened or kidnapped for ransom, and five were murdered by mobsters. Bollywood music producer Gulshan Kumar, for instance, died from gunshot wounds outside a temple in Mumbai in 1997. Producer Ajit Devani was gunned down outside his Mumbai office in July 2001. One of India's biggest heartthrobs, twenty-seven-year-old Hrithik Roshan, travels with gun-toting security guards who follow him even to the bathroom—a precaution he took after the mob tried to assassinate his producer-father in February 2001.

Mob financing took its toll on Bollywood. Pankaj Kharbanda, a publicist for several top stars like Sunil Dutt and now a producer himself, says that until recently, the toniest names in the industry were refused personal bank, housing, and car loans and even credit cards for fear they would either disregard their bills or drag in the mafia. Fortunately, the new flow of legitimate money, plus a police crackdown and the mob's own financial reversals, have loosened the underworld's grip. Police estimate that mob money is backing less than 10 percent of Bollywood films these days, and that figure will decrease as younger, more professional producers and directors enter the business.

The industry has seen an increase in institutional and private funding over the last three years, to about $110 million. Last year alone saw $40 billion in new investments—a 200 percent increase over the previous year, according to Yes Bank's Kheterpal in one of the few reports available on the industry.[7] That amounts to less than 10 percent of the total funding requirement of the Hindi film industry. Almost no venture funding is available for films in India, and the little that exists is in new theaters. Still, large business houses are eyeing the industry, and their participation could make a difference. High net worth individuals like textile tycoon Vijaypat Singhania have backed a failure or two but seem undeterred. Titans like $13 billion Reliance Industries Ltd. and $6 billion AV Birla Group are also dipping their toes into the media business, financing television ventures and planning to eventually fund movies. Some Bollywood producers dismiss such corporate efforts, saying that success in Bollywood depends on knowing the emotional pulse of India. Nevertheless, according to analysts Bollywood's excesses are so extreme that proper management alone could cut costs by 30 percent. "Corporations may not know about films, but they do know about professional management and processes," said Amit Khanna, chairman of Reliance Entertainment. "And that is what the film industry needs now."

---

7. "The Indian Motion Picture Industry: A Structural and Financial Perspective" (New Delhi: Federation of Indian Chambers of Commerce and Industry and Rabo India, 2003). See also "Indian Entertainment Industry: The Show Goes On and On . . ." (New Delhi: Federation of Indian Chambers of Commerce and Industry with Arthur Andersen India Ltd., 2002).

Under New Management

To understand what Khanna means, take the case of producer and actor Sunny Deol, the forty-three-year-old son of Bollywood heartthrob Dharmendra and a representative of the younger generation of film producers. Deol thought his Vijayeta Films productions were run too haphazardly to ever make the big time, so he hired Mumbai-based Universal Consulting to turn his business into a professional production company. Amit Dakshini, the consultant assigned to the Vijayeta job, never forgot his first day at Film City, the studio in Mumbai's distant suburbs where Deol was shooting the war action drama, *Indian*. When the shooting was scheduled to begin, 6 a.m. on that sunny September 2002 morning, Dakshini found the studio deserted save for a tea vendor. Three hours later, some production crew members rolled up and casually informed the suited consultant that shooting would begin at 2 p.m. because the lead actor wasn't feeling well. Dakshini was horrified. Postponing the shoot by eight hours, he quickly calculated, could cost $4,000—the total cost of renting the studio, equipment, and sets and paying the staff.

But Deol asked for change, and Dakshini got to work. Since then, Universal has put Vijayeta's schedule—once maintained in a tattered notebook—onto computer software. Directors and producers now order props and supplies from a list of approved vendors instead of dispatching a subordinate to pick things up at the last minute. Each scene and shot is logged onto a computer, and Deol logs on daily to view a report showing the progress of each film and a report showing how much money has been spent. "We have to rescript the way Bollywood companies run," Dakshini said. The result? Vijayeta Films has trimmed its production costs by 6 percent and expects to streamline even more.

A lot of rescripting has yet to be done. Of course, Hollywood too has generated its moments of wretched excess and produced its share of flops. But India's film industry is in a class by itself—movie stars call the shots. Hindi stars agree to make up to six films at a time and routinely flout schedules. Star salaries typically consume 40 percent of a film's budget, leaving relatively little to pay for scripts, preproduction planning, or sophisticated postproduction digitization. In Hollywood, by contrast, even the $30 million paid to Arnold Schwarzenegger for *Terminator 3* was less than 20 percent of the film's $170 million budget. And Hollywood producers spend an equal amount on the three phases of production: preparing for the film, shooting it, and processing it for screening. Bollywood scripts are written and changed on the fly, and actors receive their lines for each day's scenes just moments before filming, leading to costly extra takes as they struggle to keep up.

The results can be comical. Take *Devdas*, the hottest film of 2002 and 2003 in India. The film was a remake of a 1935 Hindi remake of a Bengali film about star-crossed lovers who defined the archetype of the lovelorn hero. *Devdas* cost $10 million and took two years to complete—twice as expensive and twice as long as planned—making it Bollywood's costliest movie ever. The culprit? A fire allegedly begun when a stray cow kicked over a kerosene lantern, destroying a $2.5 million set. Then there was the $31,000 green silk dress embroidered in gold, worn by actress Madhuri Dixit in her role as the courtesan Chandramukhi. It also did not help that producer Bharat Shah spent six months in jail, charged by Mumbai police with funneling mob money to Bollywood. Shah denies the charges and in November 2002 traveled to London to promote *Devdas* after being released on bail. Because of cost overruns the film failed to deliver the huge profits insiders had expected. (The film's extravagant sets, however, have been copied and have become the ultimate backdrop for lavish Indian weddings ever since.)

Such flaws leave many pioneering investors preaching patience to those who expect a quick return for backing Bollywood. After all, even though Bollywood hits can deliver 100 percent return on their investment, almost all Bollywood movies lose money. The industry will need the better part of a decade to reach the efficiency and production values of Hollywood. "There's too much housekeeping to do," said Vishal Nivetia, chief executive of GW Capital. The $40 million private equity fund associated with former GE Capital CEO Gary Wendt paid $5 million for a 27 percent stake in distributor Shringar Films.

Talent but No Discipline

Talent exists in abundance, but discipline and infrastructure are lacking. Indian talent has had many successes beyond Bollywood. Indian director Shekhar Kapur, who made the acclaimed *Bandit Queen*, also received praise for directing and producing the Hollywood spectacle *Elizabeth*, with Cate Blanchett. A.R. Rahman, a young *filmi* music genius, was recruited by Andrew Lloyd Webber to create the music for *Broadway Dreams*; he is now creating the music for several U.K. and U.S. films. Mira Nair, the New York–based Indian filmmaker who made *Monsoon*

Wedding on a $1.5 million budget in 2002, earned an eye-popping $35 million from its global success. In the United Kingdom, Gurinder Chadha's soccer chick-flick, *Bend It Like Beckham*, has popularized soccer with young girls like never before and transformed the film's co-protagonist, Keira Knightley, into the hottest new Hollywood find. And of course there's the evergreen partnership of Ismail Merchant, James Ivory, and Ruth Prawer Jhabvala, whose expert depictions of gracious, early twentieth century Anglo-Indian and European life (*A Room with a View*, *Howard's End*, *Shakespeare Wallah*) have always found a niche and a loyal audience in the West. Even Bollywood's technicians are finding favor with Hollywood. The Matt Damon sequel, *The Bourne Supremacy*, used local technical staff when filming in Goa earlier this year, and Goldie Hawn will share the copyright for her new movie, 60 percent of which will be shot in India, with a young local production house, Eagle Films.

Indeed, Hollywood is discovering that Indian locales like Goa, Kerala, and Andhra Pradesh are attractive destinations. State governments are vying with each other for business, and over the next few months they may start offering Hollywood producers incentives like VAT-type rebates. "They can make 85 percent of a Hollywood film at 8 percent of the cost in India," said Pritish Nandy, founder and chairman of publicly listed PNC. Still, the number of foreign producers and directors coming to India is small, and many who come recount with horror the lax safety standards. For example, technicians wander barefoot across floors crisscrossed with wires, an insurance nightmare in Hollywood. Nandy says the Indian technicians are just as good as any in the world, just undertrained and underpaid.

The infrastructure is abysmal, little more than primitive. India has no large Hollywood-style studios or production houses like Sony or Disney, and the industry is highly fragmented. Mumbai, the hub of Bollywood, has only Film City—a 500-acre stretch of hills and valleys overlooking the picturesque lakes of Powai and Vaitarna, with some pre- and post-production spaces—certainly not enough to completely service a Hollywood movie. Perched on one of the hilltops is the proverbial temple, seen in almost every Hindi movie and television serial. On another is a helipad—a Bollywood requirement, for this is where the villain lands and tells his goons to hand over the weeping heroine while the hero struggles in chains. The song sequences and love scenes are shot in the valleys among fields and flowers. The rest of Film City is decrepit. Two years ago, however, the local government, which runs Film City, decided to upgrade, and it is investing $8 million to build high-tech facilities like a station for satellite and television uplinks, digital cinemas, and more studios. In this effort to prevent the film business from going to other states, the local government is even wooing Hollywood producers to use the studio, luring them with the average 60 percent in cost savings that producing in India brings. Even the bureaucrats who run Film City understand that it must meet international standards now.

Film City does have competition. Apart from the already well-run tourism industry of Goa and Kerala, which welcomes foreigners, there are the big studios in south India, namely Ramoji Film City in Hyderabad and MGR Film City in Chennai. Ramoji Rao, the newest, largest studio in India, has 2,500 acres of land, loads of colorful temples, underground caves, trees to dance around, and modern recording and mixing pre- and post-production studios. Since it is privately run, Ramoji Rao requires fewer permissions than Mumbai's Film City for shooting films. Still, in the past few years many local filmmakers have gone to the Swiss Alps or New Zealand and Australia. Much of this can be attributed to the rise of militancy in Kashmir, regarded as the Switzerland of the East and featured in almost every popular Bollywood romance until 1989. But directors gained additional benefits shooting overseas. The Swiss and New Zealand governments are more organized and make it easy for film crews to set up shop, and the directors make actors stick to production schedules in order to finish quickly. Yash Chopra, India's most popular Bollywood producer, filmed so much in Switzerland in the late 1990s that the Swiss government awarded him a certificate for bringing the most film business to the country.

More than anything else, the Indian film industry desperately needs professionals, from the creative to the management end of films. Aspiring actors and directors have only one school from which to choose— the Film and Television Institute of India in Pune, a city a few hours from Mumbai. The institute has produced some of India's finest actors and directors, but it is government run and constantly trapped in bureaucratic meddling. The lack of large studios is directly attributable to lack of professional management. Some of the younger producers, like Deol, are attempting to corporatize their operations—but they still lack professional managers. "It requires a mind-set change," said Ronnie Screwwala, the chairman of UTV, a television and film production company that is preparing to go public and recently bought back a 30 percent stake formerly owned by Rupert Murdoch's Star network.

Mind-set Change

Ever so slowly, that mind-set change is taking place. It has happened with government policy, it is happening with banks, and now it is sinking in with the traditional industry players. Surprising industry insiders, the Indian government has also become enthusiastically proactive and ambitious for Bollywood, seeing the film industry as a large revenue earner. "India has the best film policy in Asia," said Blaise Fernandes, president of Warner Brothers India, which has been screening its Hollywood films in India for nearly a century and is considering distributing Bollywood films in India soon. Two years ago, New Delhi permitted 100 percent foreign investment in the film industry in the exhibition, distribution, studios, and production of Bollywood movies—a major move, considering that foreign investors can hold only limited stakes in other fast-growing sectors like telecommunications (74 percent) and newspapers (25 percent). It also announced a ten-year tax holiday for new investments in multiplex cinemas. While such investor-friendly policies have inspired Indian players to build 100 multiplexes across India, adding about 450 screens to the country over the next five years, foreign investors are showing little interest. Analysts say the business is not attractive enough. Still, India already has 50 new multiplexes and 250 screens, drawing moviegoers, especially in urban India, back into the theaters.

Bollywood's more ambitious players have long awaited this moment of professionalizing and government incentives. Subhash Ghai, one of India's best-known producers of grand, romantic extravaganzas, created Mukta Arts and took it public two years ago, raising $16 million. Unlike most of the one-man shows that are Bollywood producers, Ghai dreams of becoming a Hollywood-type studio and a global player. With the money raised from his initial public offering, Ghai is building what is already one of India's most professional and genuine studios, with a bank of writers and editors, a talent training school, and a team of independent directors. He also was the first in the Indian film industry to hire a professional manager as a permanent staff member. Creating a proper business plan was the first task of Pankaj Sethi, a former Unilever executive and graduate of the prestigious Indian Institute of Management.[8] "We laid out our goals as a company, as individuals within the company, computerized the operations, expanded into the television

8. In July 2004, Pankaj Sethi switched jobs and began working for the telecom sector.

business, and decided to raise funds internationally," said Sethi. While most of Bollywood logs its accounts on a ledger, Mukta Arts maintains an online, live, professional database for all its activities.

Ghai's ambitious plans are unfolding. In Mumbai's new entertainment district of Andheri, the roads are poorly paved, traffic is choked, and public transport is inadequate. In contrast, just off the main road the infrastructure in the spacious Mukta Arts complex is top-notch. Ghai has several studios and a state-of-the-art high-tech post-production facility—the most expensive in Mumbai—which is also used by the city's slick advertising industry. Ghai is also fulfilling a lifelong dream of building a film institute in Mumbai. The school, scheduled for completion in 2005 and located within Film City, started accepting its first students in the fall of 2004. Meghna Ghai, the producer's daughter, has been assigned the task of adhering to the construction schedule and opening the institute as planned. She said she hopes to make this a premier institute in Asia with teachers from film institutes across the world, especially the United States. "In five years, we will be like a large Hollywood studio," Meghna Ghai said. "India is arriving on the scene, and the West can smell it." Adding the school, Ghai believes, is helping the business become more professional; the studio has also become more professional and has better facilities than any of the other studios.

This slow transformation of the industry is giving rise to innovation, not just in film financing, but also in new business models. Most movies in India—especially the blockbusters—have pan-Indian themes and must appeal to Indians in the remotest corners of the country. That, however, is a hugely expensive proposition in India. In Hollywood, studios bear the $1,200 (per print) cost of making prints, and about 3,500 prints are distributed worldwide when a movie is released. In India, the print volumes are smaller. To release a film in 4,000 theaters requires at least 400 prints. The costs can run upwards of half a million dollars, sending producers into the arms of usurers—especially for small-budget films that cost only $1 million to make, compared to the $8 million typically spent on a big-budget movie. The prints are sent first to the urban theaters, then to smaller towns and cities, and, six weeks later, to rural theater houses, where they arrive scratched. By then the pirated version of the film has already been shown on cable, diddling producers out of their fair share of revenue. In this business model, newer and less-capitalized producers can only afford to make a few prints. Bharat Dabholkar, for example, a former ad film-maker, made just sixteen prints of his first film, *God Only Knows*.

Dabholkar physically took the prints from theater to theater, changing venues every two weeks—a hard way to make a profit.

Pushed by his professional managers, Ghai is working to overcome this obstacle by going digital. For just $75, Mukta Arts creates a digital film copy that can travel cheaply across the country, reaching many more theaters simultaneously—so rural and city audiences can watch the film at the same time. Better still, Ghai has used a $2 million savings on print costs to upgrade ninety theaters across India that will screen the digitized version—a near perfect replication—of his films. The screening rooms are provided with air conditioning, digital equipment, and a small power generator. Ghai plans to renovate another two hundred theaters and has seen interest from other production houses willing to do the same. By year-end 2004, Mukta expects to be the world's largest digital cinema chain—larger even than any in the United Kingdom, which also screens digital films.

The biggest benefit of going digital for the film industry is reduction of piracy. Ghai's digitizing equipment could be just the technological edge that Bollywood needs to become globally competitive. Developing countries across the world have the same infrastructure problems, and India's solutions would work well in Africa, Asia, and the Middle East as well, making it easier and more profitable to screen Bollywood hits.

The Vital Step to Professionalization

The move to professionalize and become technically competitive has coincided with new trends hitting the Indian film industry: the separation of rural-urban films, the rise of young producers, and the proliferation of multiplexes. According to Yes Bank's Sunir Kheterpal, "The next year will see the industry start to grow and become global."

Change began with the success of *Monsoon Wedding*, which encouraged young, first-time directors to come forward with ideas quite different from the boy-meets-girl musical extravaganzas that have defined Bollywood film. The new crop of low-budget films, with their newer, younger stars, tight schedules, and smart story lines, is perfectly timed: as India develops economically and the urban middle classes expand, tastes are becoming more sophisticated. These urban Indian viewers, who account for 80 percent of movie profits, want more realistic stories and less banal, escapist fare. Mumbai audiences, for instance, loved *Maqbool*, the contemporary version of Shakespeare's Macbeth, as well as *Jogger's Park*, the story of an older man's infatuation with a young, vibrant career woman—a typically urban theme. Both films cost less than $1 million to make—a far cry from $10 million budget films like *Kabhi Khushi Kabhie Gham* (Sometimes Joy, Sometimes Sorrow), an extravagant family drama, or *Devdas*, which played well to pan-Indian audiences, especially in rural India.

This, says Mahesh Chabbria, a director at Mumbai investment house Enam, is "the vital intermediate step to professionalization" for Bollywood: interesting story lines, bolder themes, a pre-sale of the films, and a strictly adhered-to schedule. Indeed, investors and film industry insiders are starting to take notice. A number of young producers are appearing with new story lines and new ideas, signaling a change in the industry. Since the beginning of 2004, Siddhartha Jain, a twenty-five-year-old producer and film consultant, has been receiving up to three calls a week from young directors and scriptwriters, overseas production companies, and high net worth individuals and overseas Indian investors who want to invest in small-budget Indian cinema for the first time. "They have come crawling out of the woodwork," Jain said.

Not all of these niche films are hits, of course. And the big Hollywood studios like Sony and Warner Bros are more interested in distributing the big, pan-Indian blockbusters that are screened all across India. But much-needed fresh air is seeping into Bollywood. And for a change, the young talent is setting an example—and new standards—for the old guard. For starters, their tight budgets demand that they stick to schedules —a single extra day could cost them. Many of the bigger production houses that have profitably made small-budget films see them as a way to hedge their largely mainstream portfolios. Mukta Arts, for instance, made *Jogger's Park*. The big producers are also opening the doors to young talent. Yash Chopra, the doyen of Indian cinema, has farmed out three films in 2004 to younger, untested directors and producers. Ram Gopal Verma, the Quentin Tarantino of Indian cinema, made a dozen films in 2004—ten of which have been farmed out to younger directors and producers with smaller budgets.

The younger lot is strict, too—tantrums and needless delays cannot be tolerated. While filming *Mr. & Mrs. Iyer*, a hit on the foreign film festival circuit in 2002, its thirty-year-old producer found herself playing the role of drill sergeant. Every day Rupali Mehta hauled herself out of bed at 5 a.m. to cruise the hallways of the Gorumara Jungle Camp, a forest lodge deep in the Darjeeling Hills of north Bengal, knocking on doors to rouse cast and crew members from their slumber. An hour later in the hotel dining room, she took roll as bleary-eyed stars, starlets, grips, and gaffers sipped their morning tea. "It felt like boot camp," said Mehta, who is also the co-founder of Triplecom Productions. "But if I hadn't been so tough, we would never have finished the movie on time."

On the set of a well-organized Hollywood production, such draconian measures might have been unnecessary. But in the end, Mehta's toughness paid off: the 105-member crew kept to its fifty-day production schedule and stayed inside the $1 million budget for the film, a love story set against a backdrop of communal violence in north India.

Surprisingly, the major movie stars are starting to cooperate with the professionalization effort. Small-budget films typically use less familiar names, yet the big stars sometimes accept small-budget roles because they are so much more interesting than the hero or heroine roles they play in the blockbusters. The big stars are not demanding their usual high fees either, and they are flexible with payment systems. Unlike the old days, when they were paid up front, stars now have a stake in the film's success—in lieu of a fee, they accept a percentage of the take of certain regions where the films are released. Vishal Nevatia of GW Capital attributes this shift to the background of the younger set. "These younger artists are more educated and come from India's middle classes," Nevatia explained. And good distributors like Shringar now insist on viewing rushes of the movies they will distribute as the film is being made, not twenty-four hours before release, which used to be the Bollywood norm.

The influx of young talent has opened the doors for expatriate Indians to participate in Bollywood too. Indian Silicon Valley executives are always getting hit up by Bollywood film producers. Remembering the songs and films of their youth, they invest in Bollywood and reconnect with halcyon, innocent, Bollywood-laced days. Small-budget films are enabling many expatriates to participate as well. A group of Indian doctors in the United States is jointly producing a comedy to be filmed in India based on *Two Guys, Three Girls and a Mad Professor*, a book authored by their colleague, Dr. Ravindra Godse. Silicon Valley types are also trying their hand at production. Former U.S. technology executive Vivek Wadhwa, along with a U.S. investment banker and his Indian actress wife, is scripting a Bollywood movie "on Hollywood standards," Wadhwa said. Such crossover films, which use a combination of Hindi and English and contemporary themes, are developing into a popular niche of their own.

Despite this overseas interest, little venture money is being spent on

India's film industry. Bollywood's only venture fund, GW Capital, spent $5 million for a 27 percent stake in distributor Shringar Films. And GW Capital plans not to invest in film production companies for another two to three years, until India begins to develop a proper studio system. So Bollywood films, especially the new, smaller budget ones, continue to be financed by the family and friends of producers and directors—but thankfully not the underworld!

Bollywood definitely wants to achieve a professional and global reputation. It is also realizing—and acting upon—its responsibility as a medium that can bind India as a nation. Soon after Kashmir elected its own regional government in 2002, among the first moves of the newly installed government was a trip to Mumbai to woo Bollywood and plead with the industry to return to Kashmir. Bollywood had abandoned Kashmir, a favorite spot to film romantic scenes, after terrorism seized the state in 1989. The new Kashmir government promised security, and Bollywood responded—several films have since been shot in the beautiful vale without incident. *Lakshya*, a recent Bollywood hit in India about the Indian army's heroism in Kashmir, was shot almost entirely in Ladakh, the northern-most tip of Kashmir.

Its baby steps toward professionalization could yield giant results for Bollywood. The Indian government's legitimization of the industry has been a big boost; so have the 2002 Oscar nomination for *Lagaan* and the popular and financial success of *Monsoon Wedding*. Indeed, Bollywood is already dreaming up plans to boldly invade Hollywood. Hrithik Roshan, India's hottest hero, says he'd like to star as the next James Bond, and Aishwarya Rai, India's highest paid actress, already has a Hollywood agent casting about for suitable roles in Los Angeles. Bollywood's global audience has made stars like Roshan and Rai more recognized across much of the world than Leonardo DiCaprio or Julia Roberts. Eager Bollywood directors like Vidhu Vinod Chopra, encouraged by the success of his terrorism-in-the-valley action drama *Mission Kashmir* in the U.S. market a couple of years ago, moved to Michigan for a year to write a script for an all-star Hollywood cast. And Ritesh Sidhwani, producer of urban Indian hit *Dil Chahta Hai* (What the Heart Desires) and *Lakshya*, confidently says he's waiting for the day five years from now when a Western company seeks the rights to his films.

Now that's ambition, in true Bollywood style.

Downloading India:
A Guide to Online Resources

Mary Rader

The digital revolution has dramatically changed the ways one can find information about India. The advent of e-mail and the associated news and subject-oriented listservs, the nearly universal implementation of online library catalogs and indexes, and the increasingly available digital full text of monographs, journals, newspapers, and magazines have changed not only the *where* of research on India but also the *how*. It used to be that one either had to visit large, government-funded research libraries ("PL-480" repositories), consult with experts and scholars at universities or think tanks, or travel to India itself to try and gain access to materials. One would have to delve into multiple card catalogs, printed shelf-lists, or idiosyncratic indexes to discover references to India-related material or would have to rely on interpretations and guidance from experts. While one still is better served by the people and resources of large research institutions and can gain deeper understandings and unforeseen riches through travel, and while print sources are still indispensable, the online environment has efficiently streamlined, democratized, and globalized the quest for data on India. Interested scholars, policy makers, and nonprofessionals alike have experienced a certain liberation in the move to online research.

The goal of this chapter is twofold: to examine the nature of the online medium, particularly as it pertains to the study of India, and to provide the reader with a detailed discussion of some useful sources. At the end of the chapter, a list of Web sites has been compiled for "further reading." Providing a representative list of sources is difficult, given the ever-growing and ever-changing field from which to select. Informed by work in the academic study of India and influenced by the access enabled by high-speed connections and licensing agreements, no doubt the list is idiosyncratic. Yet it should provide the reader with a solid starting point from which to explore the online world related to India.

Overarching Issues

While the digital revolution has been a boon in many regards, one must still observe and participate in it critically, particularly if one is trying to find information about India. Rather than being blinded by the comparative ease of access or the bells and whistles of some highly developed products, one must not lose sight of the limitations of the media, the influences on its production, or the restrictions of its use. The skills one has gained through years of reading and consulting printed sources should not be thrown out because of some flashy audio/video files or the high results provided by full-text searching. Information, regardless of its medium, demands evaluation.

The popular perception of digital products is that they are virtually free to produce and disseminate. Contrary to popular belief, however, the production of good online content comes at considerable cost. For example, just like print publications, online content demands significant upfront costs such as solicitation, selection, and editing of content, production and layout hard- and software, advertising networks, and the like. As any publisher will attest, these costs are the most expensive components of publishing, much more so than the paper, binding, and distribution. While digital publications do not take up warehousing space or shipping costs, good ones benefit from secure and stable server space. The benefits of updating and revision enabled by the online environment also prove their downfall; many products and initiatives with grand or impressive beginnings have become stagnant or irrelevant through lack of concerted and strategic updating. In sum, while some costs might be less prohibitive than print publications, the remaining high production costs have restricted the production of online content to two principal areas: grant-funded initiatives and cost-recovery commercial ventures.

Grant-Funded Initiatives

In academic circles, grant-funded initiatives are the norm. Existing in many forms, these initiatives have many objectives, often determined by the funding agency. For example, one extremely generous funder of digital products is the Mellon Foundation. Providing the pilot money for such projects as JSTOR, the Global Resources Network (under the Association for Research Libraries and soon to be at the Center for

Research Libraries), and the Open Archives Initiative, Mellon clearly stipulated improved access to material as a condition for receiving its funding. Because of this condition, many projects that may have preservation or development of materials as their primary aim have also included access as one of their goals.

Other funders, particularly government agencies, require universal, free access to digital content for their supported projects. While in theory this is the ideal situation, it does create complexity when one considers copyright or other restrictions on intellectual property rights that may limit potential candidates for digitization. One way projects work around copyright issues is to only digitize materials that are already within the public domain. Although oversimplifying the case, typically in the United States this means materials published more than seventy-five years ago. Realizing this strategy, it comes as little surprise to see multiple projects that focus on nineteenth- or early twentieth-century materials. It will be interesting to observe the impact of this strategy in academic circles as older material gets special attention and highlighting when presented in digital formats. While changing the experience and perhaps the context of a text, added features such as citation generators, full-text search ability, and cut and paste capability ultimately do not change the content of a text, for better or worse.

Conditions of grants can often hinder future funding for projects. For example, if an index (or part of an index) is created using U.S. federal funds, it typically must remain freely available indefinitely, even if the index may need to seek fee-based structures to remain viable in the long term (for example, some *Bibliography of Asian Studies* index records were created for the grant-funded Digital South Asia Library; those records will remain freely available even though the *Bibliography of Asian Studies* is a cost-recovery project). While not insurmountable, such restrictions do affect the possibilities for lasting digital products such as updating, server maintenance, and the like.

Commercial Ventures

Commercial ventures similarly have certain limitations, and the demands of the market determine not only the look and feel of online content but also the technical advances and possibilities of it. This is not new territory—most print publishers are driven by "the bottom line" when they select monographs or need to advertise in journals (even a cursory look at the changing landscape of the university press highlights this)—content must be marketable, speaking to or being relevant to a clearly defined audience. As any user of freely available Web-based content is all too aware, cost-recovery necessitates annoying pop-up and slow-loading flashy advertisements or payment (subscriptions or otherwise) for highly desirable content (for example, newspapers will give brief synopses of stories and magazines will provide a table of contents with one or two "teaser" articles but will not give free unlimited full text).

Commercial vendors of academic products are also very savvy with their content. In the realm of large journal, index, and e-book conglomerates, big names and high use are the deciding factors for inclusion, essentially mainstreaming the field to the detriment of small but potentially influential works. Comparatively lower circulation statistics also determine the kinds of financial investment commercial vendors will make for digitization. For an illustrative example of this phenomenon, compare how many indexes and full-text providers give access to the *Journal of Asian Studies* but not to a lesser known but perhaps no less important journal from India, *Seminar.*

Technical Constraints

Combined with the pressures of size and influence, the great investments needed to address issues of non-roman script in the online environment have privileged English-language materials. Although some individual Web publications have included access to non-roman script content (newspapers and popular magazines being the most readily available examples), one typically has to download proprietary fonts to read them. Rarely will those fonts be the same across product or source. Complicating the scene is an apparent lack of encoding standards for Indian languages (International Organization for Standardization [ISO] or otherwise). Trying to work around these technical constraints, some online publishers choose to work in transliteration (Indological sites lead the way in this regard). While this eliminates some problems, it creates others: how will the diacritics be represented? Which transliteration scheme shall one use? Will the transliterated text be meaningful to actual readers of the language? and so on. In recent years, programmers and developers have been working on and promoting the use of Unicode, a system to represent characters and scripts regardless of platform, program, or language. Tools such as Unicode inspire high hopes and expectations, and most new projects and products either address its possibilities or are in the process of implementing it. However, with no real possibility for recovery of the investment in server and programming costs to convert older datasets or programming codes, it is unlikely that we will see an explosion of cross-platform, nonproprietary, multilingual online products anytime soon.

As mentioned above, providing content in the online environment enables endless updating, revision, and migration. In many ways, this is of great benefit to authors and publishers. Rather than needing to insert errata notices or reprint a text with revisions, one can relatively easily and cheaply correct, update, or otherwise modify online content. In addition, when new technological advances are made, online publishers can upgrade their products for new enhancements. The implementation of Unicode for non-roman scripts is just one such enhancement that could be added to extant data.

These possibilities for change do present problems, however. Unlike a printed book, the format, content, and ultimately online access are always potentially in flux. Instability in this virtual world can be created through very concrete complications such as breakdowns in connectivity, the inability to maintain funding, or the limitations of server space. Changes in opinion, policy, or politics can also affect online content: an author may rethink an issue and then remove particular statements or thoughts from an online publication, or a government may remove its predecessor's doctrines or strategies from official Web addresses. Obviously, the inability to cite or rely on data that may not publicly exist from day to day reduces levels of traceability and accountability. The online environment creates problems of archiving and stability on a scale unforeseen in the print environment.

Search Engines

Locating online content is equally difficult. A number of specific tools and strategies for finding India-related information are discussed in detail below. However, for the majority of users of the World Wide Web, the primary way to find information is through a search engine. Two of the most internationally prominent search engines, Google and Yahoo, will point users to innumerable Web pages related to India that hold commercial, community, political, entertainment, and other information, not to mention blogs (Web logs), chat rooms, and other communication sources. While Google dominates most Web searching these days, Indian-based and India-focused search engines also exist (for example, Rediff, Khoj, or Jadoo).

One can gather a plethora of information through any and all of these search engines, but the results are often varied in terms of usefulness or reliability. Unlike indexes or catalogs, which also organize information, search engines are completely automated processes that lack the benefit of human interpretation. Using "crawlers" or other complex algorithms, search engines primarily index Web sites based on the words that appear on their pages or in their encoding. The indexing is based not on the meaning or context of those words, but on the combination of letters in those words. Getting a search engine to understand or interpret a query is impossible; manipulating queries is not. If the user is willing to play with keywords or constantly rethink and update search strategies, search engines open up great possibilities for freely available information. Search engines do not index the entirety of the Web, however. The majority of e-texts and indexes that exist on the Web are not "crawlable" by the search engines. It has been estimated that 400 to 500 times more information than is indexed through search engines exists in isolation, untapped by common search strategies, in what is often termed the "deep Web." In an effort to combat this obscurity, projects such as the Open Archives Initiative (OAI) have emerged. Using metadata ("data about data"), the OAI facilitates the sharing of resources across institution and community to further collaboration and accessibility. The possibilities for OAI in terms of Indian material are discussed below, but it is worth mentioning here in the context of search engines and Web searching.

Having large quantities of information freely and easily accessible through the Web is a major step forward in the democratization of information sharing. However, a pure online democracy allows everyone and anyone to share in the process, regardless of their knowledge or training. As in the printed environment, a person seeking information must remain mindful of who produced the information and the context of its distribution. Some free sites, such as those associated with governmental, nonprofit, and outreach-oriented groups, are reliable sources and have long histories of freely distributing data. Other free sites should be viewed more skeptically, especially if their authority is difficult to determine. Because of the costs and benefits associated with peer review, marketing, and maintenance, scholarly and business communities still rely on profit-based publishing and distribution, whether the data is purchased directly (such as through a subscription to an online journal) or indirectly (for example, through a full-text service such as Lexis-Nexis). Thankfully, an increasing number of public and academic libraries, as well as some private institutions, subscribe to fee-based online content for the benefit of their users, and communities are beginning to explore nonprofit mechanisms for the dissemination of information.

With this background knowledge of general patterns for the creation, maintenance, and dissemination of online sources, the next section provides more detailed discussions about particular sources related to India.

Online Sources

Organizing URLs

Given the overwhelming number of online sources related to India, we are lucky to have two sources that help manage and organize them. The first, South Asia Resource Access on the Internet (SARAI), is also one of the oldest online South Asian sources. Begun, developed, and still maintained by Columbia University's David Magier, SARAI has its beginnings in the South Asia Gopher and the International Directory of South Asia Scholars. From those humble roots, SARAI has grown into the mega link for all South Asia links. As part of the larger WWW Virtual Library project, SARAI includes annotated links to bibliographic tools, job announcements, e-newspapers and e-journals, and the scholars directory, as well as more general sources related to history, politics, literature, and religion. Of note to educators, SARAI includes links to teaching resources such as syllabi, electronic course shells, and language instruction modules. Because the field of South Asian online sources is so vast, keeping up with and annotating new sources is difficult; rather than leaving those out of SARAI altogether, Magier provides a glimpse into his workspace through the "in-process backlog," a semi-structured list of sites awaiting inclusion to the SARAI structure.

The other evolving source for online organization is the Portal to Asian Internet Resources (PAIR, formerly the Digital Asia Library). Funded through successive grants from the U.S. Department of Education, PAIR in effect is a library catalog of Internet resources. Web sites are identified and selected by subject specialists and then are described and cataloged using standards and protocols accepted by most U.S. libraries (for example, the "Dublin Core" standards for metadata). The PAIR database can be approached in many ways, for example, geographically (limiting results to "India"), by subject, or by keyword searching. The collection described in PAIR is restricted to freely available Web sites and encompasses academic, governmental, nongovernmental, and commercial information. The PAIR database should be commended for its conscious inclusion of Web sites in languages other than English; at the time of this writing, Indian languages included were Assamese, Bengali, Hindi, Kannada, Malayalam, Marathi, Oriya, Pali, Sanskrit, Tamil, Telugu, and Urdu. Surely the list of languages will be expanded in the future as the resource continues to develop and grow.

Finding and Accessing Articles

Indexes

Indexes are the best places to look for material published serially or periodically. As a librarian who often assists in reference queries, I can confidently say that the migration of indexes to the online medium has dramatically and unequivocally changed the ways people generate citations. Gone are the days of trudging through year after year of the *Readers' Guide to Periodical Literature* or the *Index to the New York Times*, trying to keep mindful of the indexing vocabularies while jotting down cryptic notes on scraps of paper. Now, one can search across years, often across sources, and by means of a keyword, often without concern for the pesky rules and structures so dear to librarians. This section highlights two kinds of indexes that offer much aid to those interested in India: simple, subject-specific indexes and indexes that also provide full text. A considerable amount of data can be gleaned from the indexes, yet it must be noted that the bibliographic databases for India specifically, and South Asia generally, are few in number and limited in scope. Whether this is an outcome of linguistic difficulty, intellectual bias, or financial constraints is the subject for another essay; the researcher must be cognizant of the limitations while remaining hopeful that this glaring lacuna will be rectified in the future.

Indexes Without Full Text: The Bibliography of Asian Studies
A number of subject-specific indexes have Indian and India-related content (for example, *Historical Abstracts*, *Anthropological Literature*, and the *Modern Language Association Bibliography*), but perhaps the

most powerful and comprehensive is the Bibliography of Asian Studies online (BAS). Courageously encompassing all of Asia in scope, the BAS began as appendices to the *Far Eastern Quarterly*, then became a regular annual issue of the *Journal of Asian Studies*, and eventually evolved into a stand-alone resource. In 1991, the BAS decided to switch to the online environment and converted its records from 1971–91. In addition to those original converted records, more than one hundred journal titles have been identified by their comparative importance to necessitate continual indexing.

The intellectual scope of the BAS covers research on and from Asia within the humanities and social sciences and some of the natural sciences (particularly medicine, public health, and the environment). At the time of this writing, the BAS indexes materials in Western European languages only, primarily English. (This is in large part due to the script difficulties presented by Asian languages, as mentioned above. However, the BAS has begun to experiment with Unicode and with a small number of Thai language sources. This writer at least hopes their experiments will prove successful and that they will branch out to other non-roman script languages in the near future.) The BAS indexes journal articles, book reviews, some entire books and, perhaps most helpful of all, individual chapters within edited volumes. Although the usefulness of its subject indexing is debatable, one cannot overemphasize the BAS's importance as one of the only sources to consistently index journals from and about India. For example, using the BAS, one can find citations to articles in journals as far ranging as: *Bengal Past and Present, Bulletin of the School of Oriental and African Studies, Contributions to Indian Sociology, Indian Anthropologist, Indian Economic and Social History Review, Indian Historical Review, Journal of Asian Studies, Journal of Indian Philosophy, Manushi, Seminar, South Asia Journal,* and *South Asia Research.*

Indexes with Full Text: JSTOR, Lexis-Nexis, and Proquest
While the usefulness of the BAS cannot be underestimated, it provides only citations, not entire articles. Thankfully, a number of full-text indexes have bridged the gap between reference and source. This section highlights three in particular: JSTOR, Lexis-Nexis, and Proquest. While none of these focuses specifically on India (or Asia, for that matter) at the time of this writing, each provides India-related material in the midst of content designed for the general researcher. The quantity of sources

may be small, but the ability to conduct full-text searching within these databases generates large amounts of India-related information.

Perhaps the most scholarly of these three databases is JSTOR. Begun as a project to help with library storage needs (hence the title: Journal Storage Project), JSTOR focuses on the back files of academic journals. The database was designed specifically not to compete with the sale of print resources, and, in most cases, JSTOR does not index or digitize issues of a journal less than five years old. JSTOR adds to its digital holdings and indexes on a moving five-year window: typically encompassing the entire back-run of a title (for over a hundred years or more in some cases). In addition, due to its digitizing apparatus, which uses PDFs to deliver files, JSTOR maintains the look and feel of the print source in its digital representation—one can see page numbers, illustrations in the positions where they were printed, and so on. Included in JSTOR are journals considered to be standard, core works in the fields of South Asian Studies: the *Bulletin of the School of Oriental and African Studies*, the *Journal of Asian Studies*, the *Journal of the American Oriental Society*, and *Modern Asian Studies*. Furthermore, because of its full-text search ability and commitment to only including authoritative journals, one can stumble upon important articles in unforeseen places (such as *Ethnohistory*, the *Journal of the Royal Anthropological Institute*, or *Past and Present*). The importance and usefulness of a database such as JSTOR, particularly for historical research and literature reviews related to India, cannot be overstated.

Lexis-Nexis will probably be familiar to readers of *India Briefing*, as it was one of the first full-text databases to encompass a vast variety of news, business, and legal sources. Although Lexis-Nexis's clunky command-driven interface is still available and it is still organized around cryptic "files," its new graphical interface and added search features make Lexis-Nexis much more user-friendly and efficient than ever before. India and India-related content abounds within Lexis-Nexis, from the immediately apparent sources such as Dataquest or *India Today*, to the ability to search full-text transcripts of NPR or PBS broadcasts, which often highlight events from India. In many ways unsurpassed as a database for current and timely information, Lexis-Nexis continues to add to its India-related news sources; at the time of this writing, full-text newspapers included in Lexis-Nexis include the *Hindu, Indian Express*, the *Statesman*, and the *Times of India*. In addition to providing the full text from Indian papers, Lexis-Nexis is also immensely helpful as a general newspaper index. Unfortunately, few newspapers from India are properly indexed, and those indexes can be difficult to obtain. Using the Lexis-Nexis database, however, one can search the Associated Press, Reuters, and other newswires; and armed with dates of major events from these sources, consulting print or microfilm copies of Indian newspapers becomes much more palatable. Unlike JSTOR, Lexis-Nexis does not maintain any of the look or feel of the original print sources; all text has been either directly keyed in to the database or manipulated through optical character recognition programs. While this changes the "experience" of reading articles and can make tracking citations difficult, it is a minor inconvenience which, given the expeditious and varied content and the ability to cut and paste directly from the text, can be quickly overcome.

The ambitious Proquest fits in between JSTOR and Lexis-Nexis. Neither exclusively scholarly nor highly popular or newsy, Proquest includes both types of information, although its searches can be restricted to peer-reviewed (therefore "scholarly") articles. In addition to providing full text in both image (PDF) and keyed in form, Proquest has added an abstracting function for further searching and consulting. Proquest has directly relevant sources (*Contemporary South Asia*, the *Hindu*, the *Statesman*) as well as indirect sources, such as the historical back files of the *Washington Post* and the *New York Times* (starting from 1877 and 1851, respectively). There is some speculation that Proquest will initiate an Asian Studies portal; in the meantime, however, the powerful full-text searching and the inclusive nature of its content make Proquest a key resource for searching and retrieving articles on India.

Web-based Articles: Newspapers and Academic and Popular Journals
The above-mentioned indexes and full-text sources are the products of third parties that manipulate data to achieve ends not necessarily envisioned by the data producers. The data producers, however, manipulate and create their own resources for the online environment as well, regardless of whether print incarnations already exist. The most obvious examples of these types of sources are the Web-based versions of newspapers and journals that exist free of charge on the Web. Often not as complete as their print versions, rarely containing much of a back file ("archives"), and subject to instability (of content as well as access), such sources are integral to keeping current with late-breaking news events and the latest thinking on particular topics. This section

highlights just a few free, Web-based sources: academic (*Economic and Political Weekly* and *Seminar*), popular (*Filmfare* and *Screen India*), and news-related (general newspapers as well as *Frontline*, *India Today*, and *Outlook*).

Academic sources are well covered in the aforementioned indexes and full-text sources, but a few have ventured to create their own unique Web presences. *Economic and Political Weekly* is one of the most critical and critically acclaimed journals from India to focus on the social sciences (especially politics, economics, and development issues) and to highlight many of the most thought-provoking and influential contemporary thinkers from and about India. The Web version of the journal is structured in much the same way as the print version, using categories such as editorials, book reviews, perspectives, commentaries, and special articles. After registering (currently no charge is associated with registration), users of the Web version can access the full text of both current and archived issues and can search the archived holdings. Another acclaimed journal from India, *Seminar*, also replicates its print content on a freely available Web page. Each issue of *Seminar* contains notable contributions addressing a particular theme or "problem," for example cinema, elections, or development. Like that of *Economic and Political Weekly*, the Web version of *Seminar* includes both the current issue (with a one-month lag time) as well as archived issues, although *Seminar*'s back issues are not searchable through its Web page. The influence of these two journals is immense—one for opinion and the other for topicality—as is their commitment to the broad exchange of ideas and debate.

Popular culture is also well-represented on the Web, especially in the area of cinema. Above and beyond the blogs and chat rooms of fans, mainstream magazines such as *Filmfare* and *Screen India* have established solid presences on the Web. Including all the juicy gossip, high-profile interviews, and glossy photos of their print versions, these Web sites keep one up to date on all the hits and flops, romances and breakups, and new releases from Bollywood. *Screen India* also provides news from the "regional" cinema (i.e., not Hindi) and some discussion of television and popular music. Both post current and archived back issues.

As anyone familiar with Indian politics knows, drama is not confined to cinema. Years ago, to keep current on news events from India one would have to either rely on international newswires and broadcasts (such as the Associated Press or BBC) or wait days, weeks, or sometimes even months for print copies of newspapers or newsmagazines to arrive at a local library. The advent of the Web has dramatically changed the speed and breadth of contemporary news from India.

Most English-language newspapers from India have decent Web versions, most are free, and many include back issues ("archives") for at least a month after publication. Although the Web versions lack some of the content of the print editions, most notably advertisements and highly local information such as event listings, most carry all significant news stories and many update their pages periodically throughout the day. Rather than listing each paper, this section directs the reader to three significant lists of URLs to Web papers: South Asian Newspapers from the University of Pennsylvania, Onlinenewspapers.com, and Sama–char.com. (Both South Asian Newspapers and Onlinenewspapers.com provide links to non-English news sources.) Newsmagazines are also well represented on the Web. Three worthy of special mention are *Front-line*, *India Today*, and *Outlook*. Paralleling such publications as *Time* and *Newsweek*, these weekly newsmagazines discuss topics such as elections, political maneuvers and upheavals, public health and development concerns, sports and entertainment, the state of business and finance, and international developments, from an Indian perspective. All contain current and back issues and although *India Today* requires a paid subscription to access more than its table of contents on the Web, *Frontline* and *Outlook* make their content freely available. Using these online sources for detailed discussions of topical issues (from the newsmagazines) and timely reports (from the newspapers), one can remain abreast and apprised of current events from India.

Electronic Books

Not too long ago, journalists and trend watchers predicted that print monographs would soon become obsolete. They claimed that the new high-tech world would not stand for single-use items, and that the paperbound, printed monograph would go the way of the handwritten letter and typeset books before it. Although the extent and scope of these predictions have yet to come true, the market has produced alternatives to the traditional book—digital content can be purchased in disk, CD, or otherwise downloadable form to be read and transported through a handheld electronic device (such as the e-book reader or a Palm Pilot or other PDA)—and many high-quality full-text monographs are now available in digital form. This section discusses a small subset of the electronic book realm, namely books that require a computer to read and view the content.

Perhaps the most immediately relevant to those interested in India will be the full-text digital books available through the Digital South Asia Library (DSAL) and the Digital Dictionaries of South Asia (DDSA). Both projects were originally funded through generous grants from the U.S. Department of Education's Technological Innovation and Cooperation for Foreign Information Access (TICFIA) programs, which focus on increasing the accessibility of foreign information to the American audience. Both projects are highly specialized and geared toward the academic community, yet their applications are widespread.

Although the DSAL includes more than just books in its purview (DSAL also provides full-text journals, maps, photographs, and indexes, among other things), its full-text books are unique. As mentioned above, many grant-funded projects need to focus on the conversion of older, public domain materials. DSAL has turned this restriction into a serious collection strategy, with the inclusion of rare and fragile titles such as the *Imperial Gazetteer of India* (all twenty-six volumes) or the *Statistical Abstract Relating to British India*, which can be easily downloaded into spreadsheet format. Also unique to the DSAL portal are the abundant pedagogical resources for language instruction, such as C.M. Naim's *Introductory Urdu* or E. Dimock's *Introduction to Bengali*. In effect creating digital facsimiles of printed texts by using relatively standard scanning and optical character recognition (OCR) techniques, the technological advances for e-texts enabled by DSAL have not been revolutionary; yet DSAL deserves high praise for its consistently high quality of content selection and commitment to reproducing texts as they were printed.

The Digital Dictionaries of South Asia (DDSA), however, has been revolutionary in its scope and impact on the full-text world. At the time of this writing, the DDSA includes one dictionary for each South Asian language from that language to English (for example, Fabricius's *Tamil and English Dictionary* or Monier-Williams's *A Sanskrit-English Dictionary*), and one English-to-English historical dictionary, *Hobson-Jobson*. In the near future, the DDSA will also include monolingual dictionaries, for example, Bengali to Bengali. Beginning with content from established print dictionaries selected by leaders in the language learning and linguistic fields, the dictionaries converted to digital form are then double-keyed into the DDSA database to minimize the complications that come from OCR. In other words, rather than creating digital facsimiles, DDSA creates e-texts. In addition to minimizing the errors that come from OCR, such e-texts allow for the inclusion of data and text from multiple scripts and language families. While this language inclusion may seem a minor point, it is highly complicated and relatively uncharted terrain in the digital world. Among the benefits innovations and standards such as Unicode can provide is the capability to not only display the multiple languages and scripts represented in the DDSA, but also search in those languages and scripts. Such innovations make the digital project at least as good as the print product; yet, in further making it entirely searchable, they enable full exploitation of the medium. As in any print dictionary, one can look up definitions by head-word or page number. With the added search ability and possible manipulations of the digital dictionary, one can also search for instances of a word throughout the dictionary to compare definitions or subtleties and semantics of particular words. Projects like the DDSA are enabling true innovations of the online medium for Indian studies to work themselves out.

Commercial and academic publishers are also charting new ground in the realm of electronic books. While the Digital South Asia Library and the Digital Dictionaries of South Asia projects both rely on text conversion for their digital monographs, many publishers are publishing print and electronic versions of a book simultaneously or, more radically, in the online medium exclusively. For example, the University of California Press recently released simultaneous (or nearly simultaneous) print and electronic versions of many of its monographs. The electronic versions of these texts are freely accessible and include titles such as S. Ramaswamy's *Passions of the Tongue*, R. Eaton's *Rise of Islam and the Bengal Frontier*, and E. Irschick's *Dialogue and History*. Electronic distribution of such titles not only increases their visibility and accessibility, it makes them full-text "searchable"—the possibilities created by the medium and the ramifications for scholarship have yet to be seen. Another publisher, Gutenberg-e, has taken a slightly different approach to the online monograph: publishing its texts *only* in electronic form. A joint project of the American Historical Association and Columbia University Press, Gutenberg-e has retained high levels of quality and respectability by maintaining many aspects of the print environment, such as peer review. Moreover, Gutenberg-e manipulates the medium by adding links to external Web sites or including audio and video files where appropriate. Gutenberg-e is small, yet it already includes titles related to India such as A. Hardgrove's *Community and Public Culture* and M. Katten's *Colonial Lists/Indian Power.*

With the cadre of online monographs expanding, it is difficult to keep track of just who is publishing what and where. That is where the Digital Book Index steps in. Basically a catalog of online books, the Digital Book Index can be searched by title, by broad subject areas, or by author, but it can also be searched by digital producer and the downloading of e-books readers. The Digital Book Index is primarily useful as a locating device, but it also benefits the isolated or independent scholar by noting format and the potential fees associated with particular titles.

Statistical and Governmental Sources

Years ago, it was difficult to get information on the government of India in the United States; the Internet has vividly changed the situation. Thanks to initiatives from the National Informatics Centre (NIC), virtually all divisions of the Indian government now have active presences on the Web. The NIC has its own listing of the Web sites (Directory of Indian Government Web sites), and a parallel list exists on the Governments on the WWW Web site. All of the sites include basic contact information (the names of important personnel, postal addresses, and some e-mail addresses), and some have substantial content as well.

For example, the branches of the Indian Parliament (president, Lok Sabha, and Rajya Sabha) share an impressive, extremely content-rich Web site. The main page directs visitors to the full text of press releases and speeches of the current Indian president, the schedules and debates of both houses, listings of the current parliamentary members, an electronic version of the Constitution, and so on. Moreover, the site archives the Lok Sabha debates in both English and Hindi: the tenth through the twelfth sessions can be browsed and the thirteenth session can be searched. The site also lists the parliamentary committees, their constitutions and memberships, and provides budgetary documentation. For those concerned with Indian legislation and high-level political debate, this Web site is a gold mine.

Other content-rich Web sites worthy of special mention are those of the Election Commission and the Finance Ministry. The Election Commission site provides significant, descriptive information about elections and the electoral process in India as well as access to searchable statistical results for Lok Sabha and state elections (in many cases, from as early as 1951). The Finance Ministry's site grants access to the most current information about the Union budget, reports about foreign direct investment, and the full text of taxation-related acts.

The Indian census also has a significant Web presence. The Web site provides basic statistical data such as tables on literacy rates, general population statistics (for example, sex ratios and urban-rural distributions), and housing and household amenities as well as basic maps based on the census data. Furthermore, the main page contains contact information for purchasing census products, such as the 1991 census data on CD. One can only imagine that as the data from the 2001 census continue to be processed, the amount of information available on the Web site will increase.

Closely related to the census Web site is the commercial product IndiaStat. Primarily comprised of statistical data from the Indian government, IndiaStat provides its subscribers with a means to search, sort, and download data. In addition to PDF files, most of the data is also available in Microsoft Word and Excel spreadsheet formats, which can be of great benefit to those trying to manipulate the data through programs such as SPSS. IndiaStat contains both state and national statistics and includes demographic, agricultural, and economic data. Although a commercial product, IndiaStat promotes itself to both institutions and individuals and has adjusted its pricing accordingly. One cannot overestimate IndiaStat's potential impact.

The U.S. government also produces a considerable amount of information about India. Furthermore, since the Government Printing Office has gone almost completely electronic, the possibilities for gathering information are immense. Two former monograph series, the Central Intelligence Agency's *Factbooks* and the Library of Congress's *Country Studies*, are now available free on the Web. Acting primarily as introductory texts to the region, both the *Factbook* and the *Country Study* provide the reader with general information on topics such as geography, demographics, governmental structures, and so on. The *Factbook* includes some statistical information (on facets of the economy, the communications and transportations sectors, and so on) while the *Country Study* discusses the region's history, religions, and social systems in greater detail. The *Country Study* is no longer updated (the most recent was 1995), yet both guides are excellent ready reference sources for novice and expert alike. (The

Library of Congress posts Congressional Research Study reports on the Web, where they can be accessed and searched. Recent reports of interest address issues such as the environment, terrorism, and nuclear proliferation.)

Perhaps not specifically germane to this discussion, the U.S. government has published significant Indian diasporic information online. Among other sources, the U.S. Census Bureau provides data on specific communities within the United States, defined by race, language spoken at home, and so on. Much of this information is available at the local, state, and national levels and is relatively easy to either map or download into spreadsheet applications. As the U.S. population continues to diversify, easy access to such information will become more and more important. As an aside, the U.S. Census Bureau Web site also links to interactive international demographic information.

A final resource for U.S. government data regarding India is Lexis-Nexis (mentioned previously in the indexes section). Enabled by full-text searching of the *Congressional Record*, committee reports, and other laws, bills, and regulations, Lexis-Nexis is a quick, powerful source for those interested in U.S.–India bilateral relations.

Keeping Current

Information sharing on the Internet is not limited to Web sites or databases. In fact, one of the earliest uses of the Internet was for something most of us engage in regularly: e-mail exchanges. Although not cutting-edge technology anymore, the uses and exchanges enabled by e-mail help create online "communities" that can quickly, broadly, and inexpensively share information. The most powerful of these broad applications is the listserv.

Listservs typically are composed of a group of members focused on a particular subject area. These areas can be academic subjects (such as Indology), geographic areas (India, for example), news topics, and so on. Listservs may be moderated (meaning each message must be approved and passed by an "editor" or "moderator") or unmoderated (meaning each member can immediately post a message without any mediation). All listservs route messages through a central server (the "host server") and then send them to the list of members. The necessity of the host server used to limit listservs to corporate, governmental, or academic institutions; new advances in commercial server space (such as at Yahoo and Excite) have democratized the possibilities for listservs immensely. The number of India-related listservs is huge, yet three deserve special mention here: Indology (for classical India and its languages), Religion in South Asia (for the academic study of India's religions), and H-Asia (for interdisciplinary information related to Asia in general).

The previous sections have highlighted just a few of the many types of online resources available for those curious about India. Other types could just as easily have been selected: general Web sites of corporations, nongovernmental organizations, or educational institutions; Web sites that provide audio files; those that have graphics, photographs, or digital movies; those with a pedagogical focus. Many of these other types are listed in the source bibliography at the end of this chapter. With so many kinds and so many venues for online content, however, the problem remains: how to keep abreast of new and innovative sources. Web pages, CD products, and full-text databases do not suddenly appear on the shelves of the neighborhood bookstore or get advertised through standard publishing catalogs. Therefore, this final section highlights two sources that keep users apprised of new online content: the *Asian Studies Monitor* and the *Scout Report.*

The Asian Studies Monitor from Australian National University and the Scout Report from the University of Wisconsin follow a similar formula: the user subscribes to receive periodic updates via e-mail about new online content. These updates typically take the form of annotated lists or direct reviews of the online product. For example, the Asian Studies Monitor sends out messages that provide the location (usually a URL), projected audience, availability of archiving, and a scholarly relevance ranking (ranging from "essential" to "marginal"), while the Scout Report sends weekly descriptive reviews of Web sites written by its staff. As apparent by its name, the Asian Studies Monitor focuses its attention on online resources related to all of Asia. The Scout Report has a much more general audience and scope, but it often highlights content from and about India (for example, the Digital South Asia Library and the Portal to Asian Internet Resources were both reviewed in the Scout Report). The automated nature of these informative services makes them invaluable for keeping abreast of new online content on and from India.

The world of online content related to India has grown immeasurably over the past decade and shows no sign of slowing down. Although one cannot predict the future, surely technological advents such as Unicode and the Open Archives Initiative and movements seeking new distribution models will only increase the amount of information available. Furthermore, given the boom in information technology infrastructure within India, we can hope to see more powerful delivery mechanisms of more varied content from India itself. While scholars, policy makers, and the general public will continue to find information about India in different ways according to their specific interests, means, and needs, this chapter has aimed to describe avenues and strategies suitable for each group's particular research in the online environment.

Sources

Audio/Visual Files

BBC, http://www.bbc.co.uk, including audio links for Bengali, Hindi, Tamil, and Urdu
Doordarshan, http://www.ddindia.net
South Asian Literary Recordings Project, http://www.loc.gov/acq/ovop/delhi/salrp/
Voice of America, http://www.voanews.com, including audio links for Bangla, Hindi, and Urdu

E-books

Classical Indian Language Texts, http://www.ucl.ac.uk/~ucgadkw/indnet-textarchive.html
Digital Book Index, http://www.digitalbookindex.com/search001a.htm
Digital Dictionaries of South Asia, http://dsal.uchicago.edu/dictionaries/
Digital South Asia Library, http://dsal.uchicago.edu
Göttingen Register of Electronic Texts in Indian Languages, http://www.sub.uni-goettingen.de/ebene_1/fiindolo/gretil.htm
Gutenberg-e, http://www.gutenberg-e.org
Making of America, http://www.hti.umich.edu/m/moagrp
Muktabodha Digital Library and Archiving Project, http://www.muktabodha.org/digital_library.htm
NetLibrary, http://www.netlibrary.com
Pali Canon, http://www.accesstoinsight.org/canon
Sacred Books of the East, http://www.sacred-texts.com/sbe/index.htm
University of California Press, http://www.ucpress.edu

Governmental Sources

Census of India, http://www.censusindia.net

CIA Factbook: India, http://www.odci.gov/cia/publications/factbook/geos/in.html

Congressional Research Service Reports, http://www.ncseonline.org/NLE/CRS (searchable but limited) and http://fpc.state.gov/c4763.htm (unsearchable)

Directory of Indian Government Web Sites, http://goidirectory.nic.in

Election Commission of India, http://www.eci.gov.in

Governments on the WWW: India, http://www.gksoft.com/govt/en/in.html

India: A Country Study, http://lcweb2.loc.gov/frd/cs/intoc.html

Indian Parliament, http://parliamentofindia.nic.in

IndiaStat, http://www.indiastat.com

Ministry of Commerce and Industry, http://commin.nic.in

Ministry of Finance, http://finmin.nic.in

U.S. Department of State Country Information, http://www.state.gov/p/sa/ci/in

Listservs

Asian Studies Monitor, http://coombs.anu.edu.au/asia-www-monitor.html

H-Asia, http://www.h-net.org/~asia

Indology, http://www.ucl.ac.uk/~ucgadkw/indology.html

Religion in South Asia, http://www.montclair.edu/risa/r-instruct.html

Magazines/Journals

Economic and Political Weekly, http://www.epw.org.in

Filmfare, http://filmfaremagazine.indiatimes.com

Frontline, http://www.flonnet.com

Global Reproductive Health Forum South Asia, http://www.hsph.harvard.edu/Organizations/healthnet/SAsia/forum.html

India Today, http://www.indiatoday.com

Labour File, http://www.labourfile.org

Manushi, http://free.freespeech.org/manushi

Outlook, http://www.outlookindia.com

Screen India, http://www.screenindia.com

Seminar, http://www.india-seminar.com
University of Pennsylvania Library's South Asian Magazines Web
    Site, http://oldsite.library.upenn.edu/vanpelt/collections/sasia/
    webmags.html

News Sources

BBC, http://www.bbc.co.uk (including BBC Hindi, http://
    www.bbc.co.uk/hindi/ and BBC Urdu, http://www.bbc.co.uk/urdu/)
OnlineNewspapers.com: India, http://www.onlinenewspapers.com/
    india.htm
Samachar.com, http://www.samachar.com
South Asia Journalists Association, including *South Asia Self-Study
    Guide*, http://www.saja.org/guide.html
University of Pennsylvania Library's South Asian Newspapers Web
    Site, http://oldsite.library.upenn.edu/vanpelt/collections/sasia/
    webpapers.html
World News Daily: South Asia, http://southasiadaily.com

Nongovernmental Sources

Asia Society, http://www.asiasociety.org
Centre for Science and Environment, http://www.cseindia.org
Confederation of Indian Industry, http://www.ciionline.org
The Energy and Resources Institute, http://www.teriin.org
Human Rights Watch, http://www.hrw.org/doc?t=asia&c=india
Indian Council for Research on International Economic Relations,
    http://www.icrier.res.in
Institute for Defence Studies and Analyses, http://www.idsa-india.org
Institute of Peace and Conflict Studies, http://www.ipcs.org/ipcs/new/
    index.jsp
M.S. Swaminathan Research Foundation, http://www.mssrf.org
National Council for Applied Economic Research, http://
    www.ncaer.org
ProPoor, http://www.propoor.org
Sarai, http://www.sarai.net
SEWA, http://www.sewaresearch.org
South Asia Human Rights Documentation Centre, http://www.hri.ca/
    partners/sahrdc/index.htm

Reference Sources

ALA-LC Romanization Tables, http://lcweb.loc.gov/catdir/cpso/roman.html

Asia Source Bibliographies, http://www.asiasource.org/features/bibliographies-south.cfm

Bibliography of Asian Studies, http://www.aasianst.org/bassub.html

Digital Dictionaries of South Asia, http://dsal.uchicago.edu/dictionaries

Digital South Asia Library, http://dsal.uchicago.edu

Ethnic Newswatch, http://enw.softlineweb.com

Gender Watch, http://gw.softline.com

Historical Abstracts, http://serials.abc-clio.com/active/start?_appname=serials&initialdb=HA

India Resources Page, http://www.clas.ufl.edu/users/gthursby/ind

India WWW Virtual Library, http://www.india.com.ar

JSTOR, http://www.jstor.org

Lexis-Nexis, http://www.lexisnexis.com

Portal to Asian Internet Resources (PAIR), http://webcat.library.wisc.edu:3200/PAIR

Project Muse, http://muse.jhu.edu

Proquest, http://www.proquest.com

SARAI, http://www.columbia.edu/cu/lweb/indiv/southasia/cuvl

South Asia Bibliographies, http://www.lib.berkeley.edu/SSEAL/SouthAsia/wsaguibi.html#anchor688404

South Asia Women's Network (SAWNET), http://www.sawnet.org

Religion Sources

ATLA Religion Database, http://www.atla.com/products/catalogs/databases/catalogs_rdb.html

Atma Dharma, http://www.jainism.free-online.co.uk

Buddhist Studies WWW Virtual Library, http://www.ciolek.com/WWWVL-Buddhism.html

Hindu Universe, http://www.hindunet.org/home.shtml

Islam in South Asia, http://www.columbia.edu/itc/mealac/pritchett/00fwp/islamlinks.html

Jain World, http://www.jainworld.com

Sikhism Home Page, http://www.sikhs.org

Search Engines

Google, http://www.google.com
Jadoo, http://www.jadoo.com
Khoj, http://www.khoj.com
Rediff, http://www.rediff.com
Yahoo, http://www.yahoo.com

Teaching Resources

Asian Educational Media Service, http://www.aems.uiuc.edu/index.las
Ask Asia, http://www.askasia.org
Project South Asia, http://www.mssu.edu/projectsouthasia
Teaching Contemporary South Asia, http://www.teachingsouthasia.org

Visual and Literary Sources

Ames Library Exhibits, http://ames.lib.umn.edu/amesex-0.phtml
Atlas of Mutual Heritage Historical Map Collection, http://
    www.atlasmutualheritage.nl
David Rumsey Historical Map Collection, http://
    www.davidrumsey.com
Devi: The Great Goddess, http://www.asia.si.edu/devi/index.htm
Digital South Asia Library Images, http://dsal.uchicago.edu/images/
    index.html
"Echoes of Freedom: South Asian Pioneers in California, 1899–1965,"
    http://www.lib.berkeley.edu/SSEAL/echoes/echoes.html
Harappa: Glimpses of South Asia before 1947, http://
    www.harappa.com/welcome.html
Huntington Archive of Buddhist and Related Art, http://kaladarshan
    .arts.ohio-state.edu
Perry Castañeda Library Map Collection, http://www.lib.utexas.edu/
    maps/india.html
ReliefWeb Map Centre: South Asia, http://www.reliefweb.int/w/
    map.nsf/Region?OpenForm&Query=SAsia
"The Sensuous and the Sacred: Chola Bronzes from South India,"
    http://www.asia.si.edu/exhibitions/online/chola/default.htm
"Silicon Raj: Making a Difference to America's Future," http://
    www.lib.berkeley.edu/SSEAL/siliconraj

Chronology

Irawati Parnerkar

2001

January 2

The main electricity grid for northern India shuts down for twelve hours, causing widespread disruption of services.

January 4

With the maiden test flight of the first indigenously manufactured supersonic light combat aircraft, India joins a select group of countries.

January 8

Film financier and diamond merchant Bharat Shah is arrested by the crime branch in Mumbai for having alleged links with underworld gangster Chhota Shakeel.

January 9

The Maharashtra government agrees to pay Rs. 1.14 billion of the Rs. 2.62 billion owed by the Maharashtra State Electricity Board to Enron Corporation's subsidiary Dabhol Power Corporation.

In Allahabad, more than 2.5 million devotees take a holy dip in the waters of the *sangam* (confluence of the Ganga and Jumna rivers) on the first day of the *maha kumbh*. On the peak day of the festival, January 14, eight million devotees participate in the ritual.

January 14

Jammu and Kashmir chief minister Farooq Abdullah escapes a grenade attack for which the Hizbul Mujahideen claims responsibility.

January 17

The first test firing of the 2,500-kilometer range Agni-II Intermediate Range Ballistic Missile (IRBM) in its final operational configuration is conducted in Orissa.

January 19

U.K.-based businessman Srichand Hinduja and his brothers Gopichand and Prakash, charged in connection with the Bofors arms deal scandal, are given bail but are ordered not to leave the country without the court's permission.

January 26

A devastating earthquake centered on the city of Bhuj in the Kutch district of Gujarat destroys three towns and hundreds of villages. The final toll of dead, determined months later, is about 20,000, with 166,000 injured and 600,000 homeless. Three days later, Prime Minister Atal Bihari Vajpayee visits some of the quake-affected areas along with Home Minister L.K. Advani and announces Rs. 5 billion of assistance from the Central Government.

February 1

The union cabinet decides to levy a 2 percent income tax surcharge on individuals and companies to mobilize Rs. 13 billion for reconstruction and rehabilitation in quake-hit areas of Gujarat.

February 6

The union cabinet decides to ban smoking in all public places and the sale of tobacco products to persons less than eighteen years old.

February 10

Darjeeling Gorkha Hill Council chairman Subhas Ghising is critically wounded after an ambush of his convoy by unidentified gunmen near Kurseong, West Bengal.

February 12

The Lucknow branch of the Allahabad High Court in Uttar Pradesh sets aside on procedural grounds the CBI charges against the eight accused in the Babri Masjid demolition case, including Home Minister Advani. On May 4, a CBI special court, holding the trial of forty-nine accused in the case, drops criminal proceedings against Advani and twenty-one other BJP and VHP leaders on "technical grounds."

February 13

Manipur chief minister W. Nipamacha Singh resigns, paving the way for a new coalition, the United Democratic Alliance, led by Samata Party leader Radhabinod Koijam.

February 23

The Economic Survey of 2000–2001 presented in Parliament reports a slowdown in economic growth from 8 percent in the previous year to 6 percent due to a decline in the service sector growth rate and a recovery in exports with foreign exchange reserves at a record high level of $41.1 billion.

February 28

The union budget announces incentives for investment such as reductions in corporate and personal income taxes, interest rates, and excise and custom duties and relaxation of foreign exchange rules.

March 1

An opposition-sponsored motion against the privatization of Bharat Aluminum Company Limited (BALCO), 51 percent of which had been sold on February 21 to Sterlite Industries, a copper and aluminum manufacturer, is defeated by the NDA coalition. Two days later, workers of the company go on strike, backed by Chhattisgarh chief minister Ajit Jogi, who argues that the disinvestment of BALCO is a violation of a Supreme Court order of 1997 that no land or mining lease in tribal areas can be transferred to nontribals. The Supreme Court on March 7 directs the Chhattisgarh government to provide full protection to BALCO workers and management. On March 12 the Rajya Sabha censures the government for the BALCO deal, and on April 4 the Chhattisgarh government, arguing in the Supreme Court that the company was not sold at a competitive price, offers to pay more than the sale price for the government's 51 percent stake.

March 8

Bombay Stock Exchange (BSE) president Anand Rathi resigns after evidence emerges suggesting he had demanded sensitive price information just before a large sell-off of shares on the BSE on March 2. On March 12 the Securities and Exchange Board of India (SEBI) suspends all seven broker members of the BSE's governing board and issues a directive to the BSE barring any broker from acting as a director on the governing board on March 28, thus ensuring that BSE directors with access to vital information are unable to use it to their advantage.

March 13

Internet news service Tehelka.com exposes corruption in the government, releasing a videotape of a sting operation conducted by its journalists over seven months. The tape shows BJP president Bangaru Laxman and Samata Party president Jaya Jaitly, a close confidante of defense minister George Fernandes, accepting wads of currency notes to facilitate the prospects of a decoy company set up by the dot-com journalists posing as arms dealers. The next day the government suspends seven officials of the defense establishment, and two days later Fernandes resigns.

March 26

The registrar general announces the provisional population total of the recently completed 2001 census: more than 1.027 billion persons.

March 28

Jammu and Kashmir police gun down Salahuddin Ayubi, the chief commander of the Pakistan-based terrorist group Lashkar-e-Toiba.

March 30

The CBI arrests Mumbai stockbroker Ketan Parikh for his involvement in a Rs. 1.37 billion fraud which caused an estimated loss of Rs. 8 billion to banks.

The Supreme Court directs that witnesses must be examined on the day they are present in a trial court, in order to end their harassment in criminal cases due to frequent adjournments.

April 3

Many office workers and school children are stranded when thousands of buses stop operating in Delhi following the Supreme Court's deadline for conversion of public vehicles to the more eco-friendly compressed natural gas (CNG) fuel. The next day, the court permits city authorities to issue provisional permits until April 14 for conversion of public vehicles to CNG.

April 4

Former U.S. president Bill Clinton visits earthquake-ravaged Bhuj and announces a plan to collect several million dollars to help rebuild the area.

April 5

The Central Government invites the All Parties Hurriyat Conference (APHC) for talks without preconditions and appoints former defense minister K.C. Pant as its chief negotiator. Hurriyat chairman Abdul Ghani Bhatt says that the government must allow the APHC delegation to visit Pakistan.

April 10

Home Minister Advani expresses regret about the demolition of the Babri Masjid in December 1992, on the first day of his testimony before the Liberhans Ayodhya commission of inquiry, but on the second day he declares that the demolished structure was actually a temple.

April 18

India successfully launches a commercial satellite in a geosynchronous orbit for the first time.

Soldiers of the Bangladeshi Rifles kill sixteen Border Security Force men in Meghalaya. Two days later, Bangladesh returns their bodies, most of them in mutilated form, and hands over two injured soldiers and the body of another on April 22. India lodges a strong protest with Bangladesh over the incident.

May 4

The Supreme Court directs the union and state governments to stringently enforce an existing law banning prenatal sex determination.

May 8

The CBI files an interim charge sheet against two former chief ministers of Bihar, Laloo Prasad Yadav and Jagannath Mishra, and 108 others accused in the animal husbandry scam case.

BALCO workers withdraw their sixty-seven-day strike following an agreement with the company's new management, Sterlite Industries, on their twenty-five points of demand.

May 9

The federal government opens up the Indian defense industry to the private sector, allowing 100 percent Indian private investment and 26 percent foreign participation in private arms manufacturing ventures. It also throws open the vital sectors of civil aviation, pharmaceuticals, real estate, and hotels and tourism to 100 percent FDI and raises FDI levels in telecom and banking.

May 13

The results of the state assembly elections in four states point to the resurgence of the Congress Party. The Congress-led United Democratic Front wins in Kerala and Assam with solid majorities. In West Bengal, the CPM-led Left Front easily defeats the Trinamool Congress–Congress alliance. In Tamil Nadu, the All India Anna Dravida Munnetra Kazhagam (AIADMK) led by Jayalalitha and allies wins more than two-thirds of the seats. Elections are also held in the union territory of Pondicherry where a Congress-Tamil Maanila Congress (TMC) alliance forms the largest bloc with thirteen of thirty seats. Jayalalitha is sworn in as the Tamil Nadu chief minister on May 14. Two days later Buddhadeb Bhattacharjee becomes West Bengal's chief minister. A.K. Antony is appointed as chief minister of Kerala on May 17 and Tarun Gogoi is sworn in as Assam's chief minister the next day.

May 21

The Samata Party–led Manipur government is defeated in a vote of confidence after twenty-four of twenty-six BJP legislators, upon whose support it had relied, vote against it. On June 2, President's Rule is imposed on the state.

May 23

The government decides to call off the six-month unilateral ceasefire in Kashmir, which had been announced in November 2000.

June 29

The Central Statistical Organisation reports that India's economic growth fell to 5.2 percent in 2000–2001 from 6.4 percent in the previous year because of poor performance in agriculture and slow growth of the industrial and service sectors.

June 30

Muthuvel Karunanidhi, former chief minister of Tamil Nadu and leader of the Dravida Munnetra Kazhagam (DMK), is arrested on a corruption charge. Two members of the union government, commerce and industry minister Murasoli Maran and environment and forest minister T.R. Balu, are also arrested.

July 2

The Securities and Exchange Board of India (SEBI), responding to increased stock market volatility, bans the system of *badla* (carryforward) trade in the stock markets.

July 16

The Agra summit meeting between Prime Minister Vajpayee and General Pervez Musharraf ends without the issue of a joint statement, tentatively termed the "Agra Declaration." The difficulty apparently is that Pakistan insisted on specifying Kashmir as the core issue of dispute between the two countries, and India insisted on the incorporation of the term "cross border terrorism."

July 25

Phoolan Devi, the "Bandit Queen" and a member of Parliament for the Samajwadi Party, is shot dead outside her home in New Delhi at the age of thirty-seven.

August 8

At a meeting chaired by the union minister for health and family welfare, C.P. Thakur, a decision is made to eliminate the excise and customs duties on AIDS drugs and to ask states to remove the sales tax on them.

August 9

An army of two hundred Naxalites attacks two police stations in Orissa, killing six policemen and taking large quantities of arms and ammunition. Two Naxalites are killed.

August 15

In his address to the nation on India's Independence Day, the prime minister emphasizes India's commitment to a dialogue with Pakistan but also reiterates its resolve to crush Pakistan-sponsored terrorism in Jammu and Kashmir and to hold "free and fair elections" there.

August 24

Enron threatens India with new American sanctions unless the company and its partners get back the full $1 billion in costs incurred in building the project in Maharashtra.

September 2

Chief ministers of non-BJP-ruled states unanimously adopt a resolution protesting the center's attempts to "saffronize" education policy without consulting with them.

September 13

The cabinet committee on security meets and decides to offer all cooperation and facilities for U.S. military operations against those responsible for the terrorist attacks of September 11.

September 21

The Supreme Court rules that the controversial appointment in May of Jayalalitha as chief minister of Tamil Nadu is not legal because she was disqualified from contesting for a seat in the assembly due to a criminal conviction for corruption.

September 22

As part of its response to 9/11, the United States lifts military and economic sanctions imposed by the U.S. Congress on India and Pakistan following the nuclear tests conducted by both countries in May 1998.

September 30

Madhavrao Scindia, deputy leader of the Congress Party in the Lok Sabha and former union minister, is killed in a plane crash.

October 1

A suicide squad of Jaish-e-Mohammed bursts into the Jammu and Kashmir assembly complex in Srinagar, throwing grenades and firing guns, leaving twenty-nine persons dead and thirty injured.

October 2

Keshubhai Patel, Gujarat chief minister, resigns and the BJP decides to elect Narendra Modi as his successor.

October 15

George Fernandes is reappointed as defense minister.

October 25

The government promulgates the Prevention of Terrorism Ordinance 2001 (POTO), replacing the 1987 Terrorist and Disruptive Activities (Prevention) Act (TADA) and banning indefinitely twenty-three mostly separatist organizations. Justifying the new ordinance, the government cites not only an upsurge of terrorist and insurgent activities in India but also the September 11 attacks on the United States.

November 2

The Supreme Court bans smoking in all public places and forms of public transport, including railways.

November 12

The Hurriyat Conference offers a three-point plan to end the Jammu and Kashmir crisis, including a "comprehensive" ceasefire by all groups involved, and trilateral talks between India, Pakistan, and the Hurriyat Conference, as representatives of the Kashmiris.

November 25

An exhaustive resolution incorporating a code of conduct for legislators is unanimously approved at an all India conference of presiding officers, chief ministers, parliamentary affairs ministers, and leaders and whips convened by Lok Sabha Speaker G.M.C. Balayogi.

December 4

The High Court of Chennai acquits former chief minister Jayalalitha and other defendants of the corruption charges that the Supreme Court had relied upon in disqualifying her from standing for office in state elections.

December 10

The Supreme Court upholds the Central Government's decision to privatize BALCO, stating that the government's economic policy should be questioned in Parliament, not in the courts.

December 13

Five terrorists, later claimed to be Pakistani by Indian authorities, armed with rifles, grenades, pistols, and explosives, barge into the premises of Parliament and gun down seven persons before security personnel kill them after a forty-five-minute gun battle. Prime Minister Vajpayee is not attending the Lok Sabha at the time, but around two hundred members of Parliament are in the building.

December 21

In major first steps that lead to a six-month eyeball-to-eyeball military confrontation between India and Pakistan over the attack on Parliament, India recalls its high commissioner to Pakistan and cuts the only land transport links between the two countries. On December 27, India bans overflights of India by Pakistani aircraft.

2002

January 5

President Pervez Musharraf offers a "genuine and sincere hand of friendship" and then walks up to Prime Minister Vajpayee with an extended hand during the opening session of the South Asian Association for Regional Cooperation (SAARC) summit in Kathmandu, Nepal. A surprised Vajpayee stands up and shakes Musharraf's hand.

January 11

Army Chief General S. Padmanabhan describes the situation along the Indo-Pakistan border as "war-like" and adds that India is prepared for both a conventional war as well as a counter-nuclear strike if anyone is "mad enough" to use nuclear weapons against it.

January 12

In a nationally televised address in Pakistan, President Musharraf condemns the terrorist attacks on the Jammu and Kashmir assembly and the Indian Parliament.

January 14

Chinese premier Zhu Rongji and Prime Minister Vajpayee meet in New Delhi and sign six agreements on fighting terrorism as well as promoting bilateral cooperation in technical and economic areas.

January 24

Jharkhand governor Pratap Kumar submits his resignation because of allegations of misconduct when he was the cabinet secretary in Delhi.

February 5

Minister for disinvestment Arun Shourie announces the first major successes in the government's privatization program with the sales of stakes in the state-owned IBP petroleum company and the VSNL international telecommunications company. On February 13, the Tata group takes over VSNL.

February 10

The VHP announces that temple construction at Ayodhya will begin on March 15 with the transfer of the carved stone pillars from a workshop to the site of the shrine.

February 16

Prime Minister Vajpayee concedes that his efforts to resolve the Ayodhya dispute through negotiations have failed. He blames both the VHP and the Babri Masjid Action Committee for being "absolutely unrelenting" in their attitudes. The next day the VHP begins consecrating the pillars of the new temple.

February 24

State assembly election results are announced, with the Congress winning a majority of seats in Uttaranchal and, with its ally the CPI, in Punjab. In a by-election, AIADMK chief Jayalalitha is elected to the Tamil Nadu assembly. Congress chief Amarinder Singh is sworn in as chief minister two days later. Jayalalitha is sworn in as chief minister of Tamil Nadu. N.D. Tiwari is sworn in as chief minister of Uttaranchal on March 2.

February 25

In Uttar Pradesh, the Samajwadi Party gains significantly in the elections, winning 145 of the 403 seats, giving it almost 50 percent more seats than the second-place BJP, which was ruling the state. The BSP comes in a close third, while the Congress comes in a poor fourth, with twenty-six seats, equal to the number of winning independents. In Manipur, the Congress wins twenty of the sixty seats. The next day Samajwadi Party leader Mulayam Singh Yadav stakes claim to form a government in Uttar Pradesh. Okram Ibobi Singh, the leader of the newly formed Congress-led Secular Progressive Front, is appointed chief minister in Manipur on March 7.

February 27

A train carrying Hindu activists returning from a visit to the disputed religious shrine in Ayodhya is attacked in the town of Godhra in Gujarat. At least fifty-eight passengers, mainly women and children, are burned to death. An indefinite curfew is imposed as large-scale violence erupts and police open fire at many places to disperse rioting mobs. There are incidents of violence in Ahmedabad and Vadodara. Chief minister Narendra Modi announces a probe into the incident and an ex gratia payment of Rs. 200,000 to the kin of those killed.

February 28

The Gujarat government imposes an indefinite curfew in twenty-six places as news of the Godhra massacre sparks retaliatory attacks by Hindus in many parts of the state the same day and continuing into the next. The Vishwa Hindu Parishad calls a *bandh* in the state and the BJP state government says that those responsible for the Godhra attack will be booked under the Prevention of Terrorism Ordinance. In the worst incident, at least thirty persons are killed when their houses are set on fire by a mob in Ahmedabad, including former Congress member of Parliament, Ehsan Jafri, and nineteen members of his family. While the government deploys security forces in riot-affected areas, the army is not brought in until three days after the Godhra incident. Reports in the days following indicate that the police in many instances had stood by and allowed the mobs to kill, burn, and pillage. Prime Minister Vajpayee cancels his visit to Australia because of the violence.

Finance minister Yashwant Sinha presents the 2002–2003 budget, which aims for a fiscal deficit of 5.3 percent of gross domestic product (GDP), reduced from 5.7 percent of GDP in 2001–2002.

March 1

Communal violence continues in Gujarat, where at least thirty-three people are burned alive at Bakor-Pandarwada village, seventy kilometers from Godhra. Chief minister Narendra Modi issues shoot-at-sight orders to the police against those committing arson and violence.

March 2

Prime Minister Vajpayee describes the communal violence in Gujarat as a "blot" on the image of the nation and appears on national television to appeal to the Indian citizenry to exercise restraint and maintain peace.

March 3

Lok Sabha Speaker G.M.C. Balayogi is killed in a helicopter crash. Balayogi was the first *Dalit* to have been elected to the post.

March 13

Addressing plans for a worship service at the site of the demolished Babri Masjid in Ayodhya, the Supreme Court orders that no religious activity be permitted on the spot. The next day, Prime Minister Vajpayee assures the Lok Sabha that the Supreme Court order would be implemented in "letter and spirit."

March 15

The New Delhi High Court overturns the October 2000 corruption convictions of former prime minister P.V. Narasimha Rao and his then cabinet colleague Buta Singh in the JMM bribery case.

March 25

In a rare joint session of both its houses, the Union Parliament passes the Prevention of Terrorism Bill 2002 with 425 votes for and 296 against. The bill had been passed in the Lok Sabha on March 19 but rejected by the Rajya Sabha on March 21. The law provides for capital punishment for terrorist killings, ninety days of detention without trial for suspected terrorists, and special courts to deal with terrorist cases.

Punjab Public Service Commission chairman Ravinderpal Singh Sidhu is arrested for allegedly accepting a bribe of Rs. 500,000 from an inspector of the excise department and promising to promote him to an executive rank in the Punjab Provincial Service.

March 31

The National Commission to Review the Working of the Constitution, chaired by former chief justice M.N. Venkatachaliah, submits a four-volume report containing 249 recommendations, including the strengthening of rights to education, religious freedom, and press freedom; the inclusion of a new right to freedom from torture; and diminishing political influence over judicial appointments. The commission does not address the controversial issue of whether a person of foreign origin should hold constitutional office.

April 1

The National Human Rights Commission accuses the Gujarat government of failing to control the violence in the state that followed the Godhra incident. In its "preliminary comments," the commission questions the claims made by the state government in its report on the riots, holding it accountable for a serious failure of intelligence and action and implying that there had been police and administrative bias against Muslims. The commission recommends several steps to "restore the integrity of the process," including the turning over of critical cases to the CBI.

April 4

On his first visit to Gujarat since the violence began more than a month earlier, Prime Minister Vajpayee makes an emotional plea to Hindus and Muslims to end the violence there.

April 12

Addressing a public rally, Prime Minister Vajpayee says that Islam has two faces: one that teaches tolerance and another that fans militancy. While condemning the violence in Gujarat and stressing India's secular and multireligious culture, he blames Muslims for sparking off the violence by asking, "Who lit the fire? How did it spread?"

The national executives of the BJP, meeting in Goa, reject Gujarat chief minister Modi's offer to resign, advising him to dissolve the state assembly and seek reelection.

April 16

The Supreme Court rules unanimously that trials in a criminal case cannot have a fixed time frame for their completion. With just over

12,000 trial court judges, the ruling will affect the nearly 13 million criminal cases pending in the trial courts.

April 29

Ram Vilas Paswan, minister for coal and mines, resigns from the cabinet on the issue of the violence in Gujarat, which he says has "tarnished India's image" both domestically and abroad, adding that the four legislators of his party would vote with the opposition on the censure motion in Parliament the next day. Omar Abdullah, minister of state for external affairs, also resigns, following his party's decision to abstain from voting.

May 1

The Lok Sabha rejects the opposition-sponsored censure motion on the Gujarat issue, with 276 members voting against the motion and 182 for it. While the five-member National Conference and the eleven-member AIADMK abstain from voting, the BSP votes against the motion.

May 2

K.P.S. Gill, former Assam police chief and well known for leading anti-terrorist operations in Punjab, is appointed security adviser to Gujarat chief minister Narendra Modi to aid in the control of communal violence in the state.

The Supreme Court directs the Election Commission to require that candidates contesting parliamentary or assembly elections furnish details of their criminal records, if any, to allow voters to make informed decisions.

May 3

In Uttar Pradesh, a Bahujan Samaj Party, Bharatiya Janata Party, and Rashtriya Lok Dal coalition government headed by BSP leader Mayawati is sworn in.

May 14

In Kashmir, heavily armed fatigue-clad militants gun down the driver and six passengers of a bus, which they use to reach an army base near Jammu. They storm the camp, killing twenty-seven more people, including eight women and eleven children from army families.

May 19

The India-Pakistan border confrontation heats up, with India warning of "befitting retaliatory action" if the border is crossed.

May 21

Abdul Ghani Lone, a veteran All Parties Hurriyat Conference leader and a moderate, is killed by unidentified gunmen a day before Prime Minister Vajpayee is to visit the Kashmir valley.

May 22

Colin Powell, U.S. secretary of state, and Jack Straw, British foreign secretary, confer on the Indo-Pakistani crisis. Straw warns of the "real and very disturbing" possibility of a nuclear conflict.

May 28

Gujarat police arrest three persons with links to the VHP, Bajrang Dal, and BJP in connection with the killings of at least eighty-six people by a rioting mob in Ahmedabad on February 28, a day after the Godhra carnage.

May 29

Implying a threat to use nuclear weapons even if India sticks to conventional arms in a conflict, Pakistan's ambassador to the United Nations says "India should not have the license to kill with conventional weapons while Pakistan's hands are tied regarding other means to defend itself."

May 31

Citing the escalation of war threat between India and Pakistan, the United States, Britain, Germany, Australia, Denmark, and New Zealand decide to reduce the levels of nonessential diplomatic staff and their families in India and advise their nationals against traveling to the region.

June 3

Manohar Parrikar is sworn in as the chief minister of a BJP-led coalition government in Goa for a second consecutive term.

June 5

The death toll in the heat wave that has gripped Andhra Pradesh for three weeks soars to 1,235, and on June 21 it reaches 1,421.

June 9

Syed Ali Shah Geelani, Jamaat-e-Islami leader and former chairman of the All Parties Hurriyat Conference, is arrested under POTA (Prevention of Terrorism Act) for allegedly channeling funds to the Hizbul Mujaheddin group from Pakistan.

June 10

Prime Minister Vajpayee proposes the name of A.P.J. Abdul Kalam, a scientist who was in charge of the country's ballistic missile program and who helped supervise India's May 1998 nuclear tests, for the post of president.

The ban on flights over India by Pakistan International Airlines aircraft is lifted, as the first step toward de-escalation of the India-Pakistan confrontation. The next day, India orders its ships of the Western Fleet to return to their base as a second step.

June 12

The People's Front alliance of the left parties, the Samajwadi Party and the Janata Dal (Secular), is dissolved following differences over the choice of a presidential candidate. The Samajwadi Party endorses the candidature of the government's nominee, Abdul Kalam, while the left parties—the CPI, CPI (M), RSP, and Forward Bloc— reject it. The next day, the Congress announces its support of Kalam, when President K.R. Narayanan, whom it had supported for a second term, says he is willing to stand only if unopposed. Two days later, the Left Front nominates Colonel Lakshmi Sahgal, a leader of the Indian National Army of World War II, as its candidate.

June 13

The Vilasrao Deshmukh government wins the confidence vote in the Maharashtra assembly.

June 22

Karnataka says that it cannot release water to Tamil Nadu from the Cauvery river because inadequate rains have caused a drop in the water level in the Krishnarajsagar reservoir. The next day, Tamil Nadu dismisses the statement as being untrue.

June 28

Complying with a Supreme Court deadline on electoral reforms, the Election Commission prescribes an affidavit to be furnished by candidates that contains full and complete information regarding educational qualifications, criminal records, and financial assets and liabilities. Returning officers will be vested with the power to reject nomination papers based on the veracity of the information provided in the affidavit.

June 29

Union home minister Advani is appointed deputy prime minister.

July 1

Prime Minister Vajpayee announces a cabinet reshuffle in which External Affairs Minister Jaswant Singh and Finance Minister Yashwant Sinha exchange portfolios.

The BJP appoints Venkaiah Naidu as party president, replacing Jana Krishnamurthi, who is appointed to the cabinet.

July 9

The police invoke POTA for the first time in Tamil Nadu, arresting eight MDMK men for their recent pro-Liberation Tigers of Tamil Eelam remarks. Two days later, MDMK General Secretary Vaiko becomes the first member of Parliament to be detained under POTA.

July 18

A.P.J. Abdul Kalam is elected India's eleventh president.

July 19

Gujarat chief minister Narendra Modi resigns, along with his government, after handing over his cabinet's resolution recommending dissolution of the assembly nine months ahead of the expiry of its term.

July 25

Water resources minister Jagdanand Singh says that floods in north Bihar have claimed over fifty lives and affected over four million people. The Indian Army takes up relief and rescue operations in ten districts. Assam is also severely affected by floods.

August 5

Following a controversy over the allotments of petrol pumps, liquefied petroleum gas agencies, and kerosene oil outlets made by the dealer selection boards to the relatives and associates of leaders of the BJP, its allies, and the RSS in various parts of the country, Prime Minister Vajpayee directs the petroleum ministry to cancel all allotments made after January 2000, except those made to families of Kargil martyrs, and auction them on the basis of competitive bidding.

August 12

NDA candidate and former Rajasthan chief minister Bhairon Singh Shekhawat is elected the country's vice president, replacing Krishna Kant, who died of a heart attack on July 27.

August 16

Following its visit to Gujarat, the Election Commission rejects state chief minister Narendra Modi's request to hold elections to the state assembly in October, saying the Election Commission is not presently in a position to conduct a free and fair election in the state, and recommends that President's Rule be imposed on the state. Two days later, having rejected the recommendation, the government requests that the Supreme Court rule on the election date. On September 2, the Supreme Court upholds the Election Commission's order.

August 25

"Sandalwood" bandit Veerappan abducts a former Karnataka minister, H. Nagappa. On December 8, Nagappa's body is found in a forest area bordering Tamil Nadu.

September 3

Having considered the Karnataka government's late June decision to reduce the Cauvery water supply to Tamil Nadu, the Supreme Court orders Karnataka to release a specified amount of water until a final decision is taken by the Cauvery River Authority. Five days later, in an emergency meeting, the authority, which is chaired by the prime minister, directs the release of water to Tamil Nadu.

September 8

Disinvestment minister Arun Shourie announces the deferral of the scheduled privatization of oil refiners Hindustan Petroleum and Bharat Petroleum, creating uncertainty about the disinvestment program, as the result of the resistance of Petroleum Minister Ram Naik and Defense Minister George Fernandes.

September 9

Nearly 150 people are feared killed in a railway accident near Gaya in Bihar.

September 11

Militants gun down the Jammu and Kashmir law and parliamentary affairs minister, Mushtaq Ahmed Lone, while he is addressing an election rally.

September 12

In their second meeting in less than a year, U.S. President George W. Bush assures Prime Minister Vajpayee that the United States will use its influence with Pakistan on the issue of terrorism and expresses concern over the killings in Jammu and Kashmir.

September 15

The first phase of voting in elections to the state assembly of Jammu and Kashmir begins. Although observers report some instances of voters being coerced by the military, in general the polling appears much fairer than in previous elections. The Hurriyat Conference on September 22 asks people to stay away from polling booths and observe a complete shutdown on the day of the second phase of voting, September 24. Despite this, turnout averages 42 percent, with constituencies in Srinagar, which has many Hurriyat supporters, recording only 11 percent turnout. Forty-one percent of the electorate votes in the third phase, which ends October 1, while turnout in the final phase, which ends October 8, is 52 percent.

September 17

Uttar Pradesh chief minister Mayawati responds to the February 12, 2001, decision of the Uttar Pradesh High Court that barred (on technical grounds that could be cured by a fresh notification by the state) the constitution of a CBI court to try Deputy Prime Minister Advani and other BJP and VHP leaders in connection with the demolition of the Babri Masjid. She rules out the issuance of a fresh notification, citing "detailed scrutiny and discussion with legal experts."

September 19

The Karnataka cabinet decides to suspend the release of Cauvery waters to Tamil Nadu after a farmer commits suicide in protest against the release of water the previous day. Two days later, Prime Minister Vajpayee orders Karnataka to release water to Tamil Nadu as per the Cauvery River Authority decision.

September 24

Thirty people are killed and nearly one hundred injured when two militants heavily armed with guns and grenades storm the famous Akshardham temple in Gandhinagar, capital of Gujarat. The attack develops into a siege that ends the next morning when national security guard commandos kill the two militants holed up in the temple.

September 29

A twelve-hour blockade of railway trains by farmers in Bangalore protesting the release of Cauvery waters to Tamil Nadu leaves thousands of commuters and long-distance passengers stranded.

October 5

The Supreme Court rules that Brahmins do not have monopoly over performing *puja* (prayer) in a temple and says that anyone well versed with the rituals can be appointed as a *pujari* (priest).

The Tamil Nadu government promulgates the Tamil Nadu Prohibition of Forcible Conversion of Religion Ordinance, 2002, which bans religious conversions by use of force and proposes a three-year imprisonment and a fine of up to Rs. 50,000 for those who "force" or "induce" conversions.

October 7

The police charge Salman Khan, one of the Mumbai film industry's leading actors, with culpable homicide for driving his car into a group of bakery workers sleeping on a pavement on September 28 in Mumbai, killing one and seriously injuring three.

October 9

Karnataka chief minister S.M. Krishna says that the October 4 Supreme Court directive to release waters to Tamil Nadu in accordance with the order of the Cauvery River Authority is "unimplementable."

October 10

In a surprise result, the Jammu and Kashmir National Conference is voted out of power in Jammu and Kashmir. On October 26, the Congress and the People's Democratic Party (PDP) agree to form a government in Jammu and Kashmir, with a common minimum program and a plan to share the chief minister's post. PDP leader Mufti Mohammed Sayeed takes the first three-year term. Sayeed says that the objective of the coalition government will be to "heal the physical, psychological, and emotional wounds inflicted by fourteen years of militancy."

October 15

Jhajjar district in Haryana is put under alert following the lynching of five *Dalits* by a mob.

October 16

After ten months of confrontation with Pakistan forces following the terrorist attack on Parliament House in New Delhi on December 13, the government decides to withdraw troops from the international border but rules out any reduction along the Line of Control in Jammu and Kashmir.

October 24

The Supreme Court issues a notice to Karnataka on a contempt petition filed by Tamil Nadu for "willful non-compliance" of its order on the Cauvery issue and directs it to release "some water" to Tamil Nadu immediately. Four days later, the Karnataka government formally and unconditionally apologizes to the court and begins the release of water.

October 28

The Supreme Court, in its response to the presidential reference (request for a ruling) on the Election Commission's controversial order on Gujarat, rejects the Central Government's arguments for holding early polls, saying that election to a prematurely dissolved state assembly can be held six months after the last meeting of the house.

The union minister of state for law and justice, Ravi Shankar Prasad, reports that 869 of the 1,734 proposed fast-track subordinate courts for speedy delivery of justice had been set up and had decided 63,581 of the 163,025 cases transferred to them. He adds that nearly 20 million of the 24 million cases pending are in subordinate courts and that 200,000 prisoners undergoing trial were in jail for several years due to a delay in the disposal of cases.

October 31

Twelve BJP dissident MLAs announce the withdrawal of their support for the BSP alliance government in Uttar Pradesh.

The Supreme Court asks the federal government to constitute a task force to consider finishing the project to link all major rivers in the country by the year 2012 instead of 2042.

November 2

PDP leader Mufti Mohammed Sayeed is sworn in as the chief minister of Jammu and Kashmir, and senior Congress leader Mangat Ram Sharma is sworn in as the deputy chief minister.

November 11

Microsoft founder Bill Gates announces a $100 million long-term initiative to arrest the spread of AIDS in India, the largest by his foundation for any country, and says the country can become an example for the world through the right prevention strategies.

November 13

In Gujarat, sectarian tensions rise in the run-up to the December elections. The Election Commission bans religious rallies in Gujarat, including the *yatra* (procession) proposed by the VHP.

November 29

The Supreme Court orders that all cases pertaining to the demolition of the disputed structure in Ayodhya on December 6, 1992, including the one against Deputy Prime Minister Advani and seven other senior Bharatiya Janata Party and Vishwa Hindu Parishad leaders, will now be tried by a special court at Rae Bareli.

December 3

President Vladimir Putin of Russia begins a two-day visit during which he signs an agreement with Prime Minister Vajpayee for the promotion of economic and scientific ties and cooperation against terrorism.

December 13

Elections to the state assembly are held in Gujarat, with a turnout of 61.5 percent. The districts that were worst affected by the post-Godhra riots register 65 percent polling.

December 15

The Bharatiya Janata Party is reelected in Gujarat with a massive two-thirds majority winning 126 seats in the 182-member assembly, bettering its tally of 117 in the 1998 election. Narendra Modi is sworn in again as chief minister on December 22.

December 16

A Delhi court convicts four persons in the Parliament attack case; three are sentenced to death. On October 29, 2003, in response to an appeal, the Delhi High Court acquits two of the accused, including Delhi University lecturer S.A.R. Geelani, but upholds the death penalty against the two others.

Parliament approves the Freedom of Information Bill, providing citizens the statutory right to access official information.

December 24

Inaugurating the first stretch of the Delhi Metro, which is elevated, Prime Minister Vajpayee says that it will help ease the traffic congestion and pollution in the capital. Portions of the system are being constructed underground.

2003

January 4

The government announces that it has set up a nuclear command authority to manage India's nuclear weapons. The statement also modifies India's "no first use" policy on nuclear weapons, saying that the country might retaliate with nuclear weapons if it is the victim of a major attack employing chemical or biological weapons.

January 7

The Central Government directs all states and union territories to deport the alleged 20 million Bangladeshi illegal migrants in the country.

January 8

Despite the growing foreign exchange reserves at almost $70 billion and a healthy GDP growth of 5.8 percent in the second quarter of the current fiscal year, global rating agency Standard & Poor's maintains its "negative" outlook and the junk "BB" rating on India's foreign currency.

January 16

The Congress Party elects Sushil Kumar Shinde as chief minister of Maharashtra, replacing Vilasrao Deshmukh.

January 29

In a major cabinet reshuffle, eight ministers are relieved of their portfolios, including Pramod Mahajan, who is made the BJP's general secretary. Arun Shourie retains the disinvestment portfolio and also gets telecom and information technology.

February 8

India expels Pakistan's acting high commissioner Jalil Abbas Jilani, accusing him of channeling funds to separatist militants in Jammu and Kashmir.

February 9

The government, in collaboration with the World Health Organization, launches a six-day polio immunization program to vaccinate about 160 million children.

February 20

The government announces that it will allow futures trading in fifty-four commodities, including gold, silver, wheat, rice, oilseeds, and pulses.

February 26

President A.P.J. Abdul Kalam unveils the portrait of Hindu Mahasabha leader Veer Savarkar in the Central Hall of Parliament today amid celebratory slogan shouting by BJP and Shiv Sena members and a walkout by the opposition.

February 28

Finance Minister Jaswant Singh presents the budget for 2003–2004.

March 1

The Congress wins decisively in the Himachal Pradesh assembly elections, defeating the incumbent BJP government. In Tripura, the ruling Left Front, in power since 1992, is reelected. In both Nagaland and Meghalaya, no party gains a majority.

March 3

The opposition Samajwadi Party (SP) releases a videotape in which Mayawati, Uttar Pradesh chief minister and leader of the Bahujan Samaj Party (BSP), asks party assembly members to make donations to the BSP from money that they had expropriated from funds for public works projects.

March 5

The Allahabad High Court in Uttar Pradesh orders the Archaeological Survey of India (ASI) to excavate the site at Ayodhya to determine whether an ancient temple existed there before the construction of the sixteenth-century Babri Masjid, which was pulled down on December 6, 1992, by Hindu fundamentalists. The court asks the ASI to start the excavation work within a week, to apprise it of progress made on March 24, and to submit its report to the court within a week of completion of the excavation process.

March 6

In Meghalaya, a new government of the Democratic Alliance of Nagaland, a conglomerate of five regional and non-Congress political parties, is sworn in.

March 13

The Supreme Court declares "null and void" a provision in the Representation of the People (Amendment) Act that was intended to dilute the court's judgment requiring candidates to declare criminal records, cases pending against them, and their financial assets.

March 18

Arjun Munda of the BJP is sworn in as chief minister of Jharkhand, after the resignation of Babulal Marandi, following the loss of his majority in the assembly on March 13.

March 26

Former BJP minister Haren Pandya is killed by two unidentified gunmen in Ahmedabad. Amid the ensuing uproar in the assembly, the Gujarat government passes seven bills in thirty-five minutes, including the controversial anti-conversion legislation.

April 27

An estimated one million people attend a rally in Warangal in Andhra Pradesh in support of the regional party Telangana Rashtra Samithi, which is demanding a separate state for the Telangana region.

April 30

Replying to a four-day debate in the Lok Sabha on the finance bill, Finance Minister Jaswant Singh rules out imposing any tax on agriculture income, waives interest on all loans to farmers in the fourteen drought-affected states, and appeals to traders by ruling out implementation of the value added tax (VAT) from June 1.

May 1

The World Health Organization declares India SARS-free, putting to rest speculation and fears about an outbreak of the disease in the country.

May 6

The Women's Reservation Bill 1999, which seeks to reserve one-third of the seats in the Lok Sabha and the state assemblies for women, is deferred once again.

June 12

Automobile giant Maruti Udyog Ltd.'s initial public offer sells out in three hours, with the issue being oversubscribed nearly 1.46 times by the end of the opening day, setting a record for a company in which the government has a sizable stake.

June 20

The union minister for tourism and culture, Jagmohan, asks the Uttar Pradesh government to stop the construction work at the Taj Heritage Corridor on the Yamuna riverbed near the Taj Mahal immediately. Senior officials in various civic bodies in Agra have maintained that the construction plan was approved straight from the chief secretary's office, and therefore no civic body in Agra thought it was necessary to ask any further questions.

June 22

Prime Minister Vajpayee begins a six-day visit to China, the first such visit in ten years. The next day, with his Chinese counterpart, Wen Jiabao, he signs a joint declaration consisting of nine agreements. One of these is a border trade pact, which includes the reopening of the ancient trade pass at Nathu La in Sikkim, apparently marking the de facto acceptance by China of Sikkim's 1975 accession to India. In return, New Delhi recognizes the Tibet Autonomous Region as part of the territory of China.

June 27

A fast-track court in Vadodara, Gujarat, acquits all 21 accused in the Best Bakery case, in which 14 people were burned alive inside the shop following the Godhra train attack. After 44 days of trial, during which 73 of the 120 named witnesses deposed, of whom 41 turned hostile, Judge H.U. Mahida says: "That a violent mob caused the death of 14 people in the incident is beyond question, but the court does not have an iota of evidence about the involvement of those accused in the crime." On July 2, the chairman of the National Human Rights Commission declares the acquittal a miscarriage of justice and calls for a retrial of the case.

July 5

Sehrunissa Sheikh, one of the main witnesses in the Best Bakery case and wife of the bakery owner, tells the *Indian Express* newspaper in a tape recorded interview that she lied in court out of fear for her life.

July 11

Bus service between Lahore, in Pakistan, and New Delhi resumes service, with one bus traveling each way.

July 27

Manipur chief minister Okram Ibobi Singh survives an attempt on his life by suspected members of the outlawed People's Liberation Army.

July 30

The National Human Rights Commission decides to file a special leave petition in the Supreme Court asking for a retrial of the Best Bakery case on the basis of the feedback from a team it sent to Gujarat on July 8 to inspect the records of the case.

July 31

Mahant Parmahans Ramchandra Das, president of the trust established to build the Rama temple, dies in Ayodhya at age ninety.

August 3

Gegong Apang is sworn in as chief minister of a United Democratic Front government in Arunachal Pradesh, after the Congress government lost a vote of confidence.

August 6

While disposing six petitions challenging the Tamil Nadu government's dismissal of 170,000 striking employees a day after it forces the Tamil Nadu government to reinstate the employees, the Supreme Court rules that government employees do not have "a legal or fundamental or equitable right" to go on strike whatever the cause, "just or unjust."

August 25

Forty-eight people are killed and at least 136 injured when two taxi-bombs explode within three kilometers of each other in Mumbai. The first bomb goes off at Zaveri Bazaar, the heart of Mumbai's diamond business, followed closely by the second one in a parking lot next to the Gateway of India opposite the Taj Mahal Hotel. Four people—Hanif Sayyed Mohammed, an electrician; his wife Fehmida and daughter Fareen; and an auto rickshaw driver Arshad Ansari—are arrested on September 1 under POTA for their alleged involvement in the blasts.

After six months of excavation at the site of the demolished Babri Masjid, the Archaeological Survey of India (ASI) submits its report to the Uttar Pradesh High Court that had ordered it. The report claims that there is evidence, including fifty pillar bases and other objects, which is "indicative" of remains associated with "temples of North India" from the tenth century A.D., predating the mosque by at least five hundred years. While the Sangh Parivar welcomes the findings, the Sunni Central Board of Waqfs calls the report's conclusion "vague and self-contradictory," sparking a controversy among eminent archaeologists and historians on the ASI's interpretation of the evidence.

August 26

Uttar Pradesh chief minister Mayawati resigns after the breakup of the ruling coalition between the BSP and the BJP.

August 29

Samajwadi Party president Mulayam Singh Yadav is sworn in as the new Uttar Pradesh chief minister, with the support of the Congress and several other parties.

September 9

Israeli Prime Minister Ariel Sharon arrives for a visit and meets with Prime Minister Vajpayee, who emphasizes the bonds in defense, agriculture, and in the fight against terrorism shared by the countries.

September 12

The Supreme Court directs the chief secretary and director general of police (DGP) of Gujarat to appear in person before the Supreme Court on September 19 and account for the state's role in the Best Bakery case, describing the state's appeal before the High Court in the Best Bakery case as "a complete eyewash."

September 13

Militants wearing police uniforms gun down Kuka Parray, chairman of the Jammu Kashmir Awami League Party. Parray was a former terrorist who formed a counter-insurgency group supported by Government of India security forces.

September 19

The special CBI court at Rae Bareli clears L.K. Advani, deputy prime minister and home affairs minister, of charges in the Babri Masjid demolition case but frames charges against seven others, including Murli Manohar Joshi, the minister for human resources development.

September 22

Dara Singh, convicted for the murder of Australian missionary Graham Staines and his two minor sons more than four years earlier, is sentenced to death by the trial court in Bhubaneswar. The other twelve convicted in the case are awarded life imprisonment.

October 1

Andhra Pradesh chief minister N. Chandrababu Naidu escapes an assassination attempt suspected to be carried out by the People's War Group.

October 7

The CBI files a charge sheet against Chhattisgarh chief minister Ajit Jogi for "dishonestly or fraudulently" using a forged document to tarnish the image of the Intelligence Bureau and the Central Government.

October 17

The authorities in Uttar Pradesh deploy thousands of security personnel, block roads, and divert trains to thwart a rally planned for October 17 by the Vishwa Hindu Parishad at Ayodhya.

November 8

Mumbai police commissioner R.S. Sharma is called in for questioning on his role in a corruption scandal, a day after the arrest of the inspector general of police, Sridhar Vagal, for watering down charges against counterfeiter Abdul Karim Telgi and allegedly accepting a bribe of Rs. 7.2 million. Telgi, a former travel agent from Belgaum, Karnataka, ran a massive business spanning seven states that printed and distributed fake revenue stamps and stamp paper. He successfully bribed policemen and politicians to evade arrest.

November 14

The Andhra Pradesh state assembly is dissolved by Governor Surjit Singh Barnala eleven months early, on the recommendation of chief minister Chandrababu Naidu.

November 21

The Supreme Court orders the halting of ten cases relating to the communal violence in Gujarat in 2002, in response to requests by the National Human Rights Commission that the cases be transferred to courts outside Gujarat because of intimidation of witnesses and inadequate investigations by the police.

November 23

Murasoli Maran, senior leader of the DMK and union cabinet minister without portfolio, dies at age sixty-nine.

November 24

The Supreme Court upholds the acquittal of Tamil Nadu chief minister Jayalalitha in the Tansi land scam cases.

December 1

Akali Dal leader Parkash Singh Badal, his son Sukhbir Singh Badal, and three of their associates are sent to jail on corruption charges.

December 4

The ruling Congress Party is decisively defeated in elections in Madhya Pradesh, Rajasthan, and Chhattisgarh by the BJP but retains the government in Delhi, although with a reduced majority. On December 8, Vasundhara Raje is sworn in as chief minister of Rajasthan—the first woman to occupy that position—and another woman, Uma Bharati, becomes chief minister of Madhya Pradesh. The day before, Rama Singh takes over as chief minister in Chhattisgarh. In Delhi, Congress chief minister Sheila Dixit retains her post, although with a slightly reduced majority. In Mizoram, the Mizo National Front retains power.

December 6

In Assam, the Bodo armed movement comes to a formal close with the disbanding of the Bodo Liberation Tigers and laying down of arms by 2,641 of its cadres, followed by the creation of the Bodoland Territorial Council.

December 9

The CBI charges former Congress chief minister of Chhattisgarh, Ajit Jogi, with attempting to bribe seventeen newly elected BJP legislators into defecting from their party after it won December state assembly elections.

December 20

A Central Bureau of Investigation court acquits former prime minister P.V. Narasimha Rao of all charges in a corruption case concerning the alleged cheating of a businessman, Lakhubhai Pathak, in 1983.

Abbreviations and Glossary

Some Common Abbreviations

AIADMK	All India Anna Dravida Munnetra Kazhagam
BJD	Biju Janata Dal
BJP	Bharatiya Janata Party
BSP	Bahujan Samaj Party
CBI	Central Bureau of Investigation
CPI	Communist Party of India
CPI(M) or CPM	Communist Party of India (Marxist)
DMK	Dravida Munnetra Kazhagam
FIR	First Information Report
IAS	Indian Administrative Service
MLA	Member of the Legislative Assembly
NDA	National Democratic Alliance
NHRC	National Human Rights Commission
NRI	Nonresident Indian
OBCs	Other Backward Classes
RBI	Reserve Bank of India
RJD	Rashtriya Janata Dal
RSS	Rashtriya Swayamsevak Sangh
SAARC	South Asian Association for Regional Cooperation
SCs	Scheduled Castes
SP	Samajwadi Party
STs	Scheduled Tribes
TDP	Telugu Desam Party
UPA	United Progressive Alliance
VHP	Vishwa Hindu Parishad

Glossary

All India Anna Dravida Munnetra Kazhagam (AIADMK). Tamil nationalist party in the state of Tamil Nadu led by Jayalalitha, one of the most powerful women in Indian politics. Although enmeshed in a series of corruption cases, she led the party to a landslide victory in the 2001 elections in Tamil Nadu and has now become, once again, chief minister of the state.

Ayodhya. A small city in east-central Uttar Pradesh believed to be the birthplace of Ram (or Rama, the god-king who is the hero of the *Ramayana*). Site of the disputed Babri mosque/Ram temple shrine. The mosque was demolished on December 6, 1992, provoking widespread rioting and a major political crisis.

Bahujan Samaj Party (BSP). Led by Kanshi Ram and Mayawati, the party of the *Dalits* and other "underclass" social groups. It is mainly an Uttar Pradesh party, but it does have significant support in Punjab and Madhya Pradesh.

Bharatiya Janata Party (BJP). Party formed from the Janata Party by elements of Jana Sangh, with support mainly in northern India. It favors a Hindu nationalist ideology, but its appeal also derives from the reputation for discipline and integrity of its core leaders. The core party of the opposition NDA coalition, it received 22 percent of the vote in the 2004 election. Its strength is greatest in the western and northern states of Delhi, Gujarat, Himachal Pradesh, Madhya Pradesh, Maharashtra, Rajasthan, and Uttar Pradesh.

Biju Janata Dal. Party named after the late Biju Patnaik, a major all-India politician, and led by his son, Naveen Patnaik, who serves as chief minister of Orissa, to which the party is confined. The party is allied with the BJP in the NDA.

Chief Minister. The head of government in the state, who serves at the pleasure of the majority party of the state legislative assembly; the equivalent of the prime minister.

Communal. Term commonly used, as in "communal conflict," to refer to Hindus and Muslims as communities with distinct feelings of identity. It often serves as a term of condemnation.

Congress Party. The dominant Indian party from Independence until 1967 at the state level, and 1977 at the national level; its coalition, the

United Progressive Alliance, won the parliamentary elections of 2004. The president of the party is Sonia Gandhi, the widow of Rajiv Gandhi, who served as Congress prime minister from 1984 to 1989, while Dr. Manmohan Singh leads the party in Parliament and serves as prime minister. Also known as the Congress (I), the name of the faction created by a party split in 1977 and initially led by Indira Gandhi (the "I" stands for Indira).

Dalit. Literally, "oppressed" or "ground down," the term for people of the Scheduled Castes, preferred by militant and educated ex-untouchables and by many others who sympathize with their aspirations.

Dravida Munnetra Kazhagam (DMK). Tamil nationalist party led by M. Karunanidhi, who served as chief minister of Tamil Nadu from 1969 to 1976, 1989 to 1990, and 1996 to 2001.

Election Commission. The constitutionally established autonomous body that is responsible for conducting national elections, including the declaration of polling dates, preparation of voter lists, certification of parties and candidates, establishment of rules for the election campaigns, and management of the polling and counting of ballots. The chief election commissioner is joined by two additional election commissioners who serve fixed terms.

Finance Commission. Established under Article 280 of the Constitution, finance commissions make recommendations (which are typically accepted unchanged) to the national government on the allocation to the states of taxes collected by the central government and grants-in-aid. The twelfth finance commission was appointed in 2002, and is chaired by C. Rangarajan, a former governor of the Reserve Bank of India.

First Information Report (FIR). The complaint that a crime has been committed entered in a ledger in the police station, either by the police or by the crime victim.

Gandhi, Indira. Daughter of Jawaharlal Nehru and prime minister from 1966 to 1977 and 1980 to 1984, when she was assassinated by her own Sikh bodyguards.

Gandhi, Mohandas K. The preeminent leader of India's fight against British colonial rule from 1919 until Independence. He was assassinated in January 1948 by a Hindu nationalist fanatic. Also known as Mahatma Gandhi and Gandhiji.

Godhra. City in eastern Gujarat state where a railway car was set on fire in February 2002, killing fifty-eight persons, presumed to be Hindus, sparking the anti-Muslim pogrom of the next few days.

High Court. The highest court at the state level, which mainly hears appeals in criminal and civil cases. A large number of judges, and a chief justice, serve until a mandatory retirement age of sixty. As in the Supreme Court of India, a given case can be heard by "benches" of different numbers of justices, from one to six or more.

Hindutva. Literally, "Hindu-ness," the term was used as the title of a book written in 1922 by Hindu nationalist leader V.D. Savarkar to argue that Hindus were a nation. It is now used as the equivalent of "Hindu nationalism."

Home Ministry. The ministry, in the central government and the states, that deals with internal security. It includes organizations such as the CBI and the police. The home minister is one of the highest ranking ministers.

India Shining. The campaign slogan–phrase of the NDA in the 2004 parliamentary election, meant to convey India's triumphant economic progress in areas like information technology.

Indian National Congress. *See* Congress Party.

Jana Sangh. Properly, the "Bharatiya Jana Sangh" (Indian People's Party), founded in 1951 with an ideology of Hindu nationalism, it developed strength in western and northern India. It reemerged as the present-day Bharatiya Janata Party after merging with other parties to form the Janata Party in the crucible of the 1977 elections that ended the Emergency rule of Indira Gandhi.

Janata Dal. A party formed from the Jan Morcha, the Janata Party, factions of the Lok Dal, and a Congress Party splinter known as the

Congress (S). In 1989, it had 141 of the 144 seats held by the National Front in the Lok Sabha that formed the government led by V.P. Singh. After several splits and mergers, it survives at present only in the state of Karnataka. *See* Rashtriya Janata Dal, Biju Janata Dal.

Kargil. A town in the Ladakh region of the state of Jammu and Kashmir. It gave its name to the crisis of a miniwar between India and Pakistan in May-July 1999 that erupted when insurgents and Pakistani troops crossed the line of control on the icy mountain heights overlooking it and other territory along the Srinagar-Leh road.

Lok Sabha. Lower house of India's bicameral Parliament, equivalent to the British House of Commons. All but two of its 545 members are directly elected from district constituencies for a five-year-maximum term.

Mahabharata. One of the two major epics of India, it describes the internecine warfare that resulted from the feud of succession involving descendants of the legendary king Bharata.

Mandal. Refers to the politics of lower caste mobilization that came to a peak during the government of V.P. Singh (1989-90), when it accepted the recommendation of the Mandal Commission (officially, the "Backward Classes Commission") that government regulations be introduced to increase the employment of "backward" class persons in government.

Member of the Legislative Assembly (MLA). The equivalent of a member of Parliament at the state level.

National Democratic Alliance (NDA). Formed just before the 1999 election, a coalition whose leader and major constituent is the Bharatiya Janata Party. It governed India as the core of a coalition of more than twenty parties until defeated in the parliamentary elections of 2004.

Nehru, Jawaharlal. Nationalist leader who served as prime minister from 1947 until his death in 1964. Policies particularly associated with him—the promotion of secularism, socialism, and planning, and nonalignment in foreign affairs—are often dubbed "Nehruvian."

Other Backward Classes (OBCs). "Backward" classes other than the Scheduled Castes and Scheduled Tribes. Typically defined in caste terms to mean the non-elite, non-untouchable castes (*jatis*).

Panchayat. Literally, a "council of five." A village or *jati* (caste) council. The *panchayati raj* system of rural local self-government introduced in 1959 was entrenched in the Constitution as the Seventy-Third Amendment in 1993, with institutions at village, block, and district levels now exercising significantly enhanced political and financial powers. A major feature of the new system is the reservation for women of not less than one-third of the seats of the village council and of chairpersons of the *panchayati raj* body at each level.

Partition. The 1947 division of British India into independent successor countries, India and Pakistan. Estimates of persons killed in ethnic cleansing, mainly in the northwest of the subcontinent, range from 300,000 to three million, and the migrants numbered at least ten to twelve million.

Planning Commission. Government body that prepares five-year plans, which provide a broad framework for public and private economic goals.

President. In India, the equivalent of a constitutional monarch with very restricted powers. The requirement of giving formal assent to bills has been used by several presidents to influence legislation by withholding assent when a bill is first sent to him (all presidents have been male). Elected by members of Parliament and the state legislatures for a five-year term in 2002, the present incumbent is A.P.J. Abdul Kalam.

President's Rule. Suspension of a state's assembly and direct rule of the state by the central government through the centrally appointed governor, typically when the state government loses its majority or is deemed unable to govern due to a "disturbed" political situation. It has sometimes been used by the central government to topple opposition-controlled state governments.

Rajya Sabha. Upper house of India's bicameral Parliament. All but six of its 256 members are elected by the state legislatures for staggered six-year terms. Roughly equivalent in power to Britain's House of Lords.

Ramayana. One of the two main epics of India, depicting the triumph of King Rama, thought to be an incarnation of the god Vishnu, in a war sparked by the abduction of his wife, Sita.

Rashtriya Janata Dal. Party led by Laloo Prasad Yadav of Bihar, with strength mainly in that state.

Rashtriya Swayamsevak Sangh (RSS). Literally, "National Volunteer Association," a militant Hindu organization founded in 1925 and associated with the Bharatiya Janata Party, the Vishwa Hindu Parishad, and the Bajrang Dal—the members of the Sangh Parivar (RSS family). The RSS draws its membership mainly from urban and lower-middle-class voters and seeks the consolidation of a Hindu nation.

Reservation. The provision for quotas in legislative bodies, civil services, educational institutions, and other public institutions, typically in proportion to the percentage in the population, for qualified members of Scheduled Castes and Scheduled Tribes, and, in some places, Other Backward Classes.

Saffronization. A term of disdain used by opponents of the BJP and the Sangh Parivar to describe the perceived introduction of Hindu nationalist ideas and persons into government, especially in education. Derives from the association of the color saffron with Hindu worship (the robes of ascetics, the color of temple penants, and so forth), as adopted by organizations of the Sangh Parivar.

Samajwadi (Socialist) Party (SP). Led by Mulayam Singh Yadav, a former defense minister of India and at present chief minister of Uttar Pradesh. The party is mainly confined to that state and draws support largely from the OBCs.

Samata Party. Confined largely to Bihar, this party is led by George Fernandes, defense minister in the BJP-led 1998 and 1999 governments.

Sangh Parivar. See Rashtriya Swayamsevak Sangh.

Scheduled Castes and Scheduled Tribes (SCs/STs). The "schedule" refers to a list of untouchables, or Harijan, castes and tribes drawn up under the 1935 Government of India Act and subsequently revised. Legislative seats as well as government posts and places in educational institutions are reserved for members of these castes and tribes. In general usage, the preferred term for Scheduled Caste members is *Dalit.*

Shiv Sena. Militant nativist communal organization founded in Bombay (now Mumbai) in 1966 to agitate against South Indian immigrants to the state of Maharashtra, which is the only state in which it has developed significant strength. Alleged to have played a major part in the riots of December 1992 and January 1993 in Bombay, following the demolition of the Babri mosque. It is the BJP's closest ally. Its founder and all-powerful leader is Bal Thackeray.

Sikh, Sikhism. The religion of Sikhism was founded in the sixteenth century by the first guru, Nanak, drawing on Hindu devotionalism and Islam.

South Asian Association for Regional Cooperation (SAARC). Organization formed in 1985 to enhance cooperation in social, economic, and cultural development. The SAARC members are Bangladesh, Bhutan, India, the Maldives, Nepal, Pakistan, and Sri Lanka.

Supreme Court. The highest court of India, which has over time carved out for itself the right to declare parliamentary legislation unconstitutional. Justices are appointed by the Government of India, typically with the advice of the chief justice, who is usually appointed on the basis of seniority. Justices retire at age sixty-five, usually after ten years of service. Depending on the significance of the case, "benches" of various sizes are constituted by the chief justice to hear appeals or cases brought directly to the court.

Swadeshi. Literally, "(one's) own country." A nationalist slogan from the early twentieth century that asked Indians to boycott foreign goods, especially cloth, in favor of Indian manufactures. More recently used to indicate an ideology of economic self-reliance.

Telugu Desam Party (TDP). Confined entirely to the state of Andhra Pradesh, where it has ruled for most of the years since its formation in 1982, this party is led by Chandrababu Naidu. A major supporter "from outside" of the National Democratic Alliance government of 1999–2004, it was defeated in the state elections held in 2004 and lost badly in the parliamentary elections as well.

Trinamool Congress. Confined to the state of West Bengal, this party split from the Congress Party in 1998. Its leader is Mamata Banerjee, one of the major women politicians who has emerged without being the widow or relative of a male politician.

Vishwa Hindu Parishad (VHP). A movement seeking to reinvigorate Hinduism. Leader of Hindu sentiment and organizer of actions in connection with the Babri mosque/Ram temple controversy. Its precise responsibility for the demolition of the mosque is not clear.

Yadav. An agrarian (cowherd) caste of the Gangetic Plain, it forms a substantial bloc within the "backward" castes; leaders of the community have governed as chief ministers of Uttar Pradesh and Bihar.

About the Contributors

Isher Judge Ahluwalia has served as director and chief executive of the Indian Council for Research on International Economic Relations in New Delhi and now sits on its board. Ahluwalia is chair of the board of the International Food Policy Research Institute, and was most recently visiting professor at the School of Public Affairs, University of Maryland at College Park. She is the author, co-author, or editor of five books, most recently, *Indian Economic Reforms and Development: Essays for Manmohan Singh*.

Alyssa Ayres is deputy director of the Center for the Advanced Study of India at the University of Pennsylvania, as well as managing editor of the journal *India Review*. She was previously assistant director for South and Central Asia at the Asia Society, and she has served on mission in Jammu and Kashmir with the International Committee of the Red Cross. She is a term member of the Council on Foreign Relations and the International Institute of Strategic Studies. She is writing a book on language, nationalism, and the nation. This is her second *India Briefing*.

Richard H. Davis is associate professor of religion and Asian studies at Bard College in Annandale, New York. He is author of *Ritual in an Oscillating Universe: Worshiping Siva in Medieval India* (Princeton, 1991) and *Lives of Indian Images* (Princeton, 1997), winner of the 1999 A.K. Coomaraswamy Award from the Association for Asian Studies. Currently he is completing work on a translation of a twelfth century Sanskrit ritual text, the *Mahotsavavidhi*, and starting work on a cultural history of early India. An edited volume on visual representations of nationhood in India, entitled *Iconography and the Nation in India*, is due out in 2005 from Orient Longman.

Niraja Gopal Jayal is professor at the Centre for the Study of Law and Governance, Jawaharlal Nehru University, New Delhi. She is the author of *Democracy and the State: Welfare, Secularism and Development in Contemporary India* (Oxford University Press, 1999), co-author of

Drought, Policy and Politics in India (Sage, 1993), and editor of *Democracy in India* (Oxford University Press, 2001). She is co-editing two forthcoming volumes to be published by Oxford University Press: *The Oxford Companion to Politics in India* and *Local Governance in India: Decentralisation and Beyond*. Her current research interests include gender and governance; ethnic inequality and the governance of public institutions; and the Indian idea of citizenship in the twentieth century. She is also director of a research project funded by the Ford Foundation, *Dialogue on Democracy and Pluralism in South Asia*.

Renana Jhabvala has a master's in economics from Yale University. She has been with Self-Employed Women's Association (SEWA) for over twenty-five years and is presently national coordinator, responsible for the spread of SEWA to the national level. She is also chair of SEWA Bank, president of SEWA Bharat, and a founding member of WIEGO (Women in Informal Employment Globalising and Organising), based at Harvard University. Ms. Jhabvala has written extensively in newspapers, journals, and books on the subject. Her most recent book was *Informal Economy Centrestage: New Structures of Employment* (Sage Publications, 2003), co-edited with Ratna Sudarshan and Jeemol Unni.

Manjeet Kripalani is the bureau chief for India for *Business Week* magazine. With a master's in international affairs from Columbia University and a degree in law and English literature from Bombay University, she has been covering India since 1996. Prior to that, she was a staffer at *Forbes* magazine in New York and served as deputy press secretary to Steve Forbes during his first presidential campaign in 1995–96. In 2004 she received a George Polk award for public service journalism, a Gerald Loeb award for distinguished business and financial journalism, a Daniel Pearl award for outstanding story on South Asia, and she was a finalist for the National Magazine Awards.

Amitabh Mattoo is currently vice chancellor of Jammu University and professor of international relations at Jawaharlal Nehru University. He is also honorary academic advisor to the Observer Research Foundation and is on the Governing Council of the Nuclear Science Center. Until recently, he was a member of India's National Security Council's Advisory Board. Mattoo received his doctorate in international relations from the University of Oxford, and he has been a visiting professor at Stanford

University and the University of Notre Dame. He has served as chair of the Centre for International Politics, Organization and Disarmament at Jawaharlal Nehru University and has written eight books and more than forty articles in leading international journals.

Philip K. Oldenburg is senior lecturer in the department of government at the University of Texas at Austin and adjunct research scholar at Columbia University. He has edited or co-edited nine previous volumes in the *India Briefing* series. He is the former director of Columbia University's Southern Asian Institute and the author of *Big City Government in India.*

Irawati Parnerkar is a doctoral candidate in political science at the University of Chicago. She has a master's degree in economics from the Delhi School of Economics.

Mary Rader has been the South Asia bibliographer at the University of Michigan since 1999 and at the University of Wisconsin since 2004. She holds graduate degrees from the University of Washington at Seattle and the University of Texas at Austin.

Index